The Crisis of the Holy

Interreligious Reflections

Series Editor
Alon Goshen-Gottstein, director of the Elijah Interfaith Institute

With the rise of interfaith relations comes the challenge of providing theory and deeper understanding for these relations and the trials that religions face together in an increasingly globalized world. Interreligious Reflections addresses these challenges by offering collaborative volumes that reflect cycles of work undertaken in dialogue between scholars of different religions. The series is dedicated to the academic and theological work of The Elijah Interfaith Institute, a multinational organization dedicated to fostering peace between the world's diverse faith communities through interfaith dialogue, education, research, and dissemination. In carrying out Elijah's principles, these volumes extend beyond the Abrahamic paradigm to include the dharmic traditions. As such, they promise to be a source of continuing inspiration and interest for religious leaders, academics, and community-oriented study groups that seek to deepen their interfaith engagement. All volumes in this series are edited by Elijah's director, Dr. Alon Goshen-¬Gottstein.

Titles in the Series

The Religious Other: Hostility, Hospitality, and the Hope of Human Flourishing, edited by Alon Goshen-Gottstein

The Crisis of the Holy: Challenges and Transformations in World Religions, edited by Alon Goshen-Gottstein

The Crisis of the Holy

Challenges and Transformations in World Religions

Edited by Alon Goshen-Gottstein

WIPF & STOCK · Eugene, Oregon

Wipf and Stock Publishers
199 W 8th Ave, Suite 3
Eugene, OR 97401

The Crisis of the Holy
Challenges and Transformations in World Religions
By Goshen-Gottstein, Alon
Copyright©2014 Rowman and Littlefield Publishing Group
ISBN 13: 978-1-5326-5925-6
Publication date 5/25/2018
Previously published by Lexington Books, 2014

Contents

Foreword   vii

Preface   ix
Alon Goshen-Gottstein

1   The Crisis of the Holy—An Overview   1
    Alon Goshen-Gottstein

2   Summary of Essays   23
    Alon Goshen-Gottstein

3   Buddhism   39
    Michael von Brück and Maria Reis Habito

4   Christianity   67
    Sidney H. Griffith

5   Judaism   87
    B. Barry Levy

6   Hinduism   111
    Deepak Sarma

7   Islam   125
    Vincent J. Cornell

8   Concluding Reflections   151
    Alon Goshen-Gottstein

Selected Bibliography   157

Index   161

About the Contributors   163

Foreword

The world's religions have evolved in response to numerous internal and external factors, but over time each has retained a solid (if constantly changing) outlook on life and the proper way to conduct it. Even throughout the political turmoil that sometimes shocked religions or their individual communities, a sense of purpose remained.

The modern era—including but not limited to the pervasive intrusion of globalizing political and economic developments; the often simplistic, polarized and morally equivalent presentations seen in the media; and the sense of surety demanded in and promised by a culture dominated by science—has cause a threat to the foundation of the world's religions and the cohesive assurances of their societies.

This cataclysmic change has stimulated all sorts of unnatural and in many ways unprecedented responses by religious, and more particularly their constituent, groups. The growth of fundamentalism and isolationism has provided strength for some, while the syncretistic search for meaning in previously unfathomed contexts moves others. Imbalance in leadership has been accompanied by the appropriation of ancient holy texts as a bulwark against change. Suspicion of all religions and their quest for meaning has increased in some circles, while globalization has suggested, for the first time, that all peoples share a common and shrinking place on earth. Some have abandoned ritual; others have opted for the routinized practice of it. Some have assimilated; others have grown increasingly xenophobic. Many have abandoned their deities; others have retreated into them.

Whatever the particular action or reaction, the totality of these unanticipated pressures and responses is pushing religious people into controversial forms. And it is sometimes stimulating unhealthy, unwanted, and, ultimately, fatal, flaws in religious thinking and living. This situation, which we have assembled to address, we call "the Crisis of the Holy."

The members of the Elijah Interfaith Institute Think-Tank see this crisis as a confluence of threats, challenges, and opportunities for the religions, indeed for religion. Some of the opportunities provided by the crisis are: providing context in which to rectify world wrongs; stimulating the rethinking of long standing religious postures, allowing for adopting inclusive rather than exclusionary positions, and providing both the means and the methods to ensure the creative and spiritual strengthening of religions.

We invite you to explore this exciting opportunity with us.

—Think-Tank of the Elijah Interfaith Institute

Preface

Alon Goshen-Gottstein

The striking topic around which this volume was penned was not our own invention. It was suggested by assembled religious leaders, who gathered in Seville at the end of 2003, for the inaugural meeting of the Elijah Board of World Religious Leaders. That gathering represented the successful implementation of the model which gave rise to the first volume in this series, *The Religious Other: Hostility, Hospitality and the Hope of Human Flourishing.* Scholars from different religions, under the aegis of the Elijah Interfaith Academy, prepared materials for religious leaders, who then engaged in conversation based upon the prepared material, with an eye to addressing global contemporary concerns. We asked religious leaders gathered in Seville: "On what would you like us to further reflect, on your behalf?" A number of the twenty or so answers that we received came neatly under the rubric of "Crisis of the Holy." It was then up to the think-tank whose work is represented in this volume to provide the parameters and definition to the intuition that our common crises are something religious leaders, and more broadly speaking, religious people, ought to be talking about.

Defining the parameters of this project turned out to be a far more complicated task than we had initially estimated. The chapters of this volume reflect a process that took place over three week-long meetings. The first was held in Barcelona in July 2004, at the invitation of the Council for a Parliament of the World's Religions. That meeting was devoted to defining how the Holy is understood in different traditions, what are the dimensions of the crisis, how crisis itself is understood in the different traditions and to initial considerations of how we might provide conceptual tools for approaching the topic in a broad comparative perspective.

The insights developed at this meeting of the think-tank take up the greater part of the opening chapter in this collection, which is an attempt to describe what we mean by the "Crisis of the Holy" and to describe the parameters and expectations that were set for the entire project. Even though I am the author of this piece, the key ideas presented in it are the fruit of the weeklong meeting described above. Additional meetings took place in Jerusalem and at the University of Arkansas, at the invitation of the King Fahd Center for Middle Eastern Studies.

The present collection is, thus, the result of collaborative thinking. While the authors of individual chapters are recognized for their work, in some way the entire project is owned by the entire think-tank, which includes some scholars who did not author chapters. Some of them were with us for only part of the process, some for the entire process. Our project benefited from the wisdom of David Chappell, who passed away after the Barcelona meeting, as well as of David Burrell, Rkia Cornell, Mona Siddiqui, Kurt Schreiber, Brenda Brasher, and Michael Weil, who played an important role in helping us to crystallize the eight moments of the crisis. The coming together of minds during this process is an academic tribute to the possible collaboration of different institutions worldwide and a testimony to the potential enrichment that deep interfaith sharing offers.

The essays presented in this book provided the foundation for a meeting of the Elijah Board of World Religious Leaders at Lingjiu Monastery in Taiwan. Dharma Master Hsin Tao, a pillar of this community of worldwide religious leaders, offered us hospitality, wisdom, and a context in which to engage the challenges of the Crisis of the Holy. Meetings of this forum seek to cultivate deep and intimate exchanges between religious leaders, rather than to make novel statements. Consequently, the benefits of this gathering of world religious leaders were felt by participating leaders and their communities, but are not communicated in the present volume, which features the work of the preparatory think-tank.

This project could not have taken place without the financial support of the following bodies: The Fetzer Institute, The von Groeben Foundation, The Guerrand-Hermes Peace Foundation, The Gerald Weisfeld Foundation, The Museum of World Religions in Taiwan, McGill University, The University of Arkansas, The Episcopal Church USA, and the Council for a Parliament of World Religions. I express my gratitude once again for their support for the work of our think-tank.

The present volume owes much to the editorial skills of Peta Jones Pellach, Director of Educational Activities at the Elijah Institute whose partnership is of immense value to me. I am also grateful for the caring attention of Emily Frazzette and Alissa Parra of Lexington Books and for their ongoing collaboration in developing our series.

All the people named above have put much time and thought into this project because they believed it would make a difference. This work has already made a difference to the religious leaders with whom it was initially shared. It is my sincere hope that with the publication of this volume our thinking will find further reception in broader circles of religious thinkers.

Chapter One

The Crisis of the Holy—An Overview

Alon Goshen-Gottstein

"The Holy" is not understood in the same way, nor does it necessarily have the same prominence in the overall economy of the different traditions. Moreover, within each of our traditions we recognize significant divergence in different attitudes to and positions regarding the Holy. Thus, to take two extreme positions, while many mystically informed stands of Judaism place a heavy premium on notions of holiness as defining the essence of religion, and see holiness as an inherent and essential quality, many schools of early Buddhism, as well as the teachings of Zen Buddhism offer an outright rejection of the notion of holiness, and its attendant divisions, hierarchies, constructs, and categories. While various forms of Buddhism, especially of the Mahayana school, did develop de facto recognition of holiness, as this attaches itself to people, places, rituals, etc., one must recognize that holiness is valued in very different ways in Buddhism compared to the Abrahamic faiths or even to Hinduism.

Even traditions that place a high premium on holiness do not necessarily exhibit a single understanding of it. At the one extreme, one may consider "holiness" to be the making of space, of setting apart, of various aspects, such as time, space, or people. "Holiness" thus understood emphasizes the human action of setting apart and its normative and sociological implications. The opposite understanding emphasizes the essential and ontological dimensions of holiness. That which is "holy" has some inherent and essential characteristic that sets it apart from that which is "profane," and even more, that which is impure and unholy. Some of the classical scholarly treatments of holiness assume some dimension of this latter, essential, sense of holiness. Thus, Rudolph Otto, in his classical work "The Holy"[1] refers to the numinous character and to the characteristic of the holy that is made manifest through acts of setting apart. Even more explicit is the treatment of holiness

1

by Mircea Eliade. Holiness serves as a core concept in his work, with "The Sacred and the Profane"[2] being but one of the many places where Eliade treats the subject. In Eliade's understanding, the holy is indeed a manifestation of another order of being, finding its expression in our life through the various forms of manifestation and revelation captured in religion. It would seem that some of our religious traditions treat holiness more along the human, legal, institutional side. Others emphasize the essential dimension. A broad generalization, misleading as all generalizations are, allows us to consider Islam as approaching holiness in the former sense, while much, though not all, of Judaism approaches holiness in the latter sense.

With such varieties in the understanding of holiness, in what sense can we refer to "the Crisis of the Holy" as something that different religions can address? It should be stated at the outset of the present project that we do not assume a uniform understanding of holiness. In one sense, "the Crisis of the Holy" is simply a catchy phrase. It points to an area of concern, rather than to a strictly conceived theological understanding that would be claimed as common to all religions. Thus, in a minimal sense, one need not conceptualize religion in terms of "the Holy," as we noted above with reference to Buddhism, to find the topic relevant. However, there may be more to the present project than simple concern for the well-being of religions and their institutions. Discussions about "religion and secularity" or "religion and modernity" abound. The overlap between the present discussion and sociologically based discussions that examine the present state of a given religion or religion in general in contemporary society is, of course, significant. Yet, our project aspires to something more than a neutral sociological description of religion in change, or even of religion in crisis.

It is recognized that the term "Holy" is not employed in equal ways by all religions. Nevertheless, it figures heavily both in most religious traditions and in much scholarly discussion of religion as a phenomenon. Hence, in using it we appeal, at the very least, to a broad, if not universal, convention. Some traditions or conceptualizations of religion may substitute terms such as "ultimacy," "transcendence," or "purpose." The point is that the choice of language suggests concerns that bridge the external perspective with the concerns that are proper to religions as systems of meaning, seeking to address that self-same external perspective from the perspective of their own mandate of providing meaning.

The present project grows out of the concerns of religious leaders, representing different religious traditions. It thus grows from within religion, or better yet: religions in dialogue. As such, it touches upon some of the ultimate concerns of religion. While survival and transformation are, of course, core concerns of any religious tradition, there are other aspects that are broached through the present posing of the problem. These concern the ultimate purpose and viability of religion. In this sense, to speak of "the Crisis of the Holy" is to suggest that the composite situation, to be described below, touches upon core issues that are deeper than the concern for continuity and transformation in religious institutions. Growing out of the initiative of religious leaders, the present project seeks to consider the relationship between religions and contemporary reality also through the lens of the ultimate purpose and significance, the *telos* of religions. As such, it is a project that combines perspectives that are both external and observation-based, such as sociology, and internal and reflection and theology-based. We thus engage in an attempt to think the complex situation of "the crisis" in terms that are not simply descriptive, in an attempt to gage the possible significance of the crisis for the religions themselves. The present project undertakes to examine the "Crisis of the Holy" from a perspective that combines the observations and the descriptions of the outsider with the intuition that seeks to bring about positive growth and transformation, appropriate to the insider. We seek to stimulate a healthy exchange and reflection among and beyond the religious leaders, who felt the need in the first instance to devote thought and attention to the "Crisis of the Holy." Thus, "the Crisis of the Holy" is more than a clever phrase inasmuch as it points to a dimension of ultimacy and of transcendence that is challenged by the "crisis."

There are several underlying assumptions that inform the present project. The first is that there is indeed a crisis. Moreover, that crisis impinges itself as a significant factor in the minds and realities of religious leaders as well as practitioners. Secondly, while each religion may live the crisis in its own terms and in ways particular to its own structures, it seems (and so much of the present project is indeed based upon impressions, even if learned ones), there is something common to the crisis of all religions. And in some sense the commonalities may outweigh the individual particularities, thereby making this crisis a subject worthy of sharing between different religions. We were wary that by attempting to offer a common definition of "the Crisis of the Holy," this project ran the risk of flattening significant differences and nuances between the traditions. However, our writing process has allowed the different voices to emerge while responding to the same set of questions. Finally, if something is common to all traditions, then how we deal with it may also be similar. We may thus reflect upon concrete strategies for dealing with the problem in a collaborative framework. We may even be able to share strategies and coping mechanisms across different traditions.

This brings us to one of the key insights that has informed our work as a group. To speak of "crisis" has negative connotations. The implied understanding is that the old is good, and that it is in some way threatened. Indeed, this may be the case and many religions may feel themselves precisely in such a position. Nevertheless, the "crisis" contains within it also seeds of growth, potentiality for transformation. Threat may be the starting point of the crisis. Yet, along with threat come challenges and opportunities as well.

Religions are challenged to address new situations and with that comes the opportunity for growth, for transformation, for purification, for discovering new forms and new meanings within religion. The crisis need not, therefore, be viewed as exclusively negative. It contains within it also possibilities for growth and transformation, opportunities and challenges for realizing the ultimate purpose of religion.

This statement is to a large extent based upon a view of religion that needs to be spelled out, namely: *religion as process*. The view of crisis in relation to religion could address religion as static or dynamic entities. As static entities they may be thought of as fixed and closed systems, given from the beginning in their wholeness and thus perfect both historically and ideally. Against such a view, to admit crisis is to acknowledge a fundamental breakdown in tradition and to recognize that deep imperfection has set in. Moreover, the only response to such an understanding of crisis would be the attempt to return to the original wholeness, short of which all else is imperfect. For such a view, crisis is a threat to be overcome.

The alternative to such a view is a dynamic understanding of religion, as capable of growing and adapting itself to changing circumstances. Accordingly, the core spiritual impetus or vision adapts and accommodates itself to changing times, circumstances, and challenges. According to such a vision, the crisis holds in it also the seeds of growth and positive transformation. What we experience as crisis may actually be the spiritual growth pangs of religion, as it becomes increasingly attuned to the will of God, or to its original purpose, given present circumstances. The history of religions is, according to such a view, a rich dialectic of stability and change, of continuity and challenge.

It is this latter view that informs the present collection of essays. In our understanding, the challenge of the crisis contains the seeds of transformation. Difficult and painful as it may be, taking a critical view of one's own religion is not necessarily a bad thing to be avoided. Rather, it is a challenge and although those most challenged by it are the religious leaders who invited us to reflect on these issues, it extends beyond them. Offering an overview of the crisis is an invitation to all members of religious communities to engage in constructive reflection upon the ways religions are called to grow in accordance with the higher design, made manifest at this point in time.

IS "THE HOLY" IN CRISIS?

Posing the question in this way points to the absurdness of taking the title of our project in the most literal sense. All would agree that the Holy itself cannot be in crisis. To the extent that "the Holy" is an epithet for divine or transcendent or ultimate reality, we should recognize that in its ultimacy this reality is not threatened by any of the factors that go into making the present "Crisis of the Holy."

Nevertheless, it may be equally false to simply state that "the ultimate" is happy in the heavens, while all problems reflect only crises in human institutions and organizations. The crisis is more significant than worring about declining church membership or increasing rates of assimilation in the Jewish community. If one is willing to accept the premise that the ultimate, the divine, is engaged in a project with humanity, and that within that project religions are formed as vehicles for education, transformation of society, and the guiding of individuals and collectives to the good life, understood also in terms of higher spiritual realities, then the crisis may be located not simply within the human dimension of religion but at the interface of the human and the divine as well. In other words: as a time of change and transformation, brought about through the conglomeration of elements to be described below, this point in time also constitutes a challenge for how ultimate reality is expressed through the vehicles of religion. If by "crisis" we refer not only to the negative expressions of the crisis but also to the challenges and opportunities that it includes, then in some sense it may be appropriate to refer to the "Crisis of the Holy" proper. In other words, there may be a sense in which the crisis is not simply a sociological matter, something to be described through the tools of sociology, but also something of metaphysical significance, calling for theological reflection and understanding.

It is here that we may locate the uniqueness of the present project. We are seeking to consider ways in which the "Crisis of the Holy" may serve as a basis for creative reflection by scholars and religious leaders. The kind of reflection we envision goes beyond the merely descriptive sociological analysis. It calls for thinking from within about the challenges and opportunities created by the crisis. As such, it maintains a perspective on religions as vehicles for "the Holy," and seeks to engage religions from the perspective of their ultimate meaning.

Let us, then, turn our attention now toward the various dimensions of that complex reality that we have chosen to address as "Crisis of the Holy." The phenomenon is broad and complex and is made up by a variety of forces and circumstances. In what follows, various phenomena will be grouped under major group headings. The first of these touches upon what has been suggested as the uniqueness of our project: reference to the ultimate purpose of religion.

"THE CRISIS OF THE HOLY" AS A CRISIS OF PURPOSE

The most important aspect of "Crisis of the Holy" touches upon the ultimate meaning and purpose of religions. Are religions able to achieve their ultimate stated spiritual purpose? Perhaps the most important area for reflection is to what extent the series of factors listed below and the accumulated pressures they exert upon the forms of religion impede the spiritual functioning of religion. It is recognized that to speak of the *telos* of religion assumes a particular spiritual worldview or vantage point, other than the purely descriptive perspective of religions *as they are*. This, however, is precisely the perspective appropriate for religious leaders and for religious thinkers. Hence, it informs the present reflections.

There are multiple levels of loss of meaning and purpose. Sometimes the loss of spiritual purpose finds expression in religions being concerned with their own physical survival. The sum total of pressures exerted upon religions may paralyze their ability to lead their believers to the stated spiritual goals of the religious traditions. Emphasis upon the concrete forms of religion and the attempt to safeguard them may lead to over-identification with these forms, at the expense of using them as vehicles to achieve their ultimate goals. Broader perceptions of religion often reinforce such loss of ultimacy and transcendence. For example, in a variety of circles, religions—individually or collectively—are configured as cultures. Emphasis upon culture is often an attempt to uphold religion as something of enduring value, despite a secular perspective from which religion is viewed. Thus, human, social, or cultural values are highlighted at the expense of those elements of religion that address the ultimate, the beyond, the transcendent. However, loss of *telos* need not be limited to the transcendental dimension of religion. Religion addresses broader social reality and contains a social vision. In certain instances an inwardness produced by the "Crisis of the Holy" leads to withdrawing from the broader social arena and to the loss of social vision particular to the tradition.

One may consider both dimensions of loss of *telos* as expressions of a yet broader phenomenon. Religions are comprehensive systems, better yet: comprehensive systems of providing meaning to life. Religion addresses both the ultimate, usually the hereafter, and the here and now in all its concrete manifestations. Ideally, religion provides meaning to all individual, family, social, national, universal—and one may go on in naming the relevant aspects—expressions of life. Whether it actively and directly controls all aspects of life or not, religions nevertheless ideally have the task of charging them with meaning. One important way of characterizing the "Crisis of the Holy" is precisely that such comprehensiveness is lost. If in former times religion was the norm, providing the canons of interpretation for life in all its diverse aspects, today religion may be considered the alternative, the break, from the norm. The norm of life is often set by market realities and the unrelenting pressures of work. These shape life, while religion is relegated to a mere break from this unrelenting pressure. Consequently, a more fragmented way of making sense of life is often the norm. Political forces, market forces, science and technology, psychology, and any number of additional forces have each carved out slices of life and provided them with an interpretive framework through which meaning is provided. Religions collectively have been challenged to either integrate a variety of competing systems of endowing meaning into their own worldview or to justify from within the resources of their own self-understanding why both control and meaning-giving should be relinquished in favor of competing systems of providing meaning. As more and more dimensions of life are seen outside the range of the interest of religion and as more and more of life is surrendered to the many forces competing for control, religion gradually ceases to be the broader factor that endows, orients, and structures life. To recognize this breakdown of the holistic and integrated function of religion and the resultant tensions, competitions, and mechanisms through which religions address the breakdown is perhaps to gain the broadest perspective upon the "Crisis of the Holy."

CREATING THE CRISIS: RELIGION UNDER EXTERNAL PRESSURE

The association of religion and crisis may not, in and of itself, be new or unique to the present point in time. One may claim that some sense of crisis is fundamental to any form of religion. If religion negotiate between ideals and realities, the strive for the ultimate and its realization in the here and now, some sense of tension, failure, and crisis is inevitable. Indeed, some of the foundational stories of different religious traditions hinge on crisis, built into the fabric of their view of life or history. Crises have been present in different forms in all religions' histories. Some of those crises are also part of the contemporary challenges facing religion. For example: issues of identity, as these play themselves out in the relations between religions today are a continuation of centuries-old tensions. The same holds true for issues of authority and group definition within the Christian world, a problem that continues to inform crisis in a Christian context. Nevertheless, there is something unique about the present point in time, when considering religions, in their plurality, and crisis. When the various factors we are about to consider are taken in their totality, they amount to unprecedented pressure upon religion. The variety of factors and their intensity suggest this situation is unique in history. What is certainly unique is the fact that the various factors are not affecting one single religious tradition, or even several. Rather, what we refer to as the "Crisis of the Holy" is affecting all our religions collectively. Despite differences in emphasis, particular to one religion over and against another, there are broad commonalities that affect *all* religious traditions, thereby making the crisis a global phenomenon. Thus, to the extent that the

"Crisis of the Holy" consists of opportunities, as much as threats, these broad phenomena, common to all of our religions, are in fact possibilities for growth for all of our religions and hence suggest new possibilities relevant to all our religions.

The following paragraphs constitute a partial catalogue of the external factors bringing pressure to bear upon our religions. While the list may not be exhaustive, it is suggestive of the breadth, variety, and intensity of factors affecting the forms religions take and the ways in which they are challenged to address contemporary challenges.

We begin this catalogue by pointing to the phenomenon of globalization. Along with the economic and the political dimensions of globalization come also strong influences in the fields of ideas, ideology, and lifestyle. While not necessarily impacting religion directly, they do impact life in society in significant ways that affect religion globally. Thus, the forces of globalization serve as carriers for many of the attitudes, habits, and new forms that religions are taking. Media and mass communication play, of course, a central role in creating a single culture around the world, thereby leading to the creation of common attitudes in parts of the globe previously separated by deep cultural divides.

Technology too is ubiquitous, its fruits being enjoyed worldwide. However, along with the spread of technology comes the challenge it presents. As technology gives control over greater areas of life, this sense of control of human creativity can potentially challenge religion. The increase in human autonomy and power may, though it need not always, create the sense that various arenas of life can be controlled and determined through human initiative and its technological feats. This could, and often does, lead to a sense of the diminished relevance of religion in providing meaning to those areas. It is not argued here that this is a necessary consequence of the spread of technology. Often it is a consequence of what may be termed "scientism," a pseudo-scientific attitude or one that exhibits excessive faith in the power of science and its rational premises in providing answers to absolute questions and providing directions in facing all contemporary challenges, simply on the basis of scientific and technological knowledge alone.

Technology initiates change in religion even when it does not threaten religion directly. Two examples suffice. Through technology, holy sites previously accessed only by means of arduous pilgrimage, are now accessible within the click of a mouse. Notions of sacred time and place are thus challenged and transformed through the possibilities provided by technology. Technology also leads to the spread of knowledge and its greater accessibility. While this might seem as a fulfillment of religious ideals to some, in other ways it threatens traditional forms of religion. The secrecy attached to certain ancient bodies of knowledge is undermined, leading to shifts in the sociology and spread of knowledge. Similarly, authority is challenged and reconfigured as knowledge spreads and the boundaries of the canon are potentially redrawn, by means of technological advance.

Further expressions of the sweeping effects of ideological trends throughout our world may be found with reference to the effects of secularization. While statistical studies do show that most societies still consider that religions play a major role, there is also a strong tendency to secularization that is affecting all religions, leading to drop in membership along with increasing distance and criticism toward religion. Often secularization is a by-product of economic progress, contact with western, perhaps better yet: European, trends. While different societies and religions experience secularism in different ways, there is a rise in secularism, especially among elites. Thus, while some forms of secularism may not be anti-religious in and of themselves, the overall dominance of secular ideologies in the western world constitutes a serious challenge to religions.

Along with an increase in secularism, we may note the effects of democracy and its spreading to new territories. This is not to suggest that democracy is inherently incompatible with a religious worldview. Nevertheless, along with democracy comes also an appreciation for the role of the individual and a potential decline in the status of traditional figures, structures, and institutions of authority. Further ideological support for these tendencies is found in the rise of a variety of related ideals and values, primary among which is the notion of human rights. In fact, universal ideals that are broader than the individual, such as environmentalism and animal rights, can potentially exert additional pressures upon religions, thereby indirectly bringing further pressure to bear upon the individual, in relation to collective religious identity. The upshot of it all is that individual choice, quest, and identity emerge as factors that must be reckoned with by religions and their structures of authority, in ways not imagined by earlier generations.

There are other, less ideologically justifiable, aspects of globalization that deeply affect religion. Consumerism is an important by-product of globalization. The primary driving force through which ideas and attitudes spread is, of course, economical. This drive creates consumer societies, wherever buying-power, coupled with the possibility of implementing a particular lifestyle, permit it. The effects of consumerism on religion can be devastating. In a culture that sees reality through the lens of consumer reality, religion too becomes a commodity. Thus buying religious objects could replace genuine spiritual practice. The rise of religious tourism, noted below, certainly contributes to this tendency. From here arises also the growing phenomenon of treating religion as one more item on a supermarket shelf, picking and choosing the appropriate brand, or the mix and match of religious practices, as though they were pieces of apparel of a (divine) designer's wardrobe. The effect of such mentality on the stability of religious institutions and on their perceived authority is obvious. Religions are forced to sell themselves, and are thus transformed in the process. Consumerist mentality, applied to religion, creates a new type of religious competition. Earlier theological competition can give way to a competition driven by market forces, as these become intertwined with religious concerns. One instance of such "commodification" of religion is the creation of religious superstars (such as certain popes or the Dalai Lama) by media and market forces. While not as ideologically motivated as some of the other movements and tendencies discussed here, the sheer power of consumerism as a way of life has profound impact upon how religion is perceived and how in turn it is made to function.

One important factor that is related to the changing landscape of growing individuality and the insistence of various groups upon their rights and claims for specific and adequate identity and recognition is the challenge of feminism. Feminism constitutes a critique of traditional forms of religion and in its secular versions provides a strong challenge, as well as strong alternative perspective, on society and reality than those often espoused by traditional religions.

Feminism, as well as scientism, are worldviews, even epistemologies in their own right. We may also consider historicism a critical epistemology, affecting the view of religion. Thus, the ability to reduce religions to historical developments and thereby to emphasize their historical contingency provides one, among several, critical epistemologies, that weaken the absolutism associated with religion, its status, truth claims, and authority in earlier periods. One particular mental attitude, common in particular in the so-called post-modern period, is that of relativism. Accordingly, all religions are but relative expressions of the same, or similar realities. Religion cannot make absolute truth claims and its institutions and authorities falsely claim absolute validity for their teachings. Relativism touches at the heart both of the relationship between one religion and another and of the relationship between religion and other systems of endowing meaning. A broader relativistic view thus undermines the public standing of religion.

Erosion of religion's authority and standing need not be direct. There are forces in society that contribute to such erosion even without targeting religion in an intentional or focused way. Two examples suffice.

The family is a primary locus for the practice of religion. It is where religion is learned, celebrated, and transmitted. Broadly speaking, society is witnessing significant changes in the understanding and function of the family. Indeed, in the present context we may refer to a crisis of the family, as a parallel crisis, that ultimately is refracted in "Crisis of the Holy." The breakdown, leading to the eventual redefinition, of the meaning of family has direct repercussions on the knowledge of, transmission of, and capacity to celebrate religion.

A second, less dramatic, but nevertheless interesting, example is that of religious tourism. This is not a reference to pilgrimage, that actually assumes new and original forms, in response to the "Crisis of the Holy." Rather, this is a reference to the unprecedented possibilities that modern travel presents for visiting religious sites, worldwide, in a context that is no longer traditional or religious. While modern travel is not in and of itself negative, the question must be posed of what are the consequences of widespread practices as these create new approaches and views of religion. In what way do traditional understandings of sacred space, sacred time, and ritual become eroded through new habits that lead to exposing the intimacy of one's religion to the gaze of the visiting other? Trivial as this case may be at first hearing, it actually portrays fundamental issues and difficulties that bring us to the heart of our crisis.

THE CRISIS AS THREAT: THE STRUCTURES OF RELIGIOUS INSTITUTIONS

Needless to say, religions cannot remain the same in view of all the above pressures. The sum total of the pressures and movements mentioned above may be considered in terms of power negotiation. Religions concentrate power and negotiate it. By power is intended both political and social power, as well as a means of guiding a variety of expressions of power in life. In fact, power and its negotiation in accordance with their own stated ideals constitutes one of the greatest of challenges for religions, as these find themselves cyclically in positions at times closer and at times further removed from a place of influence on power in the concrete spheres of life. The "Crisis of the Holy" may thus be seen as a threat to the powers of religion. Its primary challenge is to the authority of established religious structures. The processes here described amount to a challenge, at times even a denial, of the power and authority of religious traditions and their structures.

One of the immediate effects of these forces is the increasing demand on equality within religious structures. The demand for equality will, of course, find different expressions in different traditions. Thus the push for equality in face of the traditional Hindu caste system, the push for more democratic processes within ecclesiastical structures or the push for broader diffusion of knowledge within religious movements that had previously exercised control over knowledge and its dissemination.

What is under threat is thus the stability of religious institutions. And more is at stake than simply the authority of religions, measured in the degree that adherents follow the commands of religious leaders. By stability of religious institutions we refer to the very viability of religious institutions, measured in the long run. Monastic orders, both east and west, are undergoing change, but also frequently decimation. Similarly, religious traditions that depend on transmission frequently remain without the next generation to continue the tradition. While all traditions may be touched by such lack of continuity, perhaps the variety of subtraditions of Hinduism are most affected by it. Yet, the challenge of transmission of knowledge and its continuity challenges all of our traditions.

THE CRISIS: HABITS OF MIND

If the objective threats to the physical stability of religious institution is one pole through which the crisis is expressed, the subjective attitudes of mind that are brought to bear upon religion are the other. Indeed, it may be argued that at the core of the crisis are attitudes, ideas, and habits of mind, that eventually impinge upon the concrete and institutional expressions of religion. Turning our attention to the habits of mind characteristic of the crisis we may best begin with individualism as a feature of the contemporary mind. Highlighting the individual as an ideal, as witnessed by several of the forces listed above, has significant consequences for the overall standing of religion. We have already noted some of those, such as the increasing pressure for democratization and broader diffusion of knowledge, along with the pressure to increase representation and opportunity for previously under-represented groups, foremost among which are women. But there is more to the emphasis upon the individual. Here too we may consider positive and negative expressions of such individualism.

On the one hand we note a sense of distance and disconnectedness of individuals, in relation to religion. Thus, to use Max Weber's term,[3] we may speak of disenchantment with the spiritual life, having lost the power of attraction and interest, this having been taken up by some of the other forces spelled out above. A related, though not identical expression, of flailing individual relationships to the collective may be found in the recognition of alienation, as an almost all-pervading phenomenon in relation to each of our religions. Thus, there are broad segments of religions' former membership that suffer from alienation in relation to religions and their structures. The youth are prime carriers of such sentiments of alienation, but not exclusively so. In part, the sense of alienation hinges upon the fulfillment, or lack thereof, of the quest for democratization and representation, referred to above. The consequences of alienation are, of course, dropping membership in religious communities. These may be expressed in some cases in terms of lowered attendance in houses of worship and in others in terms of assimilation and of moving out of traditional religious structures.

Yet, alongside these negative expressions of individualism, we also encounter attempts at religious revival and the quest for spiritual meaning, carried out along the lines of individualism. Disenchantment with secularism, modernity, and scientism generate alternative religious responses. Primary among these is the strong quest for spirituality that has come to dominate the private, and to a certain degree public, religious landscape. Spirituality is slowly gaining standing and is becoming the appropriate buzz word through which that which is essential in religion is portrayed. The quest for spirituality finds various expressions both in and beyond religion. Within religious traditions there is any number of attempts to recast, rediscover, or configure anew the significance of established religion in light of spirituality in general, or more particularly—in light of the spiritual heritage of the individual religious tradition. Yet, spirituality cannot be contained within one particular religion. Often, the quest for spirituality leads to borrowing and sharing of religious traditions, across traditional religious lines, in an attempt to deepen religious awareness. Some contemporary phenomena such as the so-called *Jew-Bu*, that is, Jews who seek their spirituality through the practice of Buddhist meditation and other forms of practice, are expressions of the quest for spirituality cutting across religious traditions. More broadly speaking, the so-called new age is a broad and not fully defined attempt to highlight spirituality as an alternative to existing religious forms. The great suspicion with which it is met by traditional religious authorities testifies both to the need it fulfills and to the threat it constitutes. Established religions are wary both of the competition and of what they consider immature and eclectic spiritual practices. The "new age" is often, perhaps usually, syncretistic, drawing upon various mixed religious traditions. The ultimate arbiter of the value of those traditions and of how they are to be put into practice is the individual herself. Hence, one may recognize here a consumerist expression of the individual quest for spirituality.

But perhaps the most strident expression of the tension between traditional forms of religion and the contemporary quest for spirituality may be found in what originated in a slogan, but seems to be gaining the status of a movement: I am spiritual, not religious. To thus juxtapose religion and spirituality is to suggest the latter's autonomous standing. It is the height of expression of individual religion, divorced from traditional forms, seeking new expressions for individual realization, while consciously rejecting traditional religion.

THE NEW FORMS OF RELIGION

Of course, traditional religions cannot remain impervious to the challenges posed by the crisis and to the attitudes of mind that are characteristic of it. There is not one response, typical of religious traditions. Multiple responses characterize the different traditions. What they all have in common are the new forms they take in response to the crisis. Forms that religions adopt in response to crisis, be it the current aggregate of factors or earlier crises characteristic of the various stages of modernity, colonialism, secularism, and the likes, are in many ways unanticipated. They come at the expense and sacrifice of some portions of tradition that are relinquished in the process of shaping a new religious response to the perceived threat. Thus, crisis in general, and the present "Crisis of the Holy" end up shaping religions in new ways. Some of these ways may be creative, many represent a loss, and may be judged as a more imperfect form of the religious traditions compared with their own past and ideals. Let us note some examples.

As the chapters in this volume will suggest, some of our religions suffer from a form of corporate religion, or as called by other observers—syndicated religion. By this is meant a form of religion that highlights the collective, its values, and ideals at the expense of classical spiritual ideals associated with the tradition. One could see how a response to excessive individualism might be an excessive emphasis on the corporate elements of the same tradition. Thus, both Hinduism and Islam know of attempts to cast national, political collective identities, that are identified with the tradition. These attempts serve as powerful social and political forces within the respective traditions, seeking to create an ideal society, or a coherent collective identity. Yet they do so at the price of distortion and obliteration of that self-same collective memory, which should feed the collective identity. Individual smaller religious traditions, expressions of cultural diversity, a variety of mystical, hermeneutical, and philosophical traditions, are wiped out of memory, as a new collective identity is imposed upon the religion.

Such imposition would be undermined by excessive knowledge or the development of critical and historical awareness of tradition. Hence, portions of tradition are obliterated from memory in what is ultimately a failure of education on behalf of religious traditions to transmit themselves fully from one generation to the next. Uncritical traditionalism is adopted. New and exclusive paradigms are developed in an attempt to create a uniform and triumphant form of the religion.

This form of religion is triumphant both in relation to how it recasts its own past and in relation to other religious traditions. Typically, those forms of religion, cast in the context of an embattled self-awareness, seeking to express itself in the face of collective adversity, also feature the specific religious tradition as superior to other traditions. As such, they tend to be less dialogical, less open to the other, and less open to introspection and self-criticism.

While there are many dimensions to the term *fundamentalism*, and not all are necessarily relevant to the present description, much of what is called fundamentalism may be viewed in the context of the "Crisis of the Holy." The uncritical reliance upon traditions, seen in isolation from others, from broader society, and cast in ways that are ultimately distorting of the history of the individual religious tradition are marks of fundamentalism as it is relevant to the concerns of the "Crisis of the Holy." In the context of the present discussion, we may suggest that the need to respond to the crisis by creating new and appropriate religious forms, leads to the emergence of fundamentalisms, here viewed as expressions of the crisis. Fundamentalism, thus defined, is a phenomenon that cuts across religious traditions. To the extent that all our traditions are beleaguered by the challenges of the crisis, they all develop some form or another of fundamentalism, respective to their own internal understanding and the sense of authenticity and faithfulness to historical memory appropriate to those traditions.

It would be a mistake to represent the forms of religion as exclusively limited to reactionary forms generated by the crisis. Alongside those we also encounter alternative and creative forms intended to replace the forms of religion under critique. Much as the breakdown of the traditional family is accompanied by the rise of new forms and new definitions of the family, so we note the rise of alternative forms of religion. Returning to the influences of feminism upon religion, we note the rise in the role of women in all religious traditions. The rise of religious feminism leads to various new forms of religion, involving redefinition of traditional roles of authority, knowledge, and worship.

All religions also experience the rise of alternative forms of leadership and authority within them. This is true of the rise of lay leadership and the increasing shift of authority and power from religious officials and virtuosi to broader segments of society. The quest for spirituality also produces new forms of leadership, at times more capable of addressing spiritual concerns proper. The situation is in some ways analogous to the relationship between classically practiced medicine and the slow rise and increasing acceptance of alternative means of practicing medicine. The quest for health and healing seems to be pointing in the direction of the integration of alternative forms of healing within the conventional norms of medical practices. Similarly, it seems that alternative religious forms are gradually becoming integrated into traditional power structures. New emphases upon aspects of tradition coupled with the rise of alternative leadership amount to emerging new forms within the religious traditions themselves.

PRESENTING THE CRISIS OF THE HOLY

Overarching Perspectives

It should be obvious by now that it is impossible to offer a definitive analysis of all aspects of the "Crisis of the Holy." The crisis as described above is broad and encompassing. It straddles traditions, finding varying expressions in different religions and their subtraditions. It is therefore both beyond the scope of the present study and beyond the abilities of the authors of this volume to offer an exhaustive presentation of the crisis so broadly conceived. The goals we set ourselves are, therefore, more modest. The first among these is the attempt to bring together the disparate elements described above within an overarching conceptual framework. It is hoped that such grouping will allow religious leaders an overview of a broader situation, through which they may be inspired to reflect upon the crisis not simply in relation to individual components, as these present themselves, but seen in a broader scope. The challenges and opportunities for traditions could thus become more apparent when a synthetic perspective on the crisis is offered.

A second purpose of the project is to raise awareness both among religious leaders and among the thinking religious regarding the crisis as a topic worthy of consideration. Such raising of consciousness regarding the topic holds the promise of constructive thought and greater reflexivity when addressing issues related to the crisis.

But we also hope to achieve more by entering a discussion of "Crisis of the Holy." The goal of good analysis is also to provide tools through which a topic might be approached. Getting a conceptual handle on a topic is an important step in addressing it and seeking to find appropriate responses to it. Fresh insight and conceptual grasp may even pave the way to new practical initiatives and strategies in approaching the crisis. We have thus sought to enter a more detailed discussion of aspects of the crisis through particular conceptual frameworks. Two such frameworks were examined in the context of preparing the present volume. While both figure to some extent in the final presentation, one figures more heavily.

The first conceptual handle concerns comprehensiveness and totality. As noted above, one way of describing the crisis is as the breakdown of earlier comprehensive systems that offer meaning to all aspects of reality. The crisis is thus a breakdown in comprehensiveness. If that is indeed the case, one response to the crisis might be the quest to rediscover or reintroduce comprehensiveness. This, of course, would have to be done in ways that do not constitute a blind return to the past, nor reinforce fundamentalist responses, as described above. It is possible to entertain ways of restoring lost comprehensiveness without undermining those elements considered positive in and of themselves, even while recognizing the ways in which they challenge religion. Thus, the quest for a new comprehensiveness of meaning and a search for how religion might address all aspects of life, discovering a new comprehensiveness, might be one way of getting a conceptual handle on the crisis and developing responses to it.

The second conceptual handle, and one that figures more heavily in this work, concerns the relations of individual and collective. Upon analysis of the various components of the crisis we noted just how many issues and agendas are related in some way or another to the relationship of individual and collective. By this is intended more than simply the tension between individual will and autonomy and the collective mandates of tradition. Phenomena such as the quest for spirituality, the role of women, syncretism and new religious forms, alternative sources of authority, and more all hinge on some relationship of individual and collective. Thus, we considered this axis to be a helpful one in developing conversation and in encouraging new approaches to the crisis.

It should be acknowledged that certain issues that could be considered as part of the crisis will be excluded from the present project. Primary among them are politics and church-state relations. While relevant to a consideration of the crisis, to comprehensiveness, and to individual-collective relations, these subjects are too vast to discuss in the present context, and will therefore not be discussed here. Other aspects relevant to the role of religion in the public sphere will occupy our attention.

Identifying Critical Moments of Crisis

Recognizing overarching concerns through which the Crisis of the Holy may be tackled is one strategy for facilitating a conversation between different religions as they seek to recognize the commonality of their crises and to learn from each other how to better cope and how they might collaborate. The other strategy is to identify specific crises and issues that affect most, perhaps all, of our religious traditions. Identifying particular issues, or moments of crisis, allows us to focus our attention upon the concrete expressions of the broader tendencies spelled out in this overview. These chapters employ both strategies. Alongside the overarching conceptual approach, we have attempted to focus upon specific moments of crisis. These moments are deemed central to the traditions and we found a broad consensus concerning their relevance to the traditions represented in this volume.[4] Accordingly, the authors of these chapters attempted to address these critical moments in their descriptions of the crisis of the Holy in their specific traditions. Not all critical areas are highlighted in the same way in all papers. This is in part due to the difference in how each of these critical issues is experienced in each of the traditions. While the chapters do not follow a strict structure that seeks to address each of these issues, they are deeply aware of these issues, which provide the concrete framework for the entire project. Let us then offer a brief presentation of these moments of crisis.

Integrity and Change of Religious Traditions

In some sense, this is what our project is all about. The Crisis of the Holy addresses change in religions. Change may be welcome or unwelcome. It may undermine the stability of religion or push it toward greater growth. However we may view change, religions are all challenged to change and must cope with this challenge. In the process, they are challenged to identify that which is fundamental to their being, or if we are willing to use the term—essence. The dynamics of stability and change, of recognizing the essential and the changeable in religion are the subtext of the Crisis of the Holy. In this way, the crisis challenges our religions to identify their core and to establish the means appropriate to them for their presence in the world and for the achievement of their ultimate purpose, under and through conditions of change.

Individualism

We have already noted the centrality of this issue in referring to overarching concerns. Perhaps the most prominent battleground on which the Crisis of the Holy is being fought is that of the individual, or perhaps better yet—the range of relations between individual and collective. The most obvious expression is the tension between individualism and the collective structures of religions. But the formation of collective identities and the ways in which these identities are themselves distorting of the historical and spiritual reality of the traditions is but the other side of the coin. To pay attention to this axis and to the tensions brought to bear by the rise of the idea of the individual as expressed in ideology, psychology, and market forces and as these in turns produce interact with religious life, leading to new expressions of religion, is thus to address a core issue that shapes and drives the broader Crisis of the Holy.

Religious Authority

This is one of the most threatened and challenged areas. Virtually all aspects of the crisis converge in relation to religious authority. Change is often geared to changing leadership structures and entitlement to leadership roles. The conceptual rise of the individual further undermines authority. Concerns of gender and youth, spelled out below, obviously play into this issue as well. Shifting balances of religious leadership and community, of consecrated and laity, are significant expressions of the change in religious authority produced as part of the broader crisis. The chapters of this volume were initially presented to a body of religious leaders who, in and of themselves, represented classical religious authority. The purpose of doing so was not to make any specific suggestions regarding how authority should be negotiated in light of the crisis; neither to bolster it nor weaken it. We proceeded from the understanding that we had a mandate from our Board of Religious Leaders to explore challenges and opportunities associated with authority in an open and thoughtful context.

Women

With the increasingly dominant role that women play in society at large, a host of challenges have been addressed to all our religions in relation to religion and gender. These go well beyond the association of women and religious authority and the call to broaden women's position in contexts of religious leadership. Issues of practice, knowledge, representation, and position in the overall economy of religious traditions are matters that all our religions deal with on a regular basis. The convergence of threats and opportunities in the Crisis of the Holy is clearly visible in relation to gender issues.

Youth and Education

Crisis and change touch upon the survival and continuity of religious traditions. These in turn depend upon education and in particular the attitude to the youth within religions. All religions struggle with how to best transmit religion to the next generation and how to avoid the alienation and distancing from tradition that have become symptomatic of the crisis. But youth is only one component of the challenge. Proper religious education is an even broader challenge. It concerns spiritual formation, the attitude to the religious other, attitude to the world at large, and the way tradition should be taught and kept for the future. Change in educational patterns spells change for the shape of tradition to come. Propagation of successful educational patterns ensures not only the survival of traditions but the form they will take in the world and their continued relevance. Religions have always been centers of cultural, religious, and spiritual education. The task and challenge of education are as old as our religions. However, the stakes have risen, in the framework of the crisis of the Holy, and education plays a unique role both in shaping the crisis and in shaping the appropriate responses to it.

Technology

Technology is directly related to education. It has come to shape how we think and view the world. It can create a mindset opposed to that which a given religious tradition seeks to cultivate, or support it, depending on how it is used. Technology affects our knowledge base, by broadening and expanding it. Broader dissemination of knowledge opens up the treasures of traditions, while potentially shaking the ancient vessels in which they were contained. Technology further places great challenges before religion as it touches all areas of life, creating new realities to which religions must respond.

Secularism and Modernity

These are often identified with technology. An interesting symbiotic relationship exists between them, as each carries and reinforces the other. Both secularism and modernity are usually seen as threats to the classical forms of tradition. They undermine it ideologically, as do most forms of secularism, and practically, as does a lifestyle associated with modernity. Whether these contradictions are real or apparent is something that each religion must decide. Thinkers within each of the traditions are often divided on this issue, and hence differing attitudes to modernity and technology.

Media and Image

If secularism and many aspects of modernity are ideologically based, media constitutes a controlling force in contemporary reality that, at least on the face of is, does not espouse a given ideology. Nevertheless, it is a powerful force, shaping life everywhere and exerting important influences upon all religions. Part of the crisis of religion is a crisis of image. How religions are perceived shapes attitudes to their relevance, message, and meaning. It has profound influence upon religious authority and structures. If the Crisis of the Holy is, in some sense, an expression of the state of consciousness associated with religion in the world today, the media play a crucial role in shaping that state of consciousness. Thus, to meet the challenge of media has become an important concern for all religions. While media may be perceived as a threat to religions, it also provides endless opportunities for communication and for religions to reach broader audiences. Even its critical exposure of the ills of religions and their leaders could be considered a blessing, a purification of religions.

The essays explore how these different critical moments in the crisis are played out in each of the traditions, the ways in which they challenge religions, and the opportunities that these challenges present. Considering these eight topics as they are configured in the different traditions allows us to understand the uniqueness of each of our traditions as it struggles with its particular expressions of the crisis and the ways in which our traditions share in common processes of growth and transformation. It is hoped that by opening up this comparative perspective ways will be found for deeper understanding between the traditions that will allow them to move from parallel experiences to collaborative initiatives. By recognizing the deeper commonalities in the contemporary experiences and challenges of our diverse traditions we may be moved to learn from the other how to cope with challenges, to find ways of sharing in the struggle, and possibly to forge a collaborative and common front in reflection and in action in relation to key issues that confront all of our religions as part of "the Crisis of the Holy."

NOTES

1. Rudolf Otto, *The Idea of the Holy: An Inquiry into the Non-Rational Factor in the Idea of the Divine and its Relation to the Rational*, Oxford University Press, 1923.
2. Mircea Eliade, *The Sacred and the Profane: The Nature of Religion*. (New York: Harcourt-Brace, 1959).
3. Max Weber, *The Protestant Ethic and the Spirit of Capitalism*. The original German text was composed in 1904 and 1905, and was translated into English for the first time by Talcott Parsons in 1930. The Routledge edition is available online. http://www.d.umn.edu/cla/faculty/jhamlin/1095/The%20Protestant%20Ethic%20and%20the%20Spirit%20of%20Capitalism.pdf.
4. We are grateful to Mr. Michael Weil for facilitating the process of identifying eight critical issues and specific moments of crisis that are common to our traditions.

Chapter Two

Summary of Essays

Alon Goshen-Gottstein

In what follows, I offer a brief summary of each of the essays in this volume, excluding the previous chapter where the "Crisis of the Holy" was expounded. The summary brings some of the chapters into conversation with one another, drawing out common features, and highlighting the individual chapter's contribution to the ongoing conversation and to the volume's conclusions.

THE CRISIS IN BUDDHISM

Maria Reis Habito and Michael von Brück continue in the footsteps of David Chappell, whose voice is carried through this essay, even though he left for a better world before the project was completed. They devote the first part of the chapter to the meaning of the "Holy" in Buddhism, a religion that developed in large part in response to existing notions of holiness and in rejection of those notions and of the concept as a whole. Nevertheless, in various expressions of Buddhism we find notions, attitudes, and practices of holiness in relation to the three formative principles: the Buddha himself, the Teaching, and the community, and in particular the venerable character of monks. Recognition of these three foci also points to how the crisis impacts Buddhism. As is seen from the essay, the major expressions of the crisis are in relation to the Teaching and the community. The appropriateness of the Teaching and its ways of adapting to the challenges of contemporary life are one important focus of the crisis in Buddhism. The relationships between the different levels of community and in particular between the lay and monastic structures are the second major expression of the crisis. These will be seen in relation to some of the eight moments of crisis identified in the previous chapter.

Central to the analysis is the relation of individual and community. Buddhism grew in societies shaped by value systems in which the individual was subordinated to communal values. The Buddhist teaching of "No-Self" lent further support to these social patterns. Today, due to Western influences and changes that result from modernization, urbanization, and globalization, societies and their behavioral patterns are changing dramatically. This causes tension, which finds different expressions in the various Buddhist countries.

One of the important developments in several Buddhist contexts is a shifting balance between monastic and lay groups. For a variety of historical, political, and contemporary reasons, lay groups in various parts of the Buddhist world are growing in prominence and importance, thereby altering leadership and authority structures. Perhaps no less important is the Buddhist experience according to which the axis of individual-collective leads to the creation of new communities. Thus, an intermediate level exists that allows individuals to regroup in smaller communities. These provide a new face for Buddhism as it develops in different countries.

The pressures of individualism also lead to greater demands for participation of individuals in the religious life. This in turn leads to a shift from earlier emphases of the religion of the masses, such as support of the monks, merit earning, and caring for the deceased, to greater involvement in spiritual matters. A potential spiritual revival may be recognized, for example, in the case of Thailand, where we note increasing time spent in retreats and periods spent in monastic settings. However, this is also accompanied by the danger of spiritual consumerism, itself a factor that accompanies individualism as part of the broader Crisis of the Holy. In Japan, the lay movements have in many instances fully taken over the responsibilities earlier associated with monastics.

Social activism and environmental concern are another expression of new forms that Buddhism is taking. Criticizing the lack of sufficient social-awareness and appropriate response have been important factors in shaping the movement of engaged Buddhists, who broaden the classical concerns of Buddhism into new arenas. These new emphases also make more room for meaningful integration of the individual.

The relationship between individualism and spirituality is perhaps best seen in the adaptation of Buddhism in the West. Buddhism seems able to tap into the desire for spirituality more than any of the other established religions, because it is able to present itself as a spiritual resource that is not tied to particular institutions, community, dogma, or ritual. It therefore attracts many people who have become alienated from their own Christian or Jewish religious institutions. Here too, we note the danger of the quest for spirituality being too closely involved with market forces and hence the danger of the development of a set of spiritual practices that ultimately serve the opposite goal from that intended by these practices in their original context. Thus, the teaching of No-Self and selflessness is in danger of serving a mentality that is egoistic, seeking to fulfill the consumerist desires of the self, as these find expression in the spiritual arena. Thus, a reliable path which is based on proven experience and authority often is lost to many expressions of western Buddhism.

Issues of consumerism are relevant to Buddhism in a further sense. The consumerist and materialist drive are influencing large portions of Asian society, in which Buddhism is a shaping religious force. The same is true for technology, which has a strong grip upon those societies. Yet, while in the West there is also a critical perspective upon the advancement of technology, in Asia the myth of progress is still relevant. Buddhism hardly relates to the problem in consumerism in modern societies on the basis of its own analysis of egoism, greed, and hatred. Most Buddhist institutions refrain from entering a serious discussion of the meaning of their teachings in these fundamental domains that shape the lives of their own constituencies. There is thus a destructive potential in the situation according to which young Buddhists are serving, without adequate direction, two conflicting principles—the spiritual principle of selflessness and the principles of secular materialism. The movement of youth away from religion may be explained as a consequence of the inherent lure of materialism. But it also owes to the inadequate attention of religious thinkers to the balancing of the competing systems and to the ways that Buddhism should address these broader contemporary trends.

Issues of individual and society as well as the influences of western culture converge in relation to women and their position in Buddhist society. Buddhism's adaptation to prevailing social structures is responsible for the strong patriarchal sense and to the secondary role that women play in most Buddhist societies. This finds specific expression in relation to the formation of nuns' orders. While these do exist in some countries, the travails of recognition of legitimate female monastic ordination in others is a sign of the strong patriarchal resistance on the one hand, and of the contemporary pressures, from within and from without, for the broadening of women's position in religion. One direction the issue has taken is the increasing involvement of women in lay Buddhist organizations, but this is primarily true of Taiwan.

Buddhism is particularly well suited to dealing with change as a phenomenon in religion. In its deep analysis of reality, Buddhism shows that everything is change. Humans, however, want to cling to what they desire because they expect stability and unchanging security, which is impossible. This gap is experienced as suffering or better: frustration. Therefore, to realize that all is impermanent is the first insight of wisdom. Change, therefore, is nothing unwanted but a proper assessment of how things are. Consequently, tradition cannot aim at a changeless repetition of past structures and events. Integrity depends on the essentials that make Buddhism what it is, presenting the Teaching in such a way that it can be grasped as the proper means to overcome ignorance, greed, and hatred, in order to attain to wisdom accompanied by compassion. In this, Buddhism may have a Teaching to offer other traditions.

Change is something Buddhism takes for granted, because nothing that is composite is permanent. Therefore change needs neither to be welcomed nor condemned. It is the most fundamental fact of life. The Buddhist teaching of the reality of impermanence implies that one should not fear change and the dissolution of certain forms of knowledge, practice, or institution. Buddhism is highly adaptable; thus, today, laity and especially women play a greater part than in the past. It is important to see this development not as a loss and decay but as chance and opportunity for growth.

Buddhism can flourish under very different circumstances and has adapted itself to many different situations in the past. It can take any crisis as an opportunity to bring out more clearly its message of training the mind for more clarity and compassion so as to contribute to the peace of mind of sentient beings, and finally to overcome all suffering by insight or wisdom and compassion. The Buddhist emphasis on insight and compassion over dogma and institutional concerns is a much-needed resource in a world that is increasingly torn apart by religious fundamentalism.

THE CRISIS IN CHRISTIANITY

Sidney Griffith points out that from the historical perspective, it seems that in every era of their two millennia of church life Christians have been in a crisis of one kind or another about their institutions, their theological formulae, their sources of divine revelation or the exact contour their moral lives should follow. But the idea of a distinctive "Crisis of the Holy" as such seems to have arisen in the minds of modern Christians and non-Christians alike as a result of the perceived rarity on the part of many people in the modern era of an active sense of the ubiquitous power and presence of "the Holy" or even of the Holy One, in modern consciousness. Due to many modern thinkers turning away from a metaphysical awareness to a more materialist philosophy of human consciousness, the intellectual and technological successes of the modern era seem to many observers to have sprung from a psychological divorce by many modern people from the sense of the sacred in human life. This divorce was initiated in the time of the Enlightenment in the West, but it built on the ancient distinction between nature and super-nature. As a result of the success of the Reformation, the "feel" for *"The Holy,"* increasingly became a private concern and not a communal or ecclesial one. As a consequence of this development, in the view of many commentators, religion in Western Europe and America was destined to have only an individual or personal relevance, with nothing pertinent to proclaim in the public sector of human society, while in the private sphere a plurality of religious voices may be expected to be heard. In other words, one result of the perceived "Crisis" of the Holy has been the progressive marginalization of religion, not only in the formation of public policy in the Western democracies but also its disappearance as a serious intellectual concern among the well-educated elite.

From a Roman Catholic perspective, the danger in these developments is the prominence of an attitude of individualism which they promote. In the context of Christian religious life, especially among the Catholics and the Orthodox, for whom the sacraments and the liturgical life, especially the Eucharist, are the privileged moments of the sense of the Holy among them, individualism threatens communion, which is at the heart of the life of the church. The problem is acutely felt in the North American context, where individualism in one form or another, along with an encouragement to escape from older traditions represented as oppressive, has been a driving force in the evolving religious consciousness.

The separation of church and state is the political principle that eventually emerged from the course of Enlightenment thinking just described. Although Christianity has always recognized at least a theoretical separation between secular and religious authority, the church also long taught that civil rulers and states are subject to God's law as interpreted by the church. Consequently, the Catholic Church historically approved of the establishment of the church as the religion of the state in places where Catholics made up the majority of the population. But in dialogue with the modern democracies, especially in the United States, Catholics have made the doctrine of the separation of church and state their own, reserving the right of freedom of religious witness and expression. While the freedom of the individual conscience has long been church teaching, the affirmation of the freedom of choice in religion as a God-given human right of every person in every polity was articulated as such by the Catholic Church most emphatically in the decrees of Vatican II. The Catholic Church expects her faithful members to uphold that what the church teaches is true and good in faith and morals and to work for the acceptance of her moral principles as integral parts of the public policy in the countries where they live. Crises have arisen for Catholics in this connection, as they struggle to reconcile the affirmation of the truth as they see it and proclaim it with the protection of the rights of others as accorded to them by the constitutions of modern, democratic, nation states. Inevitably, in regard to certain issues, this situation of bearing witness to the truth of unpopular or countercultural social or moral values also produces a measure of dissension and disagreement, even crisis, within the church's own ranks about the best ways to achieve the goal of meeting challenges to religious values in the post-modern world. Currently there is a considerable amount of unrest, even polarization among Catholics, over a whole host of issues extending from models of church government to rules of morality, the boundaries of marriage, the importance of the nuclear family, gender "inclusivism," and relations with other religious groups, including the problem of double belonging (individuals claiming to adhere to two different, sometimes seemingly incompatible religious confessions). What is more, because of the unprecedented emigration and immigration of peoples in the twentieth century, Catholics often experience an inner tension between various ethnic groups of Catholics in the same location. There is also a tension between Catholics in America and Western Europe, where there is a sense of loss of direction and diminishment, and Catholics in Asia, Africa, and South America, where there is often a sense of confidence, growth, and increasing demographic significance for the universal church.

Globalization in the Catholic community has also brought about a number of crises in church life. One obvious instance of this phenomenon is the challenge facing the church to inculturate Catholic Christianity into languages and societies outside of the western world, where ecclesiastical thought and practice was first articulated in Greek and Latin and built on the classical heritage of ancient Greece and Rome. A number of modern theologians in the West have also been called to task by the Vatican's Congregation for the Doctrine of the Faith precisely because in a number of important instances it is difficult to see how their efforts to articulate the Catholic faith in the idiom of modern philosophies can be squared with the traditional understandings.

In the context of the globalization of Christianity and the associated problems of inculturation, the issues of missionary activity and proselytism arise in connection with the Crisis of the Holy in our day, in this instance perhaps a perceived crisis in one's readiness, or not, to recognize the holiness of the other. It is undeniable that Christian missionary activity has sometimes not been conducted in a spirit of hospitality and invitation but threateningly, under the protection of colonialist or imperialist enterprises undertaken from a position of political or military power over others. It is in this context that missionary activity becomes part of the Crisis of the Holy. And it is for this reason that in recent years Catholic theologians have been wrestling with the degree to which they might not only repent of the sins of the past, but also at the same time acknowledge in their own terms the truths of other religious cultures, without adopting an unacceptable relativism or indifferentism which would exclude the Gospel imperative to "make disciples of all nations."

Multiple issues of power and authority within the Roman Catholic community have the potential to provoke Crises of the Holy in the experience of church life. They have to do principally with what we call collegiality and

subsidiarity in the governance of the church. They include the relations between the bishops and the Holy See, bishops, and local pastors and their
congregations, and the role of theologians in the teaching ministry of the
church. On the local level, especially in Western Europe and the Americas,
the dwindling numbers of priests and professed religious has become the
occasion for the alternative growth and development of large international
lay movements. These have become very powerful, and they range from the
very conservative, like Opus Dei, to the relatively liberal, like the Catholic
Worker movement in the United States or Pax Christi international. These
groups are in many ways taking the place of the once-powerful religious
orders and congregations in the life of the church and in the process, they are
sociologically reshaping the profile of modern Catholicism.

Another sociological development in the wake of the decreased number
of clergy and religious is the growing laicization of church administration in
many places and the laicization of Catholic education, from the grammar
school level all the way up to the universities, and even in theological and
seminary education.

Gender equality has obviously become a major issue in Catholic Church
life in most countries, extending all the way from concerns for equal access
for women and men to all levels of ecclesiastical service, including the
clergy, to the use of inclusive language in translations of the scriptures and in
the official books of the liturgy. This ongoing concern is still very much a
developing issue. There is no Catholic teaching about the inferiority of wom-
en, quite the contrary, but there are various ideas about the appropriate roles
of men and women in church life.

One may speak of a Crisis of the Holy in the context of a crisis in
education in the sense that the dysfunction in the educational process obviously negatively affects the transmission of the sense of the holy to the
young. And this aspect of the matter has become a moment of crisis in the
larger society in the west, especially in the United States, where there is no
established religion and where virtually every religious tradition in the world
is present. Since by law there may not be any instruction in religion in the
public school system, save in the most generally descriptive terms, and yet
the majority of Americans are in some sense religious, the situation yields a
measure of frustration. This frustration emerges into public view in the context of controversies over educational policy. The current spate of arguments
between "creationists," supporters of an "intelligent design" theory, and "ev-
olutionists" in the United States about how biologists should teach the history of the forms of life on earth, including human life, is a case in point.

A more deeply rooted crisis in the area of education in religion involves
the emergence of relativism in the realm of epistemology and the discernment of the criteria for the perception and transmission of religious truth,
indeed of the sense of truth itself. This crisis is a philosophical one, and it

seems to be a characteristic of modernity and post-modernity. The source of knowledge in religion, in the Christian scheme of things, is twofold: reason and the deposit of revelation, the latter being enshrined in scripture and tradition. There are crises in connection with the discernment of the truth in both of these sources. In the exercise of reason, modern epistemologies and modes of discourse render the expression of truths problematic; in the study of the deposit of revelation, modern historical critical methods and the predominance of critical theory in exegesis have brought relativism into the interpretation of the foundational texts to the extent that the appeal to them for doctrinal or moral teaching has become difficult.

The challenges of interreligious and intercultural dialogue confront Catholics and other Christians at every turn of modern life, beginning within the community itself and extending outward. There is a strong sense that the church should be in communion with other Christian denominations and this calls for ecumenical dialogue. However, there is a measure of resistance to ecumenical or interreligious dialogue within the ranks of Catholics and other Christians and it is often not promoted on the local level nearly as much as it is promoted in the Catholic Church by the Vatican on an international level, or on a national level by national and regional bishops' conferences. Consequently there is a need for intrachurch education not only for the sake of promoting an understanding of the practical value of dialogue for the sake of harmonious interfaith human relations, but even for the sake of the pursuit of the fullness of the truth. The fact of the matter is that religious communities bear a large share of the responsibility for promoting justice and peace in the world, maybe even more than political or military leaders, because so many of the fault lines along which war and mayhem between peoples occur, lie along the religious divisions among them, allowing religious divisions to be exploited in the service of other interests. For all practical purposes, one might say that the best antidote to the threat of a looming "clash of civilizations" is to work to forestall the effects of a clash of theologies by promoting ecumenical and interreligious dialogue.

Griffith's chapter offers us a catalogue of some of the key issues facing the Catholic Church and the ways in which they express the broader crisis of all religions. In considering this broad survey, I am moved to thinking of it in terms of two key terms—"identity" and "mission." By "identity" I refer to a series of questions concerning the identity of the Church and the makeup of its institutions. These are inextricably linked with the question of the purpose and mission of the Church in the world. Thus, the key question would seem to be how broad, or how narrow, is the reach of the Church. Complicated antinomies have to be negotiated here. An all-encompassing message of a life along with respect for the privacy of individual processes and the autonomy of governmental structures; a profound respect for the other and a vision of sharing the perceived truth with others; a history of articulating tradition in given terms and the desire to find the suitable means of acculturating these teachings, seeking to find the balance between authenticity and adaptation; a respect for all members of a community, whose self-understanding is communal and hence inclusive, and the attempt to safeguard various means of privileging the historical forms of tradition, as it privileges religious leadership and in this context is also implicated in significant gender distinctions. In other words, what emerges from this catalogue is nothing less than a question regarding the path the Church must chart in this world, as it constitutes itself and its identity in relation to others and in response to a variety of global forces. More is at stake than simply the preservation of the Church's institutions, even though membership is of concern, at least in the West. Through all these changes and challenges one notices a struggle for articulating the broadest vision of the Church's purpose and for negotiating this vision in terms of contemporary reality.

One notices in Griffith's chapter two major forces that shape Catholic Christianity, or his view of it. On the one hand, the rise of individualism, as this finds expression in relation to issues of authority, gender, education, affiliation, and more. On the other hand, "the other," be it the Catholic other, the Christian other, or the non-Christian other, poses interesting challenges to those navigating the course of the Catholic tradition. Those challenges are both theoretical and philosophical, relating to questions of philosophy, relativism, accommodation and more and practical, relating to issues of how to engage in missionary testimony, celebrate liturgies, and more. Recognition of this dual emphasis could also point to where further reflection is needed as well as to where Catholic tradition might benefit from an exchange with other traditions.

THE CRISIS IN JUDAISM

Barry Levy conveniently breaks his own description of the challenges and opportunities facing contemporary Judaism into a catalogue of individual crises, each of which he treats independently. He does, however, point to two overarching concerns from a Jewish perspective. The first is the rise of individualism, the second is the fragmentation of the Jewish community.

The crisis of individualism manifests in the personal interpretation of religion. Many Jews end up being the ultimate arbiter of the standards of religious practice. Given the choice of varieties of Judaism and differing levels of commitment to it, the individual is ultimately placed in a situation of choosing between the different options and the different degrees of faithful adherence to them. The crisis of individualism is refracted in interesting ways in the crisis of the family. The crisis of this core institution causes a shift in the performance and celebration of religious life from the family to individuals. Thus, greater pressure is brought to bear on individuals, while they themselves are not capable of carrying the load of maintaining Jewish observance on their own. Group and community end up, consequently, playing a more prominent role in facilitating Jewish life. New forms and practices are thereby created. The situation is in some ways similar to that described above in relation to Buddhism, where an intermediate level of community ends up negotiating the broader tension between individual and community at large, producing thereby new forms of the tradition.

The second core crisis, identified by Levy, concerns fragmentation. Levy points to the lack of respect and acceptance between the different stands of Judaism. The issue here is, in a sense, the opposite of individualism. Here corporate politics between the different competing groups seeking to control individual lives encourage antagonism and divide an already small and fragmented group. Levy challenges us to consider how it is that we are able to dialogue across different religious traditions, but are unable to dialogue with our own co-religionists. Fragmentation also has geographic expressions. Different forms of religion are evolving in great centers of learning and in the periphery, where knowledge and observance are weaker. But perhaps the greatest divide is that found in the state of Israel between religious and secular. This constitutes a profound breach within the Jewish people, and ends up shaping the Jewish people, as well as their religion. The fragmentation of the Jewish people leads to great hostility toward religion. Failure to develop a strong middle ground prevents many from recognizing their own tradition. Consequently, few people ever have the option to experience the richness of Judaism in any theoretical or practical way. Thus, the crisis of the Jews has become a crisis of their Judaism, and ultimately of the Holy, inasmuch as the tradition seeks to convey it from one generation to the next and from the people beyond itself. Rather than unite the people, the Holy is enlisted to force them further apart. This, suggests Levy, is the greatest crisis for the Holy itself.

It seems to me that in some sense both crises discussed thus far point to an underlying crisis of identity, a crisis that is treated independently by Levy. Fragmentation is a function of lack of clarity of who we are and what our goal is—a question that is rending the Jewish people asunder. The ability to determine the boundaries of practice and belief in such privatized ways further illustrates the crisis of identity and the mechanisms for its establishment. The crisis of identity is itself a consequence of the complex ways in which Jewish identity is constructed. Religious, spiritual, ethnic, and local-geographic components all constitute identity and also suggest the fault lines along which various identities are to be distinguished from one another and along which competing and conflicting identities are constructed. While Levy's discussion focuses upon the ethnic, cultural, and practical dimensions of the crisis of identity, his broader discussion provides us with additional issues that are perhaps best seen as expressions of the crisis of identity. The role of the state of Israel, both for those living in it and for those outside it, is constitutive of identity. And both the crisis of Jewish education and the crisis of the alienation of women relate directly to the crisis of identity.

But they also relate to the area of spirituality, or what Levy calls "the crisis of Religion without Spirituality." The flip-side of the struggle for constituting identity seems to be its relationship to spirituality. Part of the problem to which Levy points is the entrenchment of religious forms that emphasize practice at the expense of meaning and understanding and that highlight form over its spiritual significance. The ongoing concern for identity, overcoming disunity and, in general, the overarching concern for the survival of the people take their toll on the spiritual dimension of Judaism. While this is one important way the crisis is created, it is also one of the possibilities it contains. The case of Judaism points to how growing individualism is not only a means of shirking full commitment. It is also a means of entering a quest for the deeper spiritual significance of Judaism. Thus, the situation described by Levy contains in it also the seeds for regeneration. The very issues that constitute one face of the crisis might contain in them the seeds, the opportunities, for overcoming other aspects of the crisis. Indeed, it is not inconceivable that even issues of divisiveness and disunity could ultimately be overcome through the discovery of the deeper spiritual significance of the tradition. If reaffirmation of form and boundaries have led to disunity, the spiritual vision and purpose of Judaism might contain the key to desired unity.

THE CRISIS IN HINDUISM

Many of the issues raised in Levy's chapter have close echoes in the chapters on Hinduism and Islam. The defining issue here is identity. Identity is an issue both within and without. It arises as a key issue due to a variety of external circumstances. In the case of Hinduism, as we learn from Deepak Sarma, these have colonial roots. The view of Hinduism by outsiders has led to a history of reconfigurations of the tradition, and raised the issue of reform as an important issue. But perhaps even more pressing are some of the recent changes. The relations between homeland and Diaspora play a critical role, as well as the convergence of national, political, economic, and global forces. The confluence of all these forces creates a profound identity crisis. What does it mean to be Hindu? Who speaks for Hinduism? Is there such a thing as Hinduism? All these questions are raised by Sarma.

Sarma points to ways in which Hindu identity has been constructed legally, and to its intricate relationship with the establishment of the modern state of India and of legal issues that had to be resolved in this context, for example, in the context of the marriage act. Decisions concerning who is a Hindu are thus reached by a state body, with significant disregard for the complexity of the past. Accordingly, paradoxes arise, such as the legal definition of Jains and Buddhists as Hindus. Such flattening of differences is further exacerbated by the rise of Hindu nationalism in the 1990s. This decade witnessed the attempt to create a Hindu identity, culturally, linguistically, and historically.

What all these attempts have in common is the attempt to speak of Hinduism, to some extent or another, in monolithic terms. This leads to what may be called syndicated Hinduism. We find here a corporate identity that is constructed for national or group purposes. Along the axis of individual-collective, the crisis is here located in the overemphasis upon the collective dimension. This overemphasis may come at the expense of the individual— Sarma himself does not discuss the matter. But it certainly does come at the expense of the individual tradition. Thus, individual traditions and their differences are flattened and disregarded in the process of the construction of group identity. This is, suggests Sarma, the greatest crisis for Hinduism, because in the process of attempting to create Hinduism, the very traditions upon which it draws are destroyed. This is not simply a matter of the physical survival of the traditions. Rather, it is a matter of the spiritual constitution of the conglomerate of religious traditions known as Hinduism. The individual traditions are threatened and put under a variety of pressures to change and to adapt.

One arena in which particular pressure has been exerted on individual traditions is the pressure to reform. Sarma points to the case of Madhava Vedanta, one of India's religious communities, that has upheld for centuries a method of teaching that limits access to knowledge. Legal reforms insist on the opening of Hindu religious institutions of a public character to all classes and sections of Hindus. What this means for this particular tradition is that its classical modes of teaching and dissemination of knowledge are called into question. Now, is a tradition that has been forced, due to such outside pressures, to forego a fundamental defining feature of its history and teaching the same as the earlier tradition? What changes and reforms touch upon the heart of a tradition so as to alter it? Such questions are being confronted by many of India's traditions on an ongoing basis.

Just as Levy's chapter pointed to the problems around unity and its relationship to identity, so too Sarma connects the quest for unity with the problem of religious authenticity and the definition of what it means to be Hindu. Interestingly, just as in the case of Judaism a fragmented homeland is charged with providing direction, meaning, and a unifying vision to its Diaspora, so too is the case in India. Consequently, the pressure for establishment of identity is a strong Diaspora need that is radiated back to the homeland, creating an interesting symbiosis with an existing national and political agenda. The need for unity within the community creates new forms of worship in the Diaspora, bringing traditions and means of worship alongside one another in ways never previously imagined. But the quest for unity, as an expression of the quest for identity also has significant educational challenges. How to educate? How to present Hinduism alongside other traditions? These are ongoing concerns. They, in turn, point to a deeper crisis of education and leadership, inasmuch as the local community is not able to meet these needs, due to issues related to classical forms of leadership and education.

Relations between homeland and Diaspora are further complicated by the advent of technology. With modern technology distances are bridged, which in one sense is a good thing. Yet, with this bridging comes further potential transformation of tradition. Thus, pilgrimage is changed through technology. Spatial distances are bridged and what used to be an arduous pilgrimage is now, potentially, accessible within a click of a mouse. How is one to assess the meaning of such change in tradition?

Going beyond Sarma's own chapter, one may point here to the other side of the issue, not raised by him, namely—the role of the individual, as it relates to the collective. If the historical and political movements are pressuring in the direction of group identity, at the expense of the intermediate level community, technology also permits the individual to take a central role in the shaping of religious experience. Technology functions as a means of empowering the individual. Levy's chapter discussed the explosion of knowledge and the variety of books that are suddenly available to every individual through technological means. Similarly, Sarma points to how through technology teaching that has been hitherto esoteric reaches all who are interested in it. So do the remote Temples of India. Thus, the individual is once again thrown into the process of creating, defining, and expanding the religion. If Sarma's own thesis focused upon the relationship between the individual Hindu community and the broader construction of Hinduism, his own discussion of technology allows us to bring in, once again, the tension between the individual person and the community at large. The tensions between the individual spiritual life and the pressures of broader collective identity are even greater in the framework of a religious tradition that is seeking to define itself in a corporate way. This is made explicit in the final chapter on Islam.

THE CRISIS IN ISLAM

Vincent Cornell's analysis of the present crisis of Islam pits against each other in the most explicit way two factors that we have encountered throughout the other chapters—identity and spirituality. The crisis of identity in the case of Islam is not the same as in the cases of Judaism and Hinduism. The issue does not seem to be that there is extensive argument within concerning the definition of Islam. One almost wishes more argument took place. Rather, it seems that large sections of the Muslim world have bought into a particular way of constructing Muslim identity. And this construction, argues Cornell, comes at great cost to the tradition, and ultimately falsifies it. The crisis is thus a deep crisis within, a crisis of identity and of what it means to be Muslim.

Cornell refers to this crisis as an epistemological crisis. Following Alasdair MacIntyre, Cornell uses the term to describe what happens when a tradition of enquiry—such as the theological or philosophical tradition of a religion—fails to make progress by its own standards of rationality. Dissolution of historically founded certitudes is the hallmark of an epistemological crisis and if it is to be resolved, new concepts and frameworks must be developed. The opportunity posed by an epistemological crisis lies in the prospect of coming up with new approaches to tradition that provide innovative solutions through a critical engagement with the past.

The crisis addressed by Cornell is that of Islam dealing with modernity, or with the West. How most contemporary Muslims deal with this crisis is not by engaging directly with God or with the Holy. Instead of calling for a re-enagement with the transcendent, most Muslim responses are cultural. Accordingly, submission to Islam is primarily a submission to tradition (rather than to God), where religion and culture are woven together seamlessly. The epistemological aspect of this cultural model of Islam lies in the fact that Islam is not viewed as simply one tradition, but it is seen as the *only* tradition that contains normative truth. Little or no interest is shown in the history that Islam shares with other civilizations or with the problems that it shares with other traditions in facing modernity. Rather, it is viewed as a self-contained community that exists concurrently with but in separation from other communities.

In this context, opposition to the West plays a defining role in relation to Islam. Identity is here constructed over and against the West. To this end, the West is constructed as secular and godless. Islam is defined in corporate terms, using a reified concept of culture. This is a modern creation based on the nineteenth century view of social science. Strikingly absent from the corporate dichotomy of a reified Islam versus a reified West is any mention of personal salvation or the individual spiritual relationship between the human person and God. Thus, Islam is really *Islamism*, defined through such identity politics that raise the question of whether there is any authenticity to this form of Islam.

Along with attacks on the West are found attacks on modernity, though what is modernity really is rarely if ever discussed. The view of the West as secular and worldly persists among Muslims today, despite strong evidence to the contrary in many parts of the world.

One of the expressions of corporate Islam is the almost exclusive emphasis upon *Shari'a*, Muslim law. Today corporate Islam has little to do with theology, philosophy, Sufism, or the other Islamic disciplines of the past. Such emphasis and the accompanying attempt to seal Islam off from the rest of the world are symptoms of the said epistemological crisis. What Muslim anti-modernists fail to understand is that the transcendence of the modern can only be accomplished through modernity itself, by using modern concepts and methodologies.

Epistemologically, the greatest threat posed to Islam by modernity is the valuation of empiricism above both revelation and theoretical inquiry. Similarly, Muslims have a difficult time dealing with Darwin's theory of evolution, which has become an obsession for many Muslim traditionalists. Consequently, Muslim professional in the technological fields live in two separate worlds. Their professional world is governed by an empirical epistemology while the world of the local mosque is governed by traditional views of truth that have little or no relation to what lies beyond the mosque.

For Muslims, post-modernity can create a profound crisis of the Holy because nothing can be thought of in absolute terms. A world where knowledge and truth are both contested and relativized makes it nearly impossible for the individual to make the right choices, to successfully thread his way through the moral labyrinth of the human condition. All this underlies what may be called the *mal du present* that characterizes much of contemporary Muslim mindset. It is a mindset that leads Muslims, as well as members of other religions, to find solace in a nostalgia for a time when the world was simpler and the choices easier. In Islam, this nostalgia has led to the development of a corporate religion. Believers seek refuge in a traditionalistic yet fully modern utopia that falsely offers Muslims protection from the storms of change. This is, according to Popper,[1] a tribal response to the stresses created by modern open societies, that are criticized as individualistic, while the tribal ideal is collectivistic, traditionalistic, and conservative.

Corporate Islam conceives of God less as a theological construct than as a cultural and ideological icon. Islam, a word that originally meant individual submission to the will of God, has been redefined as a system that unites culture and creed in the context of a divinely guided virtuous society. That this is modern is proven by the absence of theology and metaphysics in contemporary Islam. Personal belief has been reduced to creed and practice to the lowest common denominator. What is most important today is the engineering of society, not the spiritual development of the human being.

The individual tends to be forgotten in the sociological perspective of corporate Islam. This is a major problem of "The Crisis of the Holy," because the original purpose of Islam, like that of salvation religions in general, was to prepare individual souls to meet God. When those who stress the importance of individual salvation are routinely criticized for being socially irresponsible, one must ask whether the world has taken over Islam in the name of Islam itself. The Qu'ran states: "Thusly has Allah shown you the signs so that you may reflect upon them" (2:266). The rise of corporate Islam is one of the signs of these times.

The Egyptian Sufi Ibn 'Ata'illah of Alexandria (d. 1309) wrote a remarkable treatise on the spiritual practice of trusting in God (*tawakkul*) entitled *al-Tanwir fi Isqat al-Tadbir* (Illumination in the Abdication of Personal Agency). In this work, Ibn 'Ata'illah counseled his readers to avoid trying to be masters of their own destiny. Instead, he said, they should accept the age in which they live and see its consequences as a manifestation of the divine will. To be true servants of God they should adapt themselves to present circumstances, "go with the flow," and trust that God will see them through their travails. Ibn 'Ata'illah summarized the essence of this spiritual attitude in a way that is profoundly relevant to the situation of Muslims today:

> When I saw destiny flowing,
> And there was no doubt or hesitation about it,
> I entrusted all of my rights to my Creator
> And threw myself into the current.[2]

The practice of complete trust in God should be seen not as an obstacle to progress but as an essential Islamic attitude, the practical application on the level of the personal ego of the God-consciousness that all Muslims profess to have. Ibn 'Ata'illah's wisdom might allow us to chart a course through modernity without abdicating authentic Islamic tradition. Perhaps the root cause of the crisis is not modernity or post-modernity after all. Perhaps it is the loss of a sense of the sacred, a loss of that spirituality that makes Islam not just a tradition or an identity, but a true submission to the will of God.

NOTES

1. Karl Popper, *The Open Society and Its Enemies: Volume One: The Spell of Plato* (London and New York: Routledge and Kegan Paul, Ltd., 2003): 184-186.

2. Ahmad ibn 'Ata'illah al-Iskandari, *Kitab al-Tanwir fi isqat al-tadbir* (Cairo: al-Matba'a al-Maymuniyya al-Misriyya, 1306/1888-9): 11.

Chapter Three

Buddhism

Michael von Brück and Maria Reis Habito

The feeling of crisis is widespread today and by no means limited to religion. Political and social security, economic prosperity, ecological stability, and the family—to name but a few hot spots—all are in "crisis." Some people diagnose the situation as a change of values while others fear a loss of values, and the reactions range, on the one hand, from fear and conservative clinging to the well established in order to safeguard against waves of uncertainty to aggressive overthrow of traditional structures, on the other.

THE GROWTH OF INDIVIDUALISM

One main area of concern is the growth of individualism on a worldwide scale. In the course of modernization and urbanization, old community structures (family, village community, religious parishes, parties, etc.) are disintegrating in favor of individualism, which creates a sense of being disconnected in various social fields. All societies are affected by the pluralization processes, which change homogeneous structures into several competing substructures so that one religion and one way of life are no longer informing the lives of people; instead, competing options call for conscious choices. This does not necessarily individualize societies, but new groups and organizations are being formed in the process, and religious pluralization can therefore mean a strengthening of groups forming a specific tradition that compete with others that may have a stronger identity than the classical authoritarian and monolithic structures suggest. Some movements are subsumed under the term "fundamentalism"; "traditionalism" can be interpreted in this framework and thus is evaluated in a different light.

Concomitantly, what seems to be individual choice is not at all based on individual decision making but on fashions, trends, and highly suggestive marketing. In this case, the individual is given the illusion of making an individual decision, but in reality he/she is subject to mass manipulation. This is seen in changes of food habits (McDonald's culture), clothing habits (jeans), cultural patterns (international pop culture), etc. It is important to determine whether and to what extent religions are also subject to these quasi-individualizing trends. After all, mass media create events such as the funeral of Pope John Paul II in 2005 or the Dalai Lama's seventieth birthday, and they might do so according to standardized (and standardizing) patterns.

UNDERSTANDING "CRISIS"

Whatever the specific crisis may be, *any* experience of crisis has two aspects that must be differentiated. "Crisis," derived from the Greek verb "krino-mai," means "to separate, to differentiate."

a. Crisis is a turning point in the development of individuals and/or communities related to change. Thus, crisis means to let go of old and known paths, values, institutions etc. This is the cause for a feeling of loss and instability.
b. This change is also an advent of new opportunities, a creative break for new formation and possibility.[1]

Thus, crisis is an ambiguous experience connected with fear or anguish and as well as well as hope and expectation. This experience is also expressed by the Chinese character for crisis (Chin. *wei-ji*, Jap. *kiki*), which contains the two elements of danger and turning point/opportunity.

Talk of crisis is embedded in the Buddhist view of history as a continuous decline of the Dharma teaching. Theories about the decline and eventual disappearance of the Dharma arose in later centuries and were projected back as "predictions" of the Buddha. Buddhist scriptures distinguish between external and internal causes for the crisis. There are two categories for the external causes: incursions from without (meaning foreign invasion and persecution) and excessive state control. Both factors shape the present state of Buddhism around the world. Countries such as China, Tibet, Cambodia, Vietnam, and Laos are trying to revive Buddhist institutions and culture that have been destroyed by Communism. They struggle with the fact that one generation of learned monks has been eliminated through the persecutions and the resulting low state of education. In those countries, including Burma, Buddhism is still heavily regulated through state control.

With regard to the internal crisis, several factors can be singled out from the canonical scriptures:

1. Admission of women into the monastic community.
2. Lack of proper respect toward Buddha, the teaching (Dharma), and the community of monks and nuns and laypersons (Sangha).
3. Lack of diligence in meditation practice.
4. Carelessness in transmission of the teachings.
5. The emergence of sectarian rivalries and divisions within the community.
6. The emergence of a false, counterfeit Dharma.
7. Excessive involvement of monks with secular society.[2]

Regarding the duration of the period of crisis and decline, the belief commonly held in South, Southeast, and Inner Asian Buddhism is that that the teaching will be fully accessible until it disappears in a sudden fashion, not to reappear again for millions of years until the appearance of the future Buddha Maitreya. These traditions are therefore very conservative, trying to preserve the Buddha's teaching for as long as possible in its traditional form, and generally regarding any kind of change as change for the worse.

In contrast to this, traditions of East Asian Buddhism believe in a prolonged, far from auspicious period of decline called the period of the "Final Teaching" (*mo-fa*). Therefore, starting from the sixth century, Buddhist leaders in those countries—Pure Land teacher Tao-ch'o in China to the Kamakura reformers of thirteenth-century Japan—used this belief as an incentive to innovation and devised very creative new forms of belief and practice.[3] This openness to innovation, which generally characterizes Mahayana countries, has led to new forms of "engaged" and lay-Buddhism in more recent times.

Contrasting these two approaches suggests that tradition can be read and used in different ways: it may be a safeguarding agent against unwanted change, and it can be a source of inspiration for new approaches and ways to realize the values of tradition in changing contexts.

"HERMENEUTICS OF SUSPICION"

In India, Buddhism was a spiritual and social movement directed against the sacrificial religion and social status of the Brahmins. Thus, the classical "holy" values were put under scrutiny in a Buddhist "hermeneutics of suspicion." The general result was that individuals or objects came to be seen as not inherently holy but holy only insofar as the individual mental development makes him/her holy. The classical statement of the Buddha to this effect was, "I do not call one a brahmana because of one's origin, or one's mother. Such is indeed arrogant, and is wealthy: but the poor who is free from attachments, that one indeed I call a Brahmana . . ."[4] There is nothing holy except awakening to the true nature (*bodhi*) and, derived from that, all means and paths (*upaya*) that may be useful to attain this end, which is described as the extinction of the flame of desires (*nirvana*). Having said this, one can conclude that the advent of the Buddha itself was a Crisis of the Holy.

MONASTIC BUDDHISM: OVERCOMING DEFILEMENTS

Original monastic Buddhism knows no holy spaces and times as such, but all emphasis is laid on the mental overcoming of the *kleshas* ("defilements" or "impure conditioned things"), which are described as "of battle, because they injure self and others."[5] Defilements are states of mind such as egocentricity, anger, and hatred and in general all impermanent things, including the world, existence, opinions, suffering. "Holy" is what is wholesome for the development of mind and the overcoming of what is impermanent in order to reach liberation (*nirvana*). The terminology used is not "holy and unholy" but "*kaushalya* and *akaushalya*," meaning appropriateness to the holistic development of all aspects of the mind and life. The proper qualities curing unwholesome mental states—such as error, nondiligence, idleness, disbelief, lethargy, scatteredness, and dissipation—are to be developed by awareness and attentiveness (*satipatthana*) and all auxiliary means toward achieving this goal. The wholesome states of mind are described as faith, diligence, aptitude, respect, awe, nonviolence, absence of desire and hatred, energy.

But since its beginning, the Buddhist movement has venerated specific phenomena, and the three most important ones are:

a. The importance of relics of the Buddha and enlightened masters: After cremation, tiny bone fragments and pearl-like beads, believed to be the manifestations of the realization of the Buddha or an enlightened master were collected and housed in memorial towers (stupas). These relics are venerated as holy objects that confer spiritual blessings on those who come in contact with them.

b. The veneration of the Buddha's teaching or law (*dhamma/dharma*): Collected in the Holy Three Baskets (*tripitaka*) of scriptures (*sutta/sutra*), commentaries (*abhidhamma/abidharma*), and monastic rules (*vinaya*), the teachings of the Buddha are described as the "holy net" (*jala*, chin. *sheng-wang*) that gathers all into the liberating truth. Reciting or copying even one sentence of the teachings will bring the believer on the path to salvation.

c. The "saintly" character of the venerable monks (*samgha/sangha*): Both the renunciant monks dwelling in the forest and the scholarly monks preserving and passing on the written teachings in the monastery are traditionally regarded and treated as saints. The degree of the monk's behavioral purity (*sila*) is a central component in his relationship with the laity, because the degree of merit generated by donations is dependent on the level of sanctity of the recipient.[6]

All of the above reflect the Triple Gem (*triratna: Buddha, dharma, sangha*) in its importance for the laity.

MAHAYANA BUDDHISM: HOLINESS

While in Indian Buddhism holiness is expressed in terms such as purity (*arya*), wholesomeness (*kausalya*), and the Brahmin way (*brahmamarga*) of life, Mahayana Buddhism uses the language of Holy (chin. *sheng* , jap. *sei*) to describe everything pertaining to the Triple Gem.[7] There is an even stronger development of beings (enlightened human beings), objects (such as Sutra texts, statues, relics), and places and regions of pilgrimage, which are regarded as utterly special and "holy." This development finds its culmination in the texts of Tantric Buddhism.

Three most important instances of holiness are:

a. The Bodhisattva incarnate, who in him/herself has holy qualities as appropriated by action, as a result of a vow to reach enlightenment and to liberate all suffering beings, and of karma. In Tibetan Buddhism, the incarnated Bodhisattva becomes a social institution in the Tulku, because this institution now regulates the continuity in the line of succession of ruling monasteries and lineages. Thus the lineage of the Tulku is the carrier of the "holy." The seat of the Tulku, his monastery, is holy only insofar as it houses the Tulku.
b. In Tibetan Buddhism holiness is related to "empowerment" (tib. *Dbang, wang*), i.e., a vow or oath which is an infusion of spiritual energy by the spiritual teacher that creates a habitual quality. This energy does not flow only in humans but may also be present in dedicated statues that have been enshrined. Matter becomes empowered by or loaded with spiritual energy which again may be transmitted by sanctified (empowered) objects. These can be classified according to the triple gem: relics of the *Buddha* (or empowered Lamas), scriptures containing the *Dharma*, ash and bones of important monks representing the *Samgha*.

c. While pilgrimages to the holy places are important in all traditions of
Buddhism, the texts of the Tantric tradition describe holy or sacred
regions within the inner human microcosm that find their correspon-
dence in the outer, macrocosmic environment. The inner pilgrimage
performed during meditation finds its parallel in the outer journey to
the sacred regions.[8]

Other Mahayana traditions such as Ch'an/Zen refute any distinction between the holy and unholy, which is expressed in the words of the legendary
Bodhidharma: "Holy ones and ordinary beings are of the same nature,"[9] as
well as in his famous answer to the Chinese emperor's question about "the
highest meaning of the Holy Truths": "Empty, without holiness."[10] The
teaching of the *Vimalakirti Sutra* expresses this same idea as "The holy
liberation is the equality of all things."[11] But clearly not only are the great
figures of the Masters and the legendary monastic rule by Pai-chang[12] held in
highest esteem, they are sanctified as representing the bodhi-quality to the
aspiring practitioners.

IMPERMANENCE

In Buddhism, the basic experience toward life and the first tenet of the
teaching is expressed as *sarvam anityam duhkham:* Everything is impermanent and therefore full of suffering. The suffering is not in the circumstances
but in the mental attitude toward them, thus this attitude can be changed.
Change and loss are natural and need to be regarded as a finger pointing to
the moon (of wisdom). Change is an opportunity for growth in insight into
the impermanence of things. Impermanence needs to be realized in order to
overcome clinging. To overcome clinging is essential to realize the emptiness of all phenomena including ego, which is wisdom (*prajna*). This realization is the precondition for attaining the Buddhist goal of awakening (*bodhi*
or *nirvana*). Therefore any crisis is an opportunity for the most essential
spiritual realization. In this respect the fourteenth Dalai Lama often says:
"My enemy is my best friend, because he makes me realize my human
condition and is also an opportunity for compassion (*karuna*)."

MOMENTS OF CRISIS:
INDIVIDUAL–COMMUNITY–LEADERSHIP

Individualism has been diagnosed as one of the major factors changing today's societies and imposing greatly on religious traditions. In considering
individualism as one of the moments of crisis, we have to first examine the
notion of the individual in the Buddhist context. The next question then is to

consider the traditional relationship between the individual, the religious community, and its leadership, and how this traditional relationship is affected by modern developments. Finally, in looking at individualism, we have to ask more carefully what individualism really is. Is it a more conscious and self-responsible acceptance of the challenges of life? Or is it a way into isolation that makes individuals depend on dubious influences and unaccountable powers? Has individualism a liberating effect, or is it driving people into isolation? Do individuals leave the big religious organization in order to find individualistic answers to their questions, or do they form new and smaller communities which are closer to their psychological and spiritual needs? And since certain aspects of the Buddha Dharma appeal to people in these circumstances, is this a dilution of the dharma or an expedient means (*upaya*) to meet present conditions?

The Buddhist notion of the individual is based on the Buddhist understanding of Self as No-Self or the Selfless. The notion of an independent Self or I is held to be the root of delusion and of suffering, because it gives rise to distinction and comparison between self and other, and with that to likes and aversions, grasping, lust, greed, and anger. The Buddha denied that any Self can be found in the five conditions constituting the human being (*skandhas*), such as material form, feeling, perception, mental constituents, and consciousness, because they are subject to impermanence. What is called a Self or I is not an independent entity but dependent on the law of causality (*karma*) and interdependent arising of things (*pratitya samutpada*).[13] While individuality is recognized on a relative level, the notion of an eternal soul (*atman*) is rejected.

Buddhism has developed in societies that were shaped by Brahmanic value systems (South Asia) or Confucian value systems (East Asia). Both are arranged in hierarchical models. The individual in its rights and duties is subordinated to the group that is defined according to the different cultural patterns. Even though Buddhism with its monastic institutions provided an alternative to traditionally prescribed roles in the social hierarchy, the teaching of No-Self precluded the rise of the kind of individualistic consciousness that developed with the Enlightenment in the West. Today, due to Western influences and changes that result from modernization, urbanization, and globalization, societies and their behavioral patterns are changing dramatically even though traditional values may still be idealized. This causes tension, which finds different expressions in the various Buddhist countries. Whereas, in Southeast-Asia except Thailand, Communism destroyed most Buddhist institutions, the lifestyle of the people has largely remained traditional. This means that education emphasises subordination to family and community over the training of a critical and self-assertive attitude. In a similar vein, the post-communist rebuilding of the Buddhist institutions still largely follows the traditional monastic pattern, in which the lay community supports the monks and nuns in order to generate blessings for deceased family members and benefits for this life and future lives. In Cambodia, for example, the Buddhist revival has been spearheaded by villagers who have been in the forefront of rebuilding temples and ordaining their sons to reclaim the Khmer Buddhist way of life.

Leadership of monks or higher officials has traditionally been accepted by the Sangha without questioning, though the Sangha originally was built upon a certain democratic structure in the limits of the Vinaya. In any case, in the whole Buddhist world, monks are seen as a source of authority, a refuge for the distressed, and a noble example for the laity. In Theravada countries, monks have a high status, and this can be used for better or worse. In Sri Lanka, parts of the Sangha have been heavily engaged in political agitation heating up the emotional climate against the Tamils, but other parts of the Sangha have supported peace activities and social reforms such as the ones instigated by the Sarvodaya movement, a social action that integrates Gandhian values into economic grassroots development as adapted to the needs of Sri Lanka.

THAILAND

Thailand is being changed by Westernization and by modern industrial and financial culture. The traditional respect given to monks has in recent years been eroded by a number of problems. Fake monks are cheating people out of cash, food, and other donations; real monks have been caught in the drug-trade, prostitution, or embezzlement. Even though wayward monks are only a small minority, the damage this has done to the faith was so severe that the Supreme Patriarch had to appeal for government help to deal with the crisis.[14] According to Sulak Sivaraksa, the crisis has long been in the making, with its roots lying in the rise of materialism and state control of the religion. As a result of the government's co-opting the clergy to support the new consumer culture in the 1980s, some monks are now fulfilling the historical prediction of crisis by getting too involved with society and being heavily influenced by its materialistic culture (see above). The highly publicized immoral behavior of monks is cited by converts to Christianity as one of the reasons of their conversions.[15] Other reasons are that young people find their individual needs more adequately taken care of in one of the Christian denominations than in the Buddhist communities.[16]

The individual gains importance and has to make choices, often with regard to religion. Having to choose creates tension, but this is not necessarily a bad thing, because it can lead to an increase in taking responsibility for one's life rather than following the expectations of family and community. In Thailand, as in other Buddhist countries, the traditional role of the laity is in the process of changing, because people who are no longer satisfied with the rather passive function of donor to the institution demand more than participation in rituals and receiving of blessings. Therefore, monasteries increasingly open themselves up to lay people for instructions and retreats, especially since the traditional one-month period of time that a young man or woman would spend in a monastery before getting married is less and less observed. This, however, does not necessarily mean that the participants in these retreats develop a deeper spirituality than those who lead their lives in the more traditional form of devotions. Ven. Phra Paisan Vaisalo, a socially engaged monk, warns of the "Spiritual Materialism and Sacraments of Consumerism," saying that nowadays the differences between religious faith and consumerism are becoming increasingly thin. Instead of being measured by the continuity of religious practice, faith is now measured by the number of religious devotional items people buy. As well, people tend to expect quick fixes and instant enlightenment from a three-day retreat at a monastery that they attend and for which they pay.[17][18]

One of the fastest growing Buddhist lay movements in Thailand, the Dhammakaya movement, which holds services and retreats for large numbers of lay people at its new center Pathum Tani near Bangkok or in other centers throughout the country has also been characterized as "religious consumerism." Critics argue that it is controlled by the economic and ruling elites, that it uses overaggressive recruiting methods and a commercial approach to evangelism to further its already huge assets; and that it does little to address Thailand's increasing social and economic problems. Another criticism is that it oversimplifies Buddhist teachings.[19]

At the same time, both in Thailand and Japan the issues of world peace and environment have become a focus for practicing Buddhist compassion in structural efforts such as social change, advocacy for the downtrodden, etc. In Thailand, reformist and socially engaged monks serve as role models for some, and work together with civic groups for more just, equitable, and environmentally friendly development. For example, they lead campaigns against AIDS and for reforestation programs. This kind of social and environmental engagement is new to Buddhism and could be a source of renewing the tradition. Thus, Ven. Buddhadasa Bhikkhu (1906–1993) has presented Buddhism as a teaching that involves both personal and social transformation. Thus Buddhist practice entails not only personal purification from ego-centered delusions but social engagement that seeks to dismantle the structural evils of the corporate Ego. Sulak Sivaraksa, a lay follower of Buddhadasa and founder of the International Network of engaged Buddhists, has inspired numerous monks and lay persons in Thailand to participate in community-based projects for socio-economic betterment and ecological healing. The network links Buddhist activists for social transformation in different parts of the world, and its emphasis on social engagement makes Buddhism more attractive to many people, especially since this approach integrates the individual in a meaningful way into community-oriented practice. It also addresses the pitfall of an unhealthy individualism in young people, which is of great concern to the Buddhist leaders, namely: a lifestyle that is based on materialistic motivations created through suggestive marketing and pop culture, not mature decision making.

JAPAN

Since the end of the nineteenth century, in Japan classical Buddhist institutions and their leaders have diminished in esteem among the populace, even while serving the ritual needs of the people. In the traditional Japanese schools of Buddhism—Zen, Shingon, and Pure-Land—the lay believer is first a donor, who supports the institution by contributing to memorial and other services, by buying a very expensive burial plot and the services that go with funeral rites, by the awarding of posthumous names, etc. This system came under attack with the Meiji-persecution of Buddhism, which widely eroded the belief in the efficacy of the monks to generate merit for the ancestors. As a reaction, new religious movements arose, in which all ritual functions could be carried out by lay leaders. These modern Buddhist lay movements (Rissho Kosei Kai, Soka Gakkai, and Reiyukai) are gaining ground both in Japan and abroad. For example, the Soka Gakkai is now represented in 183 countries. With the erosion of the religious authority of the priests and monks, the lay organizations have redefined the spiritual role of the individual in a collective effort. The individual is considered fully capable of performing all religious functions, including merit transfer to deceased ancestors, funerals, and ancestral rites. Differently from the traditional institutions, the lay organizations also take care of every aspect of an individual's life, including psychological, spiritual, marital, and financial counseling; all members are asked to actively recruit other members. Leadership positions are often assumed by women. A point of appeal of the groups is their way of building community through interpersonal communication and rapports in so-called dharma circles (*hoza*) of people coming together on a regular basis. In these group-counseling sessions, people share the experiences and difficulties encountered in their lives and exchange their insights on how the teaching of the *Lotus Sutra* illuminates such situations. These personal acts of witnessing help foster the cohesiveness of the group and the allegiance of its members. Since these lay movements are based on the teachings of Nichiren, one of the reformers of the thirteenth century, their study of Buddhist doctrine is mainly focused on the *Lotus Sutra*, their practice on chanting the title of the text. Even though more traditional institutions like Zen temples have opened themselves, sometimes reluctantly, to the laity, it is predominantly the lay organizations which provide spaces for adopting modern interests and values to Buddhist ideals.

While the lay organizations were created through the individualistic effort of the founders who criticized the then-exiting institutions and sought innovations, the organizations themselves, while addressing the needs of the individuals, do not make much room for individualistic choices. In this they reflect the values of Asian culture, in which harmony and cohesion of the group are valued more than individual freedom. The new religions with their intricate leadership structures demand high involvement with and submission to the group. While it is less the case with Reiyukai and Rissho-kosei-kai, there have been allegations by former members of the Japanese Soka Gakkai association (which is different from Soka Gakkai International) that extreme pressure by the organization is applied if a member tries to leave.[20] In Japan, the affiliation of the Soka Gakkai with politics has also raised doubt about the intention of its leadership.

While the comprehensive structure of the organizations attracts many who suffer from the isolation and alienation that is part of life in modern Japanese society, it also leaves out many of the young who, as a result of having been exposed too much to pressure to conform, refuse any kind of group pressure, whether at home, in the school, in the workplace, or in a religious institution. For these young people, individualism is expressed as refusal to fulfil the high expectations heaped on them by family and society, thereby leading them deeper into personal, social, and religious alienation.

CHINA–TAIWAN

The crisis of institutional Chinese Buddhism at the beginning of the twentieth century was addressed by T'ai-hsu,[21] who started his reform movement of "Wordly Buddhism" in the 1930s. This reform has strongly shaped the development of Buddhism in Taiwan, where monks and nuns go from the monastery into the world, where they are visibly engaged in social causes together with the laity. Groups such as, for example, the very well-known Tzu-Chi (Compassion Relief) Foundation, which was founded by the Buddhist nun Cheng-yen, rely on a highly organized form of community volunteerism to accomplish their charitable goals. The backbone of Tzu-chi and other charitable Buddhist organization is housewives who have found a new mission in becoming socially involved beyond the confines of the traditionally prescribed roles of wife and mother. While the decision of these women to join these charitable foundations at the expense of some of the housework that is expected of them might be criticized as individualistic by family and in-laws, the reality is that these organizations offer individuals new ways of support and fulfilment by reintegrating them into a group. The same can be said about women who choose the religious life, often against great resistance from their families, because in Confucian culture the individualistic choice not to reproduce is condemned as "unfilial." Despite this, the Buddhist Taiwanese Sangha has the highest percentage of college-educated nuns, who often explain their decision as wanting to be of service to the community rather than just to the family.[22]

Within Mahayana Buddhism, the groups that devise the most comprehensive leadership structures as well as member participation are the modern lay movements. While in the case of Japan, the organizations are entirely unaffiliated with any traditional Buddhist ecclesiastical organization, the case is different in Taiwan, where the lay support organizations are often named after the "mountain," namely the headquarters of the monastic organization with which they are affiliated. Two examples for this are Fo-kuang shan and Ling-jiu shan. In these organizations, the recruiting of new members is jointly undertaken by the lay members and the monastics. Leadership positions in the lay organizations are often held by women, and they are much easier to attain than in the traditional monastic institutions. This may be one of the most prominent reasons for the growth and popularity of these groups.

But despite the existence of these groups, many of the young people who traditionally belong to a Buddhist household remain unaffiliated with any organization and head into isolation. Historically speaking, the roots of the modern lay movements were laid in times of stress for the religious institutions—in Japan, during the political upheavals following the forceful opening of the country at the end of the nineteenth century, in China during the upheavals of the early twentieth century, in Taiwan during the period of Japanese occupation and the ensuing tension with the Mainland and martial law after the move of the Kuomintang to the island in 1949. The situation is different today, and so are the challenges. As has been described in this section, the relationship of the individual to the community and to religious leadership is changing along with other changes in society. While individualism is often used as answer to the question of what besets religion today, the question of what individualism really means in different cultural contexts needs to be kept alive. Sensitivity to the issue will more readily open up possibilities to overcoming the crisis by seeing it as an opportunity.

THE WEST

The situation of Buddhism in the West is different from what has been described above, because the historical situation is different. Even though Buddhism was imported by Asian immigrants as early as the nineteenth century, it did not really become popular among Westerners until the 1960s, when Japanese and Tibetan masters established centers for their predominantly Western students. In both America and Europe, Buddhism is now well established among immigrants from Asian countries and Westerners. While a more traditional form of Buddhism (including regular visits to the temple and observance of Buddhist festivals and rituals) is practiced by the majority of Asian Buddhists, the younger generation is affected by the loss of traditional family traditions and native languages. This causes feelings of alienation between generations and cultures, as well as a loss of the sense of religious belonging. One great challenge Buddhism shares with other religions is that the family, formerly the backbone of handing down tradition, no longer fulfills this task.

Some Western Buddhists are creating a Western form of Buddhism. Rather than worship in temples, Westerners practice predominantly in centers. The relationship between monasticism and laity and between teacher and student, the role of women, and the nature of authority and cultural expressions of individualism in the West remain open issues in this endeavor. For example, while the teaching of No-Self (anatman) which was widely debated in the history of Indian thought[23] poses less of a problem in the traditional East-Asian context, this is different in the West, where there is so much cultural emphasis on the individual "fulfilment of dreams" and "self-realization." One approach to solving this contradiction in terms and elucidating the meaning of No-Self is not to interpret it as an ontological statement, but instead as a value-oriented prescription about how one should live. In this context, the term used is "Selflessness," rather than No-Self. While this interpretation has its appeal, the awareness remains that the Buddha's teaching cannot be reduced to a simplistic moralistic message.[24]

Especially in the West, Buddhism seems to be able to tap into the desire for spirituality more so than any of the other established religions, since it is able to present itself as a spiritual resource that is not tied to a particular institution, community, dogma, or ritual. It therefore attracts many people who have become alienated from their own Christian or Jewish religious institutions. Buddhist symbols are used, for example, to market anything from cosmetics to gardening, food, interior designing, and financial planning. Buddhist ideas appear in New Age religions, medicine, psychology, sports, and business. While many Buddhists in the West are very seriously devoted to their faith and practice, the wide appeal and positive image that Buddhism enjoys also has pitfalls. Carl Bielefeld describes the situation of Buddhism in the United States as: "We seem to be dealing not with a religion, but with something that might be called 'American secular spirituality'—a longing among many (especially the white middle and upper classes) who are still not satisfied with what they have and who want something more; who have all they can eat but are still searching for that special flavoring, some 'psycho-spice' of self-acceptance, perhaps, some rare 'inner herb' of guilt-free self-satisfaction. This longing for something more, though in most societies very often associated with religion, seems in our society to be associated with a suspicion of religion. We want something more than institutional religion—something more personal, private, more narrowly focused on "me and how I feel about myself—what might be called 'I-dolatry.'"[25] While there is certainly some creativity in this "free-floating spirituality," the problem is that a reliable path which is based on proven experience and authority no longer remains visible. Instead of overcoming the Ego, these pseudo-Buddhist teachings and symbols often serve to enhance the Ego in its greedy search for self-aggrandizement, which is contrary to the teaching of "No-Self" or "Self-lessness." Here the question arises as to whether this tendency falls into the trap of diluting the Dharma—as it had been diagnosed to be one of the major reasons for decline (see above).

The commercialization of Buddhism in pop culture is of concern to Buddhists in America, even though they do not share one unified opinion on the matter. While some feel that marketing religious objects and tools for mass consumption dilutes an important aspect of the teachings, suggesting that one can buy spirituality instead of cultivating it, others think that many people are drawn to Buddhism because of its aesthetic offerings, such as amulets, statues, mediation cushions, mandalas, calligraphy, music, incense, etc.[26] From that perspective, these items can be seen as "skillful means" to get people interested in the teachings.

The positive image that Buddhism holds, especially in the Western media, helps to further its appeal even more. It is regarded as peaceful, compassionate, and not corrupt. In international news, Buddhism is almost never blamed for problems in Asian societies. For example, no connection is made between state Buddhism and the politics of Burma, but what instead the heroism of Nobel Peace Prize recipient Aung San Suu Kyi is highlighted as an example of one courageous woman who has found in her Buddhist faith a source of empowerment and support to resist the military government. Similarly, no one implicates the Buddhists from Sri Lanka in their violent campaign against the Hindu Tamils. Nor are traditional Buddhist attitudes toward women stressed as a factor in the trafficking and prostituting of poor Asian girls and women.[27]

In the American Western context, questions of religious authority circle predominantly around the teacher-student relationship. In the Zen tradition, the teacher who has transmission is seen as an enlightened, fully attained being in the succession of the historical Buddha. Thus, the teacher's behavior is generally not questioned. This uncritical acceptance has come under scrutiny after some of the financial and sex scandals that have beset some American Buddhist centers.[28] The appropriate relationship between student and teacher and ways of safeguarding it are topics that continue to be discussed in the yearly meetings of the American Association of Zen Teachers. A certain ambivalence is created by the fact that, while on the one hand, the understanding of religious authority in the Western Buddhist context is very much influenced by democratic principles and values, on the other hand, stricter forms of authority are adopted from traditional Asia forms of Zen practice and transplanted on Western soil. This ambivalence contributes to tensions and problems that remain in some communities.

The varied histories of Buddhism in the East and the West, but especially the difference in the understanding of individuality in an Asian, hierarchical, family, and community-oriented context and in the different Western context, account for their differences in the institution and practice of Buddhism. Individualism has also reached Asian societies, and this disrupts well-established institutions of community life such as the family and the Sangha (more about this below). Nevertheless, individual self-responsibility and the need to make choices in a pluralistic situation may well be a root for the development of determination and a more accountable practice of Buddhism, both in Asian societies and in a Western context.

YOUTH AND EDUCATION

Youth is the period in human life that is critical in its double sense of both danger and of opportunity, because it is mainly in this period that the potential for either negative or positive contribution to society is formed. Today's youth are tomorrow's builders of society, and therefore their education is of prime concern to both secular and religious authorities. However, the challenges educators face in the twenty-first century are immense and unprecedented due to the explosion in knowledge and technology, and due to the impact of globalizing forces on cultures and societies. Our world today is a living paradox, in which both immense wealth and abject poverty, tremendous advances in the medical field and unnecessary deaths from easily cured diseases, billion-dollar weapon trades, and millions of children dying from hunger, and an explosion in information technology and illiteracy go hand in hand. These contradictions contribute to a feeling of insecurity, powerlessness, and apathy among youth, which makes them more vulnerable to the attractions of materialism and consumerism, which treacherously present themselves as individualistic choices and lifestyles. Bikkhu Sughananda, assistant secretary to the Supreme Patriarch of Thailand,[29] expresses the feelings of other Asian Buddhist leaders when he writes that "in the dawn of this new millennium, it can be heard that there is an increasing apathy among youth, a part of the Fourfold order (consisting of monks, nuns, male, and female lay disciples) that they are running away from religions and are more inclined toward materialism, a culture of consumerism than spiritualism (spirituality). We can always hear about youth complaining about visiting a monastery for religious purposes as an outmoded act and that it is a culture of the old people. . ."

This statement would also resound with church leaders, notably in Europe, where the disaffection of many young people with the established institutions is interpreted in the context of secularization. But secularism and secularization can mean different things in different contexts. Cultures influenced by Buddhism in Asia have not gone through processes comparable to Western secularization after the eighteenth century. Most of them were secularized by different forms of colonialism that altered or destroyed legitimation of power, changed institutional forms of education, and thus altered the process of tradition. Today, globalization seems to be a new form of colonialism insofar as economic factors gain influence on the whole of life. And economic decision making is decreasingly influenced by cultural/religious values and/or political interests in favor of anonymous financial markets. Though the forces of globalization are present everywhere, Asian Buddhism is affected especially in terms of the "capitalization" and Westernization of society and values. This influences the relation of individual and community much as it did in the nineteenth century in Europe and the United States.

Technology influences everyone. Whereas in Europe, there is a critical tendency in looking at the advancement in technology, in Asia and certain sections of America the myth of progress is still prevalent. Buddhism hardly relates to the problem of consumerism in modern societies on the basis of its own analysis of egoism, greed, and hatred (the three fundamental klesas). With the exception of Sulak Sivaraksa and members of the International Network of Engaged Buddhism, most Buddhist institutions refrain from thoroughly discussing the issue or in raising their voices, probably on the basis on non-involvement in political and economic affairs (cf. above). But the rise of a materialistic worldview and consumerism has been one of the most detrimental factors threatening Buddhism, because it forces people to balance two sets of mutually contradictory principles, on one hand, the spiritual principles of Selflessness grounded in Buddhist teachings and, on the other, the principles of secular materialism, according to which the achievement of worldly success is upheld as the ideal of an accomplished individual. According to Bhikkhu Sughananda, this situation "contains within it a seed of very destructive potential," because, "it is when the contradiction is pushed down to the next generation, the youth of today, that the inherent incompatibility of the two perspectives comes into the open as a clear cut choice between two alternative philosophies of life—one proposing a hierarchy of values which culminates in the spiritual and sanctions restraint and renunciation, the other holding up the indulgence and gratification of personal desire as the highest conceivable goal. Since the latter appeals to strong and deep-seated human drives, it is hardly puzzling that so many young people today have turned away from the guidance of the Buddhist teachings to pursue new paths to instant pleasure opened up by the consumer society or, in frustration at missed opportunities, to take the path of violence."[30]

The path of violence is, in many cases, a path of violence that young people inflict upon themselves in the form of suicide. Suicide among youth is a problem in Asian Buddhist countries, very notably so in Japan, Hong Kong, and Taiwan, where publicized suicides of movie or media personalities have brought waves of youth suicides in their wake. Especially in Japan, suicide pacts among young people who meet on the Internet has become fashionable. One has to ask what the responsibility of the Buddhist institutions are in addressing this particular aspect of the crisis.

But to return to the original question of how to educate youth in a materialistic, secularist environment, there are various ways in which the Buddhist vision could make an impact on their lives. The original impulse of Buddhism was an open quest for spiritual knowledge, i.e., training the mind to become free from the fetters of defilements (*klesha*). Thus, Buddhist emphasis is on educating the mind to become aware of its own functioning. The investigating spirit of early Buddhism meant that nothing should be taken for granted unless it is established by experience and reason. This teaching puts the responsibility of discernment of truth on the individual person, not on the institution. Like other religions, Buddhism has become dogmatized, and different schools use their established knowledge to satisfy their claims for identity.

The youth life of the Buddha can serve as model for youth today to reflect upon. The Buddha's search for realization started as an individual journey. He was as surrounded by the material pleasures and distractions of his time in his palace as most youth are today in their homes. The image of the palace does not need to be taken literally. It can be read as a parable for complacency and self-delusion. The signs of the time that the Buddha saw on his first journey outside of the palace—old age, suffering, and death are those that spurred him on his quest for enlightenment. The same sights can be seen even more readily by youth today, by one look into the newspaper or one click on the Internet or TV news. And while the sight of a wandering ascetic showed the Buddha the direction in which he would start his quest, young people nowadays could easily find similar hints if they left their palaces to look. The problem today is that young people live in a virtual world of constant overstimulation. The content of their video games or TV shows is more real to them than the "real world" outside. Their heroes tend to be fictional or media stars. The question to ask is whether religious institutions and religious education are able to present real "heroes" that can inspire young people to start on a spiritual journey.

The fact that the Buddha taught at different times and places to people with different abilities of understanding produced a great variety of Buddhist teachings. Some of them were directly given to youth and expressed in a way that children and young people could understand. According to tradition, the Buddha's son Rahula was seven to ten years old when he became a novice and was exhorted by his father to observe the fundamental precepts of truthfulness and practicing mindfulness. The threefold training of morality, cultivation of mind, and wisdom could be used as a systematic training for youth according to their age.[31]

A model currently implemented in religious education in Germany could further serve as an example. It is based on the following three steps:

1. a training of youngsters in the rituals, lifestyles, and tenets of their own religious tradition;
2. a training in comparative religion, in order to realize similarities and differences of tradition, so as to be strengthened in the realization that there is more to life than just material gains and profits;
3. a training in dialogical debate based on 1 and 2, in order to find out the best solutions for oneself that are individually tested and verified by dialogical argument.

To these could be further added the approach which is already practiced by the members of the International Network of Engaged Buddhism and the Sarvodaya movement:

- training in awareness of social issues, such as poverty, discrimination, exploitation, degradation of environment, etc., and application of Buddhist teachings to this situation;
- training in networking with religious and grassroots groups and institutions engaged in those issues.

This method, it seems, would strengthen commitment to one's own resources, which are consciously appreciated, while, at the same time, teaching a recognition of other traditions as meaningful ways to fulfilment and cooperation. A basis for this training is the interest and involvement of the young people. It is therefore important to address young people where they are, to be aware of their life situations and problems. This approach is successfully used by some of the lay Buddhist organizations in Japan that have adapted methods from evangelical movements in Korean Christianity. Buddhist institutions could profit from studies and handbooks on lay leadership training that use the cell-group and lifecycle model. One very extensive study in this regard is being developed by Ven. Thitadhammo Bhikku of the Chinese Young Buddhist Association in Taiwan, with the intention of making it available as reference to other Buddhist Institutions as well.

A model of teaching school children both about both their own religion and those of others has been set by the educational programs of the Museum of World Religions in Taiwan. This model could also be more widely used in other countries. For Buddhism in the West, educational programs in centers should offer more study of basic texts of Buddhism in order to address the superficial adaptation of Buddhism to psychological needs as mentioned above. In order to train Buddhist leaders, Buddhist centers could—in cooperation with universities—offer regular, systematic, and certified studies in Buddhist history, scripture, and meditation, which would improve knowledge and competence of Buddhists in all walks of life.

WOMEN AND GENDER

The Buddhist analysis of mind and its path to train it and reach enlightenment is independent of gender, language, and culture but applicable for every human being endowed with mental discernment. However, the forms of transmission of the Dharma depend on social conditions. Buddhism has adapted a great deal when meeting new cultures. The very translation from Sanskrit and Pali language in India into Chinese and other East Asian languages has been a tremendous process of change in terms of transformation, adaptation, and cultural assimilation. Wherever Buddhism took root, it had to take into account the social and cultural matrix of a society in order to build suitable institutions for transmission of the Dharma. This created difference and multiplicity, and one only has to look into the difference of the monastic structures and Tibet and China or Japan. In most cases, Buddhism developed in patriarchal cultures or at least male dominated public spheres. This is changing today.

With the exception of present-day Taiwan, women still play a secondary role in all Buddhist hierarchies. Even though women have been active participants in the formation of the Buddhist traditions since the founding of the nun's order through the Buddha's aunt Mahaprajapati, the male-dominated culture in the societies in which Buddhism took hold had deep influence on the institution. The passage in the Pali canon predicting the crisis and decline of Buddhism because of the establishment of the nun's order is most probably an interpolation by later monks at a time when early Indian Buddhism was challenged and threatened by the rise of Mahayana Buddhism around five hundred years after the founding of Buddhism.[32] The fact that the direct monastic line of ordination of women died out in Sri Lanka in the eleventh century still affects the place of women in Theravada countries today. Since, until recently, there has been no line of ordained *bhikkhunis* in the Theravada tradition, women were able only to lead a quasi-monastic and quasi-lay style of life without the spiritual benefits, respect, and financial support that a fully monastic institution could provide. This situation equally affects women in Tibetan Buddhism. In Sri Lanka, prominent Buddhist leaders and intellectuals have been advocating a revival of the women's order since the beginning of the last century, but their efforts were thwarted by the official Sri Lankan Buddhist hierarchy. However, with support from Mahayana Buddhist countries, the first ten Sri Lankan women were ordained in India in 1996. One of them is the Ven. Bhikkhuni Kusuma, who has established an international center that is open to nuns and lay women alike and emphasises study, practice, and social involvement. [33]

In Thailand, there has been a similar resistance to the ordination of women, even more so, because, unlike Sri Lanka, a Buddhist monastic order for women had never existed in Thailand. Therefore, the Thai Buddhist hierarchy refused to recognize the full ordination of Voramai Kabilsingh (died in 2003) which she received in Taiwan in 1972. Her pioneering efforts toward reestablishing a nun's order in Thailand are continued by her daughter, Chatsumarn Kabilsingh, an internationally well-known academic and activist, who, in 2003, was fully ordained as the Ven. Dhammanada Bhikkuni in a ceremony in Sri Lanka that was covered by international media but caused opposition in her native country. [34]

Western Buddhist women are actively involved in supporting the efforts of Buddhist women in these countries. Ven. Karma Lekshe Tsomo is the current president of Sakyadhita, an international Buddhist women's organization established in 1987 in India. One of the organization's many goals is to help establish the Buddhist nun's order in countries where it is not present. In this regard, the 1993 meeting of Sakhyadhita held in Colombo was instrumental in advancing the cause of *Bhikkhuni* ordination there. [35] Ven. Lekshe Tsomo is also president of the Yamyang Foundation that supports education for Buddhist women. Women leaders in Asia and the West are also calling for attention to the experience and situation of Buddhist lay women in male–dominated Asian societies. Andro-centric biases in the writing of Buddhist texts that depict women as temptresses and unable to achieve enlightenment leads to negative self-images that are easily perpetuated among the women.

An issue that has been raised in connection with this is the large number of prostitutes in Thailand and the trafficking of Buddhist girls from Nepal. [36] These issues have to be more actively worked on by the Buddhist leadership in Asia. The importance of women in family, religious institutions, and the public sphere has to be recognized in order to build up more healthy and gender-balanced structures and attitudes in Buddhist societies.

In modern Buddhist societies, there is a strong sense both among the leaders and the practitioners that Buddhism should not be limited to the walls of the temple or institution but be actively involved in outreach to the laity and in social issues. This means that a mere revival of the old hierarchical and paternalistic monastic model cannot be a solution to the crisis. Rather, following in the footsteps of some reformers, such as Nichiren, T'ai-hsu,

Buddhadasa, Cheng-yen, Kusuma, and Dhammananda, both monks and nuns could be trained in providing access to the religious tradition to all laity. One of the problems is that even monks (and nuns) usually do not know much more than what they have learned in limited (liturgical) textbooks of their respective tradition. They know very little about other Buddhist traditions and the history of Buddhism, and they hardly have any reliable information about other religions or the philosophical and social sources and resources of modernity. Monks and nuns better educated in traditional and modern knowledge as well as trained laity could take up leadership in the spiritual and moral education of the society. A more "free-floating" spirituality among young people needs to be linked creatively to the Buddhist institutions that still can provide access to tradition. Unless this problem is solved, Buddhism will hardly gain a more thorough influence on youth.

The other crucial issue is the establishment of a more balanced relationship between the monk's order and the nun's order. The rules submitting the nuns to the monks have to be understood from their historical context that does not apply any longer. Like other monastic rules, these have to be creatively reinterpreted. Both monks and nuns have to be trained in critical readings of Buddhist texts. Drawing on the spiritual and leadership capacities of women as well as men will be crucial in addressing and solving the problems of Buddhist societies in South-East Asia.

INTEGRITY AND CHANGE OF RELIGIOUS TRADITION

In its deep analysis of reality, Buddhism shows that everything is change (*anitya*). Humans, however, want to cling to what they desire because they expect stability and unchanging security, which is impossible. This gap is experienced as suffering or better: frustration (*duhkha*). Therefore, to realize that all is impermanent is the first insight of wisdom.

Change, therefore, is nothing unwanted but a proper assessment of how things are. The question of integrity of a religious tradition in Buddhist perspective cannot aim at a changeless repetition of past structures and events. Integrity depends on the essentials that make Buddhism what it is: to present the dharma in such a way that it can be grasped as the proper means to overcome ignorance, greed, and hatred in order to attain to wisdom accompanied by compassion. Already in early Buddhism, the teaching was adopted to different conditions: village monks had a different calling from forest monks, laity was differently committed than were monks, etc. But all kept the precepts and practiced according to their roles in society. What was appropriate and what was not had to be worked out by the community itself and by councils, which took place in order to formulate and present the dharma in a way most suitable to the respective conditions.

Modernization

According to our analysis, there are two basic challenges today: modernization and pluralization. Modernization has to do with the technological age expressed in economization, mobility, urbanization, globalization, and the factor of mass media. The rhythm of life in industrialized societies is very different from the past. According to experiences all over the globe we are entering into a culture of events that are drummed up and amplified by the media. They are connected with persons who are made international stars (such as the Dalai Lama and the Pope), especially at important times (the death of Pope John Paul II.; the death of Lady Diana; the Dalai Lama's seventieth birthday), and also with places (holy places of pilgrimage). Both give rise to new pilgrimages that have both religious connotations and tourism value. Religious and secular tourism often cannot be clearly separated, because any center or place in space and any event in time can become a source of meaning, according to its interpretation. The international film and pop stars are icons for a good life in beauty and health, and this is what people seek. Expectations are high, but they will not be satisfied in this realm. Buddhism can point to the beauty of such events without clinging to them; it appreciates all but demonstrates how proper awareness can respond to the transitory nature of everything.

It is not only in the classical festivals (especially the days of memory of the dead) but in these events that Buddhism *does* contribute to a heightened awareness of the individual in modern society. The rhythm of work-time and holiday is so decisive for modern life-experience that special Buddhist pilgrimages connected with mental training should be organized during holiday seasons. Indeed, some Buddhist institutions organize family retreats during holiday seasons in order to give families some meaningful way of spending time together and finding new and creative ways of interacting. This is one of the ways in which Buddhist institutions try to strengthen the family as the backbone of the tradition.[37]

Pluralization

Pluralization expresses itself in the competition of different life styles, the meetings of religions and hybrid mixtures of formerly distinct traditions. One important response to this situation is the movement of interreligious dialogue. Buddhism has engaged in interreligious dialogue from its beginnings. There are many scriptural sources recording the debates between Buddhist followers and adherents of the different schools of Indian thought. When Buddhism was transmitted to the other cultures of Asia, notably to China, Buddhist concepts needed to be translated into the native language, and translators used already familiar Taoist and Confucian terms for key Buddhist concepts. It was only after a few centuries that Buddhists attempted to draw clearer demarcation lines between their own Buddhist notions and elements of the Taoist and Confucian traditions. Debates between the adherents of these different traditions are addressed in treatises that compare the standpoints of the three religions on particular issues. Nevertheless, Buddhism absorbed Taoist elements in its formation of the Zen-Buddhist tradition, and the harmony of Confucianism, Taoism, and Buddhism was held up and practiced as the ideal way of life.

In similar ways, Buddhism integrated elements from the Shinto tradition in its formation in Japan. The native Shinto deities were incorporated as protectors of the Dharma, and to this day it is common to find a small Shinto Shrine in a Buddhist temple compound and vice versa. In a similar manner, elements from the Bon tradition were integrated into the formation of Tibetan Buddhism.

There have also been interfaith encounters with Muslims as early as the seventh century in Eastern Persia, Afghanistan, and China. Muslim scholars—for example, Al Sharistani—discussed Buddhism with a great sympathy and understanding in the twelfth century. Buddhist-Christian dialogue also started as early as the sixteenth century in both China and Japan with the advent of the Jesuit missionaries there. [38]

In Theravada countries like Sri Lanka, Buddhism and the veneration of Hindu deities go hand-in-hand. Borrowing elements from Christian (hymns, textbooks, sources, catechisms, social services, etc.) began in the nineteenth century and has been successful, but, as with the veneration of the Hindu deities, this is generally not perceived as a mixing of the traditions. Buddhism has always considered the integration of elements of other traditions to be "skilful means (*upaya*)" in the propagation of the Dharma, without considering those elements as compromising the basic truth of the Buddha's teaching. Therefore, syncretism is not an issue that fills the Buddhists with concern.

In the twentieth and twenty-first centuries, Buddhism has continued its spread into different parts of the world; and its deepened encounter with the Abrahamic traditions is an important factor in shaping its future direction, especially since many of the teachers now spreading the Dharma are from a Jewish or Christian background. [39] For Buddhists, engagement in this more recent form of dialogue has mostly been motivated by three considerations:

- to express goodwill and compassion (*karuna*) towards all sentient beings;
- to engage communism and materialism on a common platform;
- to learn from others about social engagement and practice of *karuna* in modern societies.

It is a well-established experience that contemplatives of different religions have an easier time to understand each other than often with people of their own tradition who are not contemplatives. This shows that a deeper spiritual experience frees the mind from mental limitations and clinging to words and expressions. But even the contemplative needs to be grounded in a well-established tradition in order to avoid individualism. Buddhism has experiential resources to understand the relation between individual spiritual experience and grounding in a community of practitioners, and this is especially important today.

Dialogue will not lead to a blurring of identities but to a conscious acceptance and reconfiguration of traditionally inherited identities. Dialogue means sharing and mutual participation on all levels of life: in social relations, in emotional encounter, and in intellectual debate. The Buddhist model is that of *kalyanamitra*, the spiritual friend who is companion on the path. It is important to bring dialogue down from conference culture to grassroots activities. Leaders should educate and encourage their people to take courage in creative ways of sharing with neighbours in faith. They should especially protect those activities from those who accuse dialoguers of syncretism and betrayal of the purity of tradition. Coalitions of dialogue should be built between religions, and leaders should themselves be in the forefront and mediate their concerns publicly. Examples of Buddhist practitioners of dialogue are the Dalai Lama and other Buddhist leaders, such as Thich Nhath Hanh, Ven. Sheng-yen, and Dharma Master Hsin Tao. One also recalls the late Pope's activities for the peace prayer meeting in Assisi in 1986.

Intrareligious dialogue, even though not new among Buddhists, has also significantly increased in the last fifty years or so. And while mixing of Mahayana practices has been a feature of especially Chinese Buddhism, in which it is not uncommon to find a combination of Pure Land, Zen, and Tibetan practice within the walls of the same monastery, this feature seems to have become more widespread in the process of globalization and now to include the Theravada and Japanese Buddhist tradition. For example, a service of the Japanese Pure Land School (*Jodoshinshu*) in the United States, performed by a Japanese monk in flowing black robes and attended mainly by elderly Japanese people, closed with a loving-kindness meditation (*metta*) from the Theravada tradition embedded in a form of Yoga practice. The performing monk explained that he had picked up this form of *metta* meditation through living in New York City and found it helpful for his parishioners as a mindfulness practice.[40] Many other examples for mixing of practices from the different Buddhist traditions could easily be found.

One may ask if the economic and cultural globalization processes are also contributing to a globalized form of Buddhism in Asia; perhaps it is already there. In Dharamsala, the main seat of the Tibetan refuge community in India, Vipassana courses and Yoga classes are offered together with the courses and practices of the Mahayana and Tibetan tradition. It also has Internet cafes. Similarily, international meditation centers in Thailand and Burma are built to adapt to Western needs. The Asia visited by Western students of Buddhism is in many ways Western influenced and as such quite different from the Asia of forty years ago.

While inter- and intrareligious dialogues help create a basis on which mutual understanding and solidarity can be established, the challenge in to-day's globalized world is to keep the distinctions alive without falling into religious fundamentalism, and thereby to contribute to a culture of creative analysis, healthy critique, and disagreement, without which religions cannot flourish.

CONCLUSION: FROM SOURCE TO RESOURCE

The first part of this chapter presented the two aspects of crisis as both danger and opportunity and the historical Buddhist view of seven moments of crisis as constitutive of a continuous decline of the Dharma. Next it at-tempted to analyze the meaning of the Holy in Buddhism. We have shown that the Buddha's teaching was a critique of any static or exclusivist notion of holiness that does not involve a dynamic personal transformation in the overcoming of ignorance, greed, and anger. This dynamic is exemplified in the holy Bodhisattva, an enlightened being who acts selflessly in the fulfill-ment of his/her vow to save all sentient beings from ignorance and suffering.

In the next part of the chapter, we focused on moments of crisis in Bud-dhism as they affect the relationship of individual, community, and leader-ship both in Asia and in the West. We have shown that the various crises of traditional monastic institutions have been an opportunity for monks and nuns to reevaluate their mission and to become more socially engaged. The crises of the institutions have also been an opportunity for the laity to assume more responsibility and build new forms of community and leadership. But as the discussion of Youth has shown, neither the traditional monastic institu-tions nor the modern lay movements are able to address sufficiently and guide the youth in crisis. And while the Buddhist lay movements in Japan and Taiwan have given women greater access to religious involvement and leadership, women, especially in the Theravada and Tibetan tradition, contin-ue to struggle with issues of religious and cultural discrimination. In the final section, we have focused on Buddhist responses to the challenges of plural-ization in the continuous encounter and dialogue with other religious tradi-tions.

In conclusion, we would like to ask if there are also any insights from the Buddhist experience of crisis that could be helpful, or provide a resource for other religions. The present situation of the world is marked by dramatic changes in all aspects of life, both on individual and community levels. Change is something Buddhism takes for granted, because nothing that is composite is permanent. Therefore change needs neither to be welcomed nor condemned. It is the most fundamental fact of life. The Buddhist teaching of the reality of impermanence implies that one should not fear change and the dissolution of certain forms of knowledge, practice, or institution. Buddhism is highly adaptable; thus, today, laity and especially women play a greater part than in the past. It is important to see this development not as a loss and decay but as chance and opportunity for growth.

Buddhism can flourish under very different circumstances and has adapted itself to many different situations in the past. It can take any crisis as an opportunity to bring out more clearly its message of training the mind for more clarity and compassion so as to contribute to the peace of mind of sentient beings, and finally to overcome all suffering by insight or wisdom and compassion. The Buddhist emphasis on insight and compassion over dogma and institutional concerns is a much needed resource in a world that is increasingly torn apart by religious fundamentalism.

Buddhism as mental training can offer a more balanced and relaxed view on all our traditions including Buddhism as tradition. Some of the main training areas are mind and speech. We can become aware of the hidden agendas in our arguments and functioning, and Buddhism teaches how to do it without losing our specific identities and concerns. Buddhism balances content and mode of speech, and this is important in all communication processes including interreligious ones—it is so important that speech transports always a gentle sympathy toward the other even in disagreeing over certain arguments.

Earlier in the chapter, we raised questions about the meaning and impact of individualism in the context of Asian and Western societies, but we have refrained from rushing to answer these questions, because general answers are not possible. Each situation is different and needs clear analysis and accurate understanding. Buddhism may contribute an analytical approach and a refutation of ideological evaluations in those cases where modernity in general is rejected and too simplistic traditionalist or fundamentalist answers are constructed. Fundamentalist tendencies within the religions always strive to take the responsibility of mature thinking and decision making away from the individual person by presenting ready-made answers instead. The Buddha warned his disciples to never let this happen. His last word, spoken to his disciple Ananda on his deathbed, might be worthy of universal reflection: "Therefore, Ananda, be lamps unto yourselves. Rely on yourselves, and do not rely on external help. Hold fast to the Dharma as a lamp. Seek salvation alone in the Dharma. Look not for assistance to anyone besides yourselves."[41]

NOTES

1. Editor's note: See parallels in the Jewish perspective on page 87.

2. Jan Nattier, *Once Upon a Future Time. Studies in Buddhist Prophecy of Decline* (Berkeley: Asian Humanities Press, 1999): 120–29.

3. Nattier, 136–37.

4. Dhammapada, ch 26.

5. Louis de la Vallee poussin, transl. *Abhidharma Kosa Bhasyam*, (Asian Humanities Press, Berkeley 1988): ch.1.

6. Reginald Ray, *Buddhists Saints in India* (Oxford University Press 1994):16.

7. For details, see William E. Soothill: *A Dictionary of Buddhist Terms* (London 1930): 411, 412. There are thirty-four entries for holiness and its composites.

8. Ngawang Zangpo; Sacred Ground. Jamgon Kongtrul on Pilgrimage and Sacred Geography (New York: Snow Lion, 2001): 59–69.

9. "Treatise on the Two Entrances and Four Practices," quoted in Ruben Habito, *Experiencing Buddhism. Ways of Wisdom and Compassion* (New York: Orbis Books, 2005): 112.

10. Thomas Cleary, transl., *Secrets of the Blue Cliff Record* (London and Boston: Shambala, 2000): 1–2.

11. Thurman, Robert, *The Holy Teaching of Vimalakirt. A Mahayana Scipture.* (University Park: Penn State University Press, 1967): 59.

12. Pai-chang (720–814) was the first one to lay out a clearly formulated rule for Zen-monks. The original manuscript of the rule is not preserved.

13. For an explanation of the key Buddhist notions of "Selflessness" and "Interdependent Arising," see Habito, 47–55.

14. Robert Horn, "Buddha Boys," *Time Magazine*, Asia, May 6, 2002 (on the Internet).

15. Herb Swanson, "The Wiang Pa Pao consultation on Evangelism in the Northern Thai context," p. 17 (on the Internet).

16. Editor's note: Compare to the Christian experience on page 71.

17. Phra Paisan Visalo, Spritueller Materialismus und die Sakramente des Konsumismus," Publication by Buddha-Netz Info (on the Internet).

18. Editor's note: For description of the christian experience page 75.

19. Donald K. Swearer, *The Buddhist World in Southeast Asia* (Albany: State Unisversity of New York Press, 1995): 114, 115.

20. According to "The Victims of the Soka Gakkai Association" website.

21. M.v. Brueck/Whalen Lai, *Christianity and Buddhism* (Maryknoll: Orbis 2001): 84 ff.

22. Editor's note: Compare to the Jewish experience on page 93.

23. Steven Collins, *Selfless Persons: Imagery and Thought in Theravada Buddhism* (Cambridge: Cambridge University Press, 1982).

24. See discussion in Habito, op.cit.: 47–51.

25. "Tensions in American Buddhism," in *Religion and Ethics Newsweekly*, July 6, 2001: 2 (on the Internet).

26. Sumi Loundon, ed. *Blue Jean Buddha, Voices of Young Buddhists* (Somerville, MA: Wisdom Publications, 2001): 208–209.

27. See note 19.

28. For one example, see Michael Downing, *Shoes Outside the Door: Desire, Devotion and Excess at San Francisco Zen-Center* (Washington, D.C. : Counterpoint Publications 2001).

29. Lumbini in the New Millenium: Youth in Buddhism (a theme paper for the International Buddhist Conference at Lumbini, Nepal, Febuary 1–2, 2001): 8.

30. Ibid, 15.

31. For details, see Bhikkhu Sughananda, op.cit.: 5–6.

32. This development is analyzed in Kajiyama Yuichi, "Women in Buddhism", Eastern Buddhist, New Series No.2 (1982): 53–70. See also Rita Gross, *Buddhism after Patriarchy. A Feminist History, Analysis, and Reconstruction of Buddhism* (Albany: State University of New York Press, 1993): 33ff.

33. Editor's note: Compare to Christianity on page 76.

34. Habito, 100.

35. Ranjani de Silva, "Reclaiming the Robe: Reviving the Bhikkhuni Order in Sri Lanka," in Karma Lekshe Tsomo ed., *Buddhist Women and Social Justice* (Albany: State University of New York Press, 2004): 134.

36. On these issues, see Chatsumarn Kabilsingh, "Prostitutes and Buddhism," in *Thai Women in Buddhism* (Berkeley: Parallax Press, 1991): 67–86; and Khandu Lama, "Trafficking in Buddhist Girls: Empowerment through Prevention," in Tsomo, 165–191.

37. Editor's note: See similar examples in Hinduism on page 119.

38. See M.v. Brueck/Lai, op.cit.

39. A detailed account of the Buddhist-Christian dialogue during the last two centuries in the different part of the world is given by M.v. Brueck/Whalen Lai, *Christianity and Buddhism,* (Maryknoll: Orbis, 2001), much more detailed in the German and French editions.

40. Sumi Loundon, *op.cit.*, 214.

41. Digha Nikaya, XVI, 2.26.

Chapter Four

Christianity

Sidney H. Griffith

THE DYNAMICS OF THE HOLY

The mention of "the Holy" immediately puts the Catholic[1] in mind of the *Trishagion* in the Christian liturgy, the *Sanctus, Sanctus, Sanctus*, the acclamation of the all Holy One, the God of Abraham, Isaac, and Jacob, the God and Father of Jesus of Nazareth, the only son of the living God (cf. Matthew 16:14). The Christian knows of no crisis or critical turning point which could possibly confront the Holy One, to whom be glory and praise, the One to whom, in the Christian view, all creation testifies and whom the scriptures, the Word of God, the most fully reveal. The Roman Catholic Christian readily speaks of a crisis only among human beings in their perception of or awareness of "the Holy One" or in their acquiescence to His will for them as expressed in the revealed law and explicated for them in the authoritative teachings of the church. This human crisis is what one takes to be the subject of the present inquiry.

From the historical perspective, it seems that in every era of their two millennia of church life Christians have been in a crisis of one kind or another about their institutions, their theological formulae, their sources of divine revelation or the exact contour their moral lives should describe. Often these crises arose in the course of the encounter of Christians with non-Christians or in connection with the Christians' reaction to intellectual and spiritual challenges coming from within their own communities. But the idea of a distinctive "crisis of the Holy" as such seems to have arisen in the minds of modern Christians and non-Christians alike as a result of the perceived rarity on the part of many people in the modern era of an active sense of the ubiquitous power and presence of "the Holy" or even of the Holy One, in modern consciousness.[2]

Due to many modern thinkers turning away from a metaphysical awareness to a more materialist philosophy of human consciousness, the intellectual and technological successes of the modern era seem to many observers to
have sprung from a psychological divorce by many modern people from the
sense of the sacred in human life.[3] This divorce was initiated in the time of
the Enlightenment in the West, but it was built on the ancient distinction
between nature and super-nature. Some in the Christian community have also
found the remote preparation for the divorce in the hyper-rationalization of
theology in the western high Middle Ages.[4] Many Christians thought that the
Protestant Reformation would provide an antidote for this problem. But from
a Roman Catholic point of view, the *sola scriptura* doctrine of the Reformation, along with its twin doctrine of the "private interpretation" of scripture,
seems in the sequel simply to have referred the subsequent problems of
religious epistemology back into the hands of the Enlightenment's preferred
reference to the "human sciences," even for the discernment of meaning in
the texts of divine revelation and the solution of pressing theological problems. In other words, as a result of the success of the Reformation, the "feel"
(*Gefühl*) for *Das Heilige*, as Rudolf Otto spoke of it, increasingly became a
private concern and not a communal or ecclesial one. As a consequence of
this development, in the view of many commentators, religion in Western
Europe and America was destined to have only an individual or personal
relevance, with nothing pertinent to proclaim in the public sector of human
society, while in the private sphere a plurality of religious voices may be
expected to be heard. In other words, one result of the perceived "Crisis of
the Holy" has been the progressive marginalization of religion, not only in
the formation of public policy in the Western democracies but also its disappearance as a serious intellectual concern among the well-educated elite.[5]

From a Roman Catholic perspective, the danger in these developments is
the prominence of an attitude of individualism which they promote. In the
context of Christian religious life, especially among the Catholics and the
Orthodox, for whom the sacraments and the liturgical life, especially the
Eucharist, are the privileged moments of the sense of the Holy among them,
individualism threatens communion, which is at the heart of the life of the
church.[6] This dimension of the Crisis of the Holy among Christians will
appear as a crucial consideration under a number of the subject headings to
be discussed below. The problem is acutely felt in the North American context, where individualism in one form or another, along with an encouragement to escape from older traditions represented as oppressive, has been a
driving force in the evolving religious consciousness.[7]

THE INDIVIDUAL IN COMMUNITY

The separation of church and state is the political principle that eventually emerged from the course of Enlightenment thinking just described, perhaps in large part in response to the horrors of the religious wars in Europe after the sixteenth century. Although Christianity has always recognized at least a theoretical separation between secular and religious authority, reasoning from the Gospel dictum in which Jesus counsels his followers to "Render to Caesar what is Caesar's and to God what is God's" (Mt. 22:21), the church also long taught that civil rulers and states are subject to God's law as interpreted by the church. Consequently, the Catholic Church historically approved of the establishment of the church as the religion of the state in places where Catholics made up the majority of the population. But in dialogue with the modern democracies, especially in the United States, Catholics have made the doctrine of the separation of church and state their own, reserving the right of freedom of religious witness and expression.[8] While the freedom of the individual conscience has long been church teaching, the affirmation of the freedom of choice in religion as a God-given human right of every person in every polity was articulated as such by the Catholic Church most emphatically in the decrees of Vatican II, especially in the conciliar document, "Declaration on Religious Freedom" (*Dignitatis Humane*), promulgated on December 7, 1965.[9] Subsequently, Roman Catholic authorities, the post-conciliar popes and local bishops in particular, have tirelessly promoted this principle throughout the world.

The Catholic Church expects her faithful members to uphold that what the Church teaches is true and good in faith and morals and to work for the acceptance of her moral principles as integral parts of the public policy in the countries where they live. In Western-style democracies, the church does not dispute the right of others to do the same, but in these circumstances Catholics themselves are expected to promote the values they know to be true. Crises have arisen for Catholics in this connection, as they struggle to reconcile the affirmation of the truth as they see it and proclaim it with the protection of the rights of others as accorded to them by the constitutions of modern, democratic, nation states. One could say that for Catholics there is something of a "Crisis of the Holy" in this state of affairs, as they struggle with maintaining their own religious allegiance in the context of modern democracies which often espouse policies opposed to church teaching, especially in right to life issues and family values. Catholics do not believe that moral truth can be determined by plebiscite or simply by the will of the majority, so they struggle to commend to the public what on the basis of their faith and church teaching they know to be true and to make the case for its veracity among the people with whom they live. Inevitably, in regard to certain issues, this situation of bearing witness to the truth of unpopular or countercultural social or moral values also produces a measure of dissension and disagreement, even crisis, within the church's own ranks about the best ways to achieve the goal of meeting challenges to religious values in the post-modern world.

Within the Western world, where Catholics often feel a sense of alienation from what they perceive to be an increasing relativism, materialism, and secularization in the dominant thought-patterns of the larger society, they are aware that many contrary "winds of doctrine" also affect many members of their own churches. Currently there is a considerable amount of unrest, even polarization among Catholics, over a whole host of issues extending from models of church government to rules of morality, the boundaries of marriage, the importance of the nuclear family, gender "inclusivism," and relations with other religious groups, including the problem of double belonging, individuals claiming to adhere to two different, sometimes seemingly incompatible religious confessions. What is more, because of the unprecedented emigration and immigration of peoples in the twentieth century, Catholics often experience an inner tension between various ethnic groups of Catholics in the same location. There is also a tension between Catholics in America and Western Europe, where there is a sense of loss of direction and diminishment, and Catholics in Asia, Africa, and South America, where there is often a sense of confidence, growth, and increasing demographic significance for the universal church.[10]

The challenge of Islam in particular is increasingly perceived by Catholics as one of the most important cultural and religious challenges facing them both at home and abroad in the twenty-first century; they are divided over the healing of historical memories in this connection as well as over the appropriate modes of present day encounter with Muslims. From the time of the immediate aftermath of the Islamic conquests in the seventh century until the first quarter of the twentieth century, Christians and Muslims had been in an almost continuous state of hostility toward one another in the context of the mutual rivalries between the countries in which one or the other religious community was dominant, a hostility which was exacerbated toward the end of the period by the experiences of colonialism and imperialism. Then in 1965, in Vatican II's "Declaration on the Relation of the Church to Non-Christian Religions" (*Nostra Aetate*), the following, somewhat surprising admonition was published:

> Since in the course of centuries not a few quarrels and hostilities have arisen
> between Christians and Moslems, this sacred synod urges all to forget the past
> and to work sincerely for mutual understanding and to preserve as well as to
> promote together for the benefit of all mankind social justice and moral wel
> fare, as well as peace and freedom.[11]

Ever since the days of Vatican II, the Catholic Church has been a tireless promoter of interreligious cooperation and dialogue, not least among the Muslims.[12] Nevertheless, it still remains the case that outside of Europe and the Americas, wherever Christians and Muslims live together and increasingly in India even between Hindus and Christians, tensions and even instances of persecution and loss of life are growing in number, especially in countries where Muslims are strongly in the majority. In these situations the "Crisis of the Holy" takes on a whole new dimension, one in which the issue is no longer theoretical or epistemological but has become a matter of faithful witness in a hostile environment. In the era of terrorism, the Crisis of the Holy has become a life crisis. In this context, the church is faced with the task of commending the doctrine of the freedom of religion as a basic human right not only to Christians but to members of other religions as well, joining with leaders of other religions to discern the truth and to promote justice and peace, a process that immediately raises the difficult question of whose justice is adequate and which rationality is to prevail.[13] The pertinence of these questions is immediately evident and it underlines the need for a continued, interreligious dialogue as a practical means of addressing the numerous Crises of the Holy which confront people of faith in the twenty-first century,[14] a topic to which we shall return at the conclusion of this chapter.

FORCES AFFECTING INDIVIDUAL AND COMMUNITY

Many forces currently affect the relations between the individual and the larger community within the Catholic Church, but the issues vary in different parts of the world. One of the most pressing issues in the United States and parts of Europe is the tension resulting from the ongoing crisis sparked by the exposure in the national news media of cases of clerical sexual abuse of children and the perceived subsequent cover-up of these crimes, allegedly engineered by church leaders. Church people have been troubled by the large sums of the church's financial resources expended in compensation to victims, coming to the point of bankrupting some American dioceses. This crisis has become the occasion for some disillusion, and it has revealed the different sets of assumptions held by church leaders and some church members about accountability and responsibility in the governance of church communities and their resources. It is an instance of a "Crisis of the Holy" on a practical and pastoral level within the present-day Roman Catholic Church in that it dramatically calls attention to the want of a lived holiness on the part of some of the church's ministers and faithful in the locales where the problem has come to light. In response, the perception of this want can then itself become a catalyst for the Catholics in the milieu of the crisis to re-dedicate themselves to the goal of living a holy life as the best and only socially perceptible opportunity for them to incarnate the Holy in the life of their communities, in accordance with their profession of faith in Jesus of Nazareth as Lord and Messiah. Periodically crises of this proportion have arisen in the history of the church, and traditionally they have prompted church leaders to inaugurate programs of repentance and reform. The present crisis is no exception in that amid efforts to promote justice for all concerned, church members are challenged once again to transform sinfulness into an occasion for grace, even as they seek to improve the structures which allowed the crisis to come about in the first place.[15]

Globalization in the Catholic community has also brought about a number of crises in church life. One obvious instance of this phenomenon is the challenge facing the church to inculturate Catholic Christianity into languages and societies outside of the western world, where ecclesiastical thought and practice was first articulated in Greek and Latin and built on the classical heritage of ancient Greece and Rome. Theoretically, the church is committed to the proposition that its message can be presented in any language and culture and that its doctrines can be parsed into any adequate philosophical system. Nevertheless, the principal doctrines and articles of faith have historically been enunciated in Greek and translated into Latin, and, especially in the west, presented in the Greek idiom of Neo-Platonic and Aristotelian philosophies. These formulae have become normative and all other expressions of Christian teaching have been measured against them.[16] The result is that, for the most part, efforts to articulate the principle doctrines of the faith in other idioms have historically been found wanting and ultimately disallowed. The long history of this struggle extends from the sixteenth and seventeenth centuries, involving famous figures such as Matteo Ricci (1552–1610) in China and Roberto de Nobili (1577–1656) in India, up to the present day, in Asia and Africa in particular.[17]

A number of modern theologians in the West have also been called to task by the Vatican's Congregation for the Doctrine of the Faith (the former Holy Office) precisely because in a number of important instances it is difficult to see how their efforts to articulate the Catholic faith in the idiom of modern philosophies can be squared with the traditional understandings of the Greek formulae of orthodoxy as they have been authoritatively taught by the ordinary magisterium of the church over the centuries.

In the context of the globalization of Christianity and the associated problems of inculturation, the issues of missionary activity and proselytism arise in connection with the Crisis of the Holy in our day, in this instance perhaps a perceived crisis in one's readiness, or not, to recognize the holiness of the other. While most Christians seem willing to renounce proselytism, in the sense of an aggressive, disrespectful, and disdainful effort to win converts from other religious traditions that are regarded as simply false or even Satanic, Christians are certainly not prepared to forego missionary activity.

The Catholic Church in fact regards the *missio ad gentes*, or mission to the nations, to be an integral part of her divine charge to "Go therefore and make disciples of all nations, baptizing them in the name of the Father and of the Son and of the Holy Spirit" (Matthew 28:19).[18] But such a mission is not conceived as an unwarranted or wrongful intrusion into the lives of peoples of other religious traditions. Rather, it is considered to be an invitation issued to others out of a love for them to embrace the truth proclaimed in the Gospel and preached by the church. And in virtue of the church's own espousal of the principle of freedom of religion in all human societies and cultures, this understanding of the church's missionary mandate carries with it the corollary that Catholics should be prepared to recognize the right and duty of members of other "missionary" religions (e.g., Islam) to invite them to consider the religious truth claims of their proclamations.

Pope John Paul II spoke of the church's missionary enterprise as a process of inculturation: "Through inculturation the Church makes the Gospel incarnate in different cultures and at the same time introduces peoples, together with their cultures, into her own community."[19] Missionary activity in this sense is conceived as arising from a charitable respect for other cultures and recognition of their potential for receiving new religious truths and expressing them in their own cultural idiom. It is based on the idea that cultures are not static but that by nature they change in response to stimuli coming from other cultures, and precisely in terms of their reactions to new ideas presented by others.[20] Nevertheless, it is undeniable that Christian missionary activity has sometimes not been conducted in a spirit of hospitality and invitation but threateningly, under the protection of colonialist or imperialist enterprises undertaken from a position of political or military power over others. It is in this context that missionary activity becomes part of the Crisis of the Holy. And it is for this reason that in recent years Catholic theologians have been wrestling with the degree to which they might not only repent of the sins of the past, but also at the same time acknowledge in their own terms the truths of other religious cultures, without adopting an unacceptable relativism or indifferentism which would exclude the Gospel imperative to "make disciples of all nations." It is in the context of this struggle, still very much underway, that one must read the controversial declaration of the Vatican's Congregation for the Doctrine of the Faith known as *Dominus Jesus*, signed by Joseph Cardinal Ratzinger and Archbishop Tarcisio Bertone on August 6, 2000.[21] It appeared at a time when careful theologians were exploring the ways in which Roman Catholic thinkers might positively evaluate, in the very terms of Catholic theology, the truths enshrined in other religious traditions.[22]

The Crisis of the Holy that manifests itself in the Christian encounter with non-Christian religions in the context of globalization calls especially for a renewed effort to educate Christians about other religious traditions in the context of interreligious dialogue, a topic addressed in the last section of this paper. In the present context, it seems that discussions of the encounter with other religions cannot usefully be conducted only in general terms. Rather, they must be religion-specific and relevant to particular traditions within a given religion. In this way the project of comparative theology[23] might be brought to the service of the church's need not only to acquire an accurate knowledge of another tradition on its own terms but in response to another religion's formulations to elaborate a Catholic theology, in Catholic terms, of any given, particular tradition's postulates, with a view to dispelling caricatures and polemical portrayals and to fostering mutually profitable exchanges.

There has been an interesting development in the matter of accommodating Catholic doctrine and practice to non-Western cultures in which there are no ancient Christian usages to be adapted to the requirements of relatively new Christian populations. It is the phenomenon of the Vatican itself, or priests and teachers from the West, after the second Vatican Council's theological and liturgical renewals, becoming more vocal in promoting the so-called indigenization of the expression of Christian faith in a given locale than the local people among whom they work would welcome on their own initiative. In the context of globalization, this phenomenon represents the intrusion of western cultural values into the sphere of another culture well within the parameters of the Christian communities themselves.

Modern technology, methods of communication, and cyberspace have also presented interesting problems. For one thing, they have enhanced the central control of church affairs much more than was the case in the past. This is not just a matter in the Roman Catholic community of easing Vatican control over the affairs of local churches. Some more local media, because of their technological power and financial support can now dominate church thinking on a popular level. For example, the Roman Catholic TV network, EWTN in Birmingham, Alabama, which is owned by a very conservative religious congregation of women, operates largely independently of the American church hierarchy, and it has an enormous influence among American Catholics. Their programs focus attention away from the local dioceses and their bishops and highlight the role of Rome and of the Holy Father more immediately in the lives of individual Catholics. While a development such as this is not exactly an instance of the Crisis of the Holy, it is nevertheless indicative of the power of globalization to reach within a Christian community and significantly to alter the sense of ecclesiastical communion by means of which Catholics and other Christians experience their Christian identities.

Furthermore under the heading of globalization there is also the matter of virtual space and virtual reality. The very existence of these newly discovered dimensions of human experience raises all sorts of interesting canonical questions, some of which may well spark a Crisis of the Holy in the concrete experience of religious life. One such question might be: are sacraments valid when conducted through cyber media, without the participants being immediately physically present to one another? Within the Roman Catholic Church the sacraments are individually both the representation and the very realization of the Holy, so the determination of the conditions in which their celebration is valid is an important undertaking. Much remains to be explored in this connection, but already it is common practice for shut-ins and others to attend Mass via television. [24]

LEADERSHIP, INDIVIDUAL, COMMUNITY

Multiple issues of power and authority within the Roman Catholic community have the potential to provoke Crises of the Holy in the experience of church life. They have to do principally with what we call collegiality and subsidiarity in the governance of the church. They include the relations between the bishops and the Holy See, bishops and local pastors and their congregations, and the role of theologians in the teaching ministry of the church. On the local level, especially in Western Europe and the Americas, the dwindling numbers of priests and professed religious has become the occasion for the alternative growth and development of large international lay movements. These have become very powerful, and they range from the very conservative, like Opus Dei, to the relatively liberal, like the Catholic Worker movement in the United States or Pax Christi internationally. These groups are in many ways taking the place of the once-powerful religious orders and congregations in the life of the Church and in the process, they are sociologically reshaping the profile of modern Catholicism.

Another sociological development in the wake of the decreased number of clergy and religious is the growing laicization of church administration in many places and the laicization of Catholic education, from the grammar school level all the way up to the universities, and even in theological and seminary education. The number of clergy receiving higher degrees in ecclesiastical subjects has decreased, while the number of lay people receiving these degrees, even ecclesiastical degrees, has dramatically increased in Europe and the Americas. Lay people are more and more to be found on the faculties of seminaries. In other words, there is a dramatic change in the ways in which Catholics are educated in their religion; often these lay teachers have higher degrees from non-Catholic institutions. There is both challenge and opportunity in this situation; at the very least it provides a re-shaping of the processes of transmitting Catholic teaching. One hopes that the de–clericalization of Catholic education may bring a readier openness to ecumenical and interreligious dialogue, even at early grade levels in the religious

education programs of the local parishes. But it is already clear that laicization does not automatically bring a more open approach to church issues.
Often lay church workers are more conservative than the clerics were in the
days of their predominance. [25]

In some quarters, especially in higher education, the laicization of the
faculties in departments of religion in Catholic institutions and their espousal
of secular measures of academic competence and freedom has had the effect
of estranging many of them from the leadership of the church, thereby intro-
ducing a crisis of Catholic identity in a number of these institutions. Some of
them are no longer considered Catholic colleges or universities by their local
bishops; some of them have divested themselves of a Catholic identity by
their own corporate decisions. These developments, which actually follow a
trend in the history of colleges and universities in the United States, [26] pose
both a challenge and an opportunity to the Church. They raise the question
about the very possibility of there legitimately being a religiously confessing
university in any academically respectable sense of the institution. [27] The
issue amounts to a Crisis of the Holy because of the implication that the Holy
cannot be academically perceived in an experiential way; it can only be
described from the perspective of the behavioral sciences looking on it from
the outside, much in the manner put forward now more than a century ago by
William James (1842–1910) in his classic work, *The Varieties of Religious
Experience*, first published in 1902. [28]

Gender equality has obviously become a major issue in Catholic Church
life in most countries, extending all the way from concerns for equal access
for women and men to all levels of ecclesiastical service, including the
clergy, to the use of inclusive language in translations of the scriptures and in
the official books of the liturgy. This ongoing concern is still very much a
developing issue. There is no Catholic teaching about the inferiority of wom-
en, quite the contrary, but there are various ideas about the appropriate roles
of men and women in Church life. [29] In many instances these ideas are determined by the circumambient cultures in which the church is implanted,
where the church's doctrine of the radical equality of all people is called
upon to bring healing to hurtful and basically uncharitable practices. But in
terms of the Crisis of the Holy, the gender issue that has been the most
contentious in the Roman Catholic community in recent times has been the
controversy over the restriction of the sacrament of Holy Orders to male
candidates. While the Church's teachers at the highest level have declared
that the Church has no biblical or traditional warrant to admit women to Holy
Orders, and the Holy See has declared the discussion of this possibility
closed, [30] there is still unrest about it in the community at large and many
theological questions are raised about the adequacy of the reasons given for
the refusal to admit women to the priesthood. Some scholars insist that the
data of revelation can be rightly interpreted to support the ordination of

women. For some Catholic people this situation precipitates a grave crisis because the sacraments, and particularly the sacrament of the Eucharist, are the very moments in Church life in which the Catholic community experiences most acutely the presence of the Holy One living and acting among them. An uncertainty, a wrong perception in the celebration of the sacrament of the Eucharist, thus affects most readily the community's sense of communion with their Lord and with one another. It is for this reason that Church leaders and theologians put such a high priority on issues concerning the celebration of the Eucharist and the other sacraments. [31]

There is some tension in the Catholic community over sexual ethics, but the Church's moral teaching in this area is clear. Basically all Catholics are called to the same sexual morality, whatever their innate sexual inclinations may be. The Church teaches that marriage between man and woman is the only legitimate place for full sexual engagement, and within marriage it becomes a duty to carry out the biblical injunction to increase and multiply as well as to foster mutual love and affection between the spouses. Some controversy and different understandings exist in connection with the control of births; it is largely a controversy over the legitimacy or illegitimacy of the various means to be used in the process. [32] Currently there is a concern among Catholics for the preservation of the sanctity of marriage by legally restricting it to one man and one woman, ruling out any notion of a homosexual marriage. At issue here from the perspective of a Crisis of the Holy is once again the fact that a marriage between a baptized man and a baptized woman is a sacrament. For Catholics the sacrament is the locus of the irruption of the Holy into everyday life. There is a Crisis of the Holy when the validity or integrity of the sacrament's celebration is threatened.

Youth movements have been a prominent part of Catholic life in recent years, especially during the long years of Pope John Paul II's term in the Vatican when the celebration of World Youth Day became a yearly event. There is every indication that this trend will continue, and indeed it has already continued under Pope Benedict XVI. The concern in this event is to encourage young people to become more cognizant of the power and presence of the Holy in the universe and in their individual lives. In the modern world, in which the young live under a constant barrage of distractions from even a rudimentary awareness of the holy, they are often unaware of the means available to them to gain a sense of it in a practical way. This situation poses a crisis not only for individual young people but for the larger community of the church, too.

Education and Continuity

The Catholic education system is undergoing a considerable change at the present time. Heretofore, the Catholic Church in many countries has had

control of elementary education, either in the parochial school system, as in
the United States and elsewhere, or in state-supported "Catholic" schools, as
in some other western countries. In Africa and Asia, schools under Church
auspices have often been an important part of evangelization. Not long ago in
the United States, Church leaders pressed for every Catholic child to be in a
Catholic school. This campaign has largely disappeared in recent years. The
older parochial school system, which was largely subsidized by parishes and
religious orders of men and women in the past, has now given way to a
network of private schools under diocesan auspices, still in many instances
located in parishes, but which are now, due to the costs involved in running
them, often out of the economic reach of most Catholic families. This development is one of the consequences of the dramatic fall in the number of
clergy and professional religious who are available to serve as the administrative staff and faculty members for these institutions. Now Catholic education in the sense of education in the Catholic faith is largely a matter of
"Sunday School" arrangements, sometimes in the hands of eager but poorly
prepared teachers. There are programs to train people for ministry in religious education, but they are of very uneven quality, depending on their location, degree of funding, and the level of encouragement they receive from
Church leaders.

One may speak of a Crisis of the Holy in the context of a crisis in
education in the sense that the dysfunction in the educational process obviously negatively affects the transmission of the sense of the Holy to the
young. And this aspect of the matter has become a moment of crisis in the
larger society in the west, especially in the United States, where there is no
established religion and where virtually every religious tradition in the world
is present. Since by law there may not be any instruction in religion in the
public school system, save in the most generally descriptive terms, and yet
the majority of Americans are in some sense religious, the situation yields a
measure of frustration. This frustration emerges into public view in the context of controversies over educational policy. The current spate of arguments
between "creationists," supporters of an "intelligent design" theory, and "ev-
olutionists" in the United States about how biologists should teach the history of the forms of life on earth, including human life, is a case in point. It is a
crisis which, in its own way and on a lower level, mirrors the problems
discussed earlier in connection with the universities and the role of religion
in the academic world. Should public education be religion free to the point
that the Holy would simply have no place at all in academic discourse?[33]

A more deeply rooted crisis in the area of education in religion involves
the emergence of relativism in the realm of epistemology and the discernment of the criteria for the perception and transmission of religious truth,
indeed of the sense of truth itself. This was a major concern addressed by
Pope John Paul II in his encyclical *Fides et Ratio*, published in 1998,[34] and it

has emerged as one of the principal concerns of Pope Benedict XVI.[35] To what degree are the data of divine revelation to be taken into account? This crisis is a philosophical one, and it seems to be a characteristic of modernity and post-modernity. The source of knowledge in religion, in the Christian scheme of things, is twofold, reason and the deposit of revelation, the latter being enshrined in scripture and tradition. There are crises in connection with the discernment of the truth in both of these sources. In the exercise of reason, modern epistemologies and modes of discourse render the expression of truths problematic; in the study of the deposit of revelation, modern historical critical methods and the predominance of critical theory in exegesis have brought relativism into the interpretation of the foundational texts to the extent that the appeal to them for doctrinal or moral teaching has become difficult. This situation in turn produces difficulties of crisis proportions in the educational enterprise. But once again the problem emerges as an effect of the crises discussed earlier in this chapter.

Integrity of Community Life

The integrity of community life patterns among Christians has undergone considerable change in the churches in modern times. In western countries in particular, in the twenty-first century this seems to be due at least in part to the fact that virtual assembly in cyberspace in place of physical, bodily assembly is challenging the ways in which community is formed on a radical level. But, in some places in the immediate past, national or political ideologies, especially in the twentieth century, seem to have supplanted religion as the basis of communal life and this development produced disastrous results. At least in part, the crimes against humanity abetted by Marxist Leninism in the Soviet Union and National Socialism in the German-speaking world in the last century might plausibly be said to have become socially possible due to the failure of the churches to keep peoples' social consciences in these places well-formed according to the values of the Gospel. And this failure in turn might plausibly have been due to the breakdown of the integrity of the Christian communities in these countries and their failure effectively to counter the spread of the influence of the destructive ideologies which subverted Christian teaching and forbade effective Christian community building.

For Catholics and other Christians there is also a Crisis of the Holy in the breakdown of community integrity, because there is a strong sense in Christianity of the assembled community, the church, being the "body of Christ" in the world and the primary focus of Christian belonging, even prior to any worldly political allegiance. Excessive individualism, which is at the heart of a number of modern philosophies and ideologies, threatens this important dimension of Christian life and removes that communion among Christians which is the necessary theological basis of the church's identity. For Christians, the church and her sacramental life are the very locus of the Holy in this world; any substantial threat to the integrity of her community life is therefore a Crisis of the Holy in a major way for Christians and one which potentially has disastrous consequences in the church's ability to commend the right and proscribe the wrong in human moral behavior.

Bridges between Communities

The challenges of interreligious and intercultural dialogue confront Catholics and other Christians at every turn of modern life, beginning within the community itself and extending outward. There is a strong sense that the church should be in communion with other Christian denominations and this calls for ecumenical dialogue. Similarly, there is a strong impetus to dialogue with non-Christian religions, especially after Vatican II, as we have discussed above. And the Catholic Church has been and is now a strong supporter of this enterprise at its highest levels. However, there is a measure of resistance to ecumenical or interreligious dialogue within the ranks of Catholics and other Christians and it is often not promoted on the local level nearly as much as it is promoted in the Catholic Church by the Vatican on an international level, or on a national level by national and regional bishops' conferences. Consequently there is a need for intrachurch education not only for the sake of promoting an understanding of the practical value of dialogue for the sake of harmonious interfaith, human relations, but even for the sake of the pursuit of the fullness of the truth. The fact of the matter is that religious communities bear a large share of the responsibility for promoting justice and peace in the world, maybe even more than political or military leaders, because so many of the fault lines along which war and mayhem between peoples occur, lie along the religious divisions among them, allowing religious divisions to be exploited in the service of other interests. For all practical purposes, one might say that the best antidote to the threat of a looming "clash of civilizations"[36] is to work to forestall the effects of a clash of theologies by promoting ecumenical and interreligious dialogue.

The consideration of the Crisis of the Holy that underlies the imperative for dialogue immediately raises the question of the grounds for dialogue; what is to be the criterion of rationality, the measure of justice between different communities with different religious traditions and different authoritative texts? From the Roman Catholic perspective, the answer has to be that the truth is the necessary criterion.[37] But this answer itself raises further questions. What are the criteria of the truth and can there be an absolute truth told in human words? If one claims in response that such a truth is told in a divine revelation couched in words intelligible to human beings, the question then becomes, how rationally to recognize the signs of credibility in favor of a particular revelation and how to measure the verisimilitude of any proffered interpretations of a revealed text?

In other words, in the end ecumenical and interreligious dialogue on a practical level inevitably begs for a dialogue of philosophies. This step down, as it were, from the level of revelation to the level of reason, implies no contradiction between reason and revelation. But it does suggest that on the human level the truths of revelation must be mediated to human minds with the help of reason, especially in the interreligious context where the claims of revelation are not immediately granted by all of one's dialogue partners. In the Roman Catholic community this concern has been most notably addressed in Pope John Paul II's encyclical *Fides et Ratio*, signed on September 14, 1998.[38]

The recognition of a need for a dialogue of philosophies in the context of interreligious dialogue entails the acknowledgement of a concomitant requirement for participants in such a dialogue to converse with their partners apologetically, in the sense of being prepared to offer an *apologia* for their own faith, a reasoned defense of the truth they propose in the light of the objections brought to it by their partners.[39] The enterprise presumes that all partners in the dialogue would have it as a high priority to gain an accurate, even experiential knowledge of one another's religious confessions, in the original idiom of their expression. The charge is to study one another's traditions appreciatively. For a person of Catholic faith this would mean looking for what the Holy Spirit has chosen to bring to the church's attention in the teachings of non-Christian religions. It is in this spirit that Vatican II's *Nostra Aetate* teaches Roman Catholics as follows:

> The Catholic Church rejects nothing that is true and holy in these religions. She regards with sincere reverence those ways of conduct and of life, those precepts and teachings which, though differing in many aspects from the ones she holds and sets forth, nonetheless often reflect a ray of that truth which enlightens all men.[40]

Such an idea of interreligious dialogue calls for open conversations, even debates about religion between the scholars of the several world religions in those countries of the world in which the political realities would allow them. The purpose of such debates would not be the conversion of the other, as if someone could be argued into or out of religious faith, but the mutual clarification and explication of confessional formulae and moral principles, in the hope that in the long run such conversations would allow religious leaders to find a mutually agreed ground on which together they could espouse a rationality for justice and peace in our shared world.

Of course, one should be wary of public arguments about religion; history teaches us of the many ways in which power structures in the past have staged public debates about religion, not for promoting clarity and mutual understanding, but for the persecution of some religions, particularly in medieval, western Christendom, and most notably in that context to the detriment of Jews and Muslims. But in the modern democracies, with the separation of church and state and the guarantee of religious freedom as a basic civic right, religious groups themselves might usefully promote such conversations within their own parameters and far away from the seats of political or military power that could pose a threat to some participants in such an enterprise. In this connection one might even be encouraged by the experience of Hindus, Buddhists, and Muslims in India in former times, among whom debate in both the civic and religious spheres was for a time a way of life.[41] For modern religious leaders the challenge would be actively to promote within their own communities the sympathetic, even appreciative study of other religions in the context of the apologetic presentation of the truth claims of their own faith.

From a Roman Catholic perspective, philosophical or theological controversy should not be the only or even the major sphere of interreligious dialogue. The dialogue of everyday life and the search for wisdom wherever it may be found, especially within the so-called Abrahamic family, is particularly important. In this connection, one recalls the experience of notable individuals whose Christian faith was reawakened, deepened, and made more communicable to others precisely in the encounter with other religions and on their own ground. Jules Monchanin, Henri Le Saux, and Bede Griffiths had such an experience among Hindus;[42] Enomiya La Salle, Donald Mitchell, and many others have had the same kind of experience among Buddhists.[43] Even among Muslims, with whom Christians often have a more difficult dialogue, there are the powerful examples of Louis Massignon and Kenneth Cragg.[44] On the other side, within the Islamic world, one might cite the examples of the Royal Institute for Interfaith Studies in Amman, Jordan, the efforts of the followers of Fethullah Gülen in Turkey,[45] and in North Africa the ongoing enterprise of the Christian and Muslim members of the interfaith study group known by the acronym GRIC (Groupe de Recherches Islamo-Chrétien), who seriously discuss issues of divine revelation with one another.[46]

In conclusion, one might observe that most of the Crises of the Holy discussed in the present chapter involve, in some way or another, peoples of different religious traditions with one another. In the discussions between the religious leaders from different traditions one expects that similar moments of crisis will be seen to affect all the religious communities in the world today. In the context of this observation, the encouragement and promotion of interreligious dialogue might well emerge as the single most practical step forward any religious leader can take to help address the multiple crises their communities face. And in this enterprise, perhaps the single most important principle to defend might well be the inalienable, God-given human right to freedom of conscience and freedom of religion.

NOTES

1. This chapter represents one Christian perspective—that of Roman Catholicism. Other Christian voices were part of the conversation during the writing process.

2. One is thinking here of the human perception of the numinous and of religious awe in response as discussed in Rudolf Otto, *The Idea of the Holy* (2nd ed., trans. Jown W. Harvey; Oxford: Oxford University Press, 1950).

3. See Hans Urs von Balthasar, *The God Question & Modern Man* (trans. Hilda Graef; New York: Seabury Press, 1967).

4. See Michael J. Buckley, *At the Origins of Modern Atheism* (New Haven: Yale University Press, 1987). See also Michael J. Buckley, *Denying and Disclosing God: The Ambiguous Progress of Modern Atheism* (New Haven: Yale University Press, 2004).

5. One recalls in this connection an engaging passage in *The Education of Henry Adams*: "Of all the conditions of his youth which afterwards puzzled the grown up man, this disappearance of religion puzzled him most. . . . The religious instinct had vanished, and could not be revived, although one made in later life many efforts to recover it. That the most powerful emotion of man, next to the sexual, should disappear, might be a personal defect of his own; but that the most intelligent society . . . should have persuaded itself that all the problems which had convulsed human thought from the earliest recorded time, were not worth discussing, seemed to him the most curious social phenomenon he had to account for in a long life." Henry Adams, *The Education of Henry Adams* (New York: The Library of America, 1983): 751.

6. For an important Orthodox statement on this topic, that has been widely influential among Roman Catholics as well, see John Zizoulas, *Being as Communion: Studies in Personhood and the Church* (Crestwood, NY: St. Vladimir's Seminary Press, 1985). From a Roman Catholic perspective, see also the Vatican's "Letter to the Bishops of the Catholic Church on Some Aspects of the Church Understood as Communion—*Communionis Notio*," issued by the Congregation for the Doctrine of the Faith, 28 May 1992, available on the Vatican's Website.

7. See Harold Bloom, *The American Religion: The Emergence of the Post-Christian Nation* (New York: Simon & Schuster, 1992); Leigh Eric Schmidt, *Restless Souls: The Making of American Spirituality: From Emerson to Oprah* (San Francisco: Harper San Francisco, 2005).

8. See John Courtney Murray, *We Hold These Truths: Catholic Reflection on the American Proposition* (New York: Sheed and Ward, 1960); John T. McGreevy, *Catholicism and American Freedom* (New York: W.W. Norton, 2003).

9. See Marianne Lorraine Trouvé (ed.), *The Sixteen Documents of Vatican II* (Boston: Pauline Books & Media, 1999): 481–503.

10. See Philip Jenkins, *The Next Christendom: The Coming of Global Christianity* (Oxford: Oxford University Press, 2003).

11. Trouvé, *Sixteen Documents*, 397.

12. See, e.g., Byron L. Sherwin & Harold Kasimow (eds.), *John Paul II and Interreligious Dialogue* (Maryknoll, NY: Orbis Books, 1999).

13. See Alasdair C. MacIntyre, *Whose Justice? Which Rationality?* (Notre Dame, IN: University of Notre Dame Press, 1988).

14. These concerns are at the heart of theologian Hans Küng's promotion of the "Declaration of Religions for a Global Ethic." See Hans Küng, *A Global Ethic for Global Politics and Economics* (Oxford: Oxford University Press, 1998).

15. Editor's note: Compare to some Buddhist experiences on page 46.

16. There is a certain credibility to the privileging of Greek. For the Christians, Greek is the language of revelation in the New Testament, and the Greek Septuagint (underlying the Latin Vulgate) was the authoritative Bible in the earliest Christian communities. The earliest church councils proposed the orthodox formulae of the creeds and the basic dogmas of the faith in Greek. Inevitably then these formulae in Greek became the measure of verisimilitude for

expressions of the faith in other languages. But as Pope John Paul II wrote, "In preaching the Gospel, Christianity first encountered Greek philosophy, but this does not mean at all that other approaches are precluded." John Paul II, *Fides et Ratio*, 91.

17. See, e.g., Thomas C. Fox, *Pentecost in Asia: A New Way of Being Church* (Maryknoll, NY: Orbis Books, 2002).

18. See the Encyclical Letter, signed on December 7, 1990, of Pope John Paul II, *Mission of the Redeemer / Redemptoris Missio* (English trans.; Boston: Pauline Books & Media, 1990).

19. John Paul II, *Mission of the Redeemer*, 69.

20. See J. Ratzinger, "Faith, Religion, and Culture," in Joseph Cardinal Ratzinger, *Truth and Tolerance: Christian Belief and World Relitions* (Trans. Henry Taylor; San Francisco: Ignatius Press, 2004): 55–109.

21. Congregation for the Doctrine of the Faith, *On the Unicity and Salvific Universality of Jesus Christ and the Church / Dominus Jesus* (English trans.; Boston: Pauline Books and Media, 2000).

22. See, e.g., Jacques Dupuis, *Toward a Christian Theology of Religious Pluralism* (English trans.; Maryknoll, NY: Orbis Books, 1997); J. Dupuis, *Christianity and the Religions: From Confrontation to Dialogue* (English trans.; Maryknoll, NY: Orbis Books, 2002).

23. One has in mind in connection with this expression such efforts as are represented in the work of Francis X. Clooney, *Hindu God, Christian God: How Reason Helps Break Down the Boundaries between Religions* (Oxford: Oxford University Press, 2001); F. X. Clooney, *Divine Mother, Blessed Mother: Hindu Goddesses and the Virgin Mary* (Oxford: Oxford University Press, 2005).

24. Editor's note: See parallels in the Hindu experiences on page 118.

25. Editor's note: For the description of a Buddhist experience see page 47.

26. See George M. Marsden, *The Soul of the American University: From Protestant Establishment to Established Nonbelief* (New York: Oxford University Press, 1994).

27. See George M. Marsden, *The Outrageous Idea of Christian Scholarship* (New York: Oxford University Press, 1997).

28. William James, *The Varieties of Religious Experience: A Study in Human Nature* (Centenary Edition; London & New York: Routledge, 2002).

29. See, e.g., the encyclical letter of Pope John Paul II, September 30, 1988, *Mulieris Dignitatem*, on the dignity and vocation of women in the Church.

30. See the declaration of the Congregation for the Doctrine of the Faith, *Inter Insigniores*, January 27, 1977; the apostolic letter of Pope John Paul II, *Ordinatio Sacerdotalis*, May 22, 1994, and the response of the Congregation for the Doctrine of the Faith on October 28, 1995, regarding the binding authority of the previously mentioned apostolic letter. The position is reiterated in *The Catechism of the Catholic Church*, par. 1577.

31. Editor's note: Compare to Buddhism on page 57.

32. See John T. Noonan, *Contraception: A History of its Treatment by the Catholic Theologians and Canonists* (Cambridge, MA: Harvard University Press, 1986).

33. Editor's note: See parallels to Judaism on page 99.

34. John Paul II, *Encyclical Letter: Fides et Ration; On the Relationship between Faith and Reason* (English trans.; Boston: Pauline Books and Media, 1998).

35. See, in particular, the essays collected in Joseph Cardinal Ratzinger, *Truth and Tolerance: Christian Belief and World Religions* (trans. Henry Taylor; San Francisco: Ignatius Press, 2004).

36. In the sense of the phrase as it has been used by Samuel P. Huntington, *The Clash of Civilizations and the Remaking of World Order* (New York: Simon & Schuster, 1996).

37. See esp. Ratzinger, *Truth and Tolerance*.

38. See John Paul II, *Encyclical Letter: Fides et Ratio*.

39. See Paul Griffiths, *An Apology for Apologetics: A Study in the Logic of Interreligious Dialogue* (Maryknoll, NY: Orbis Books, 1991).

40. Trouvé, *Sixteen Documents*, p. 396. See also *Catechism of the Catholic Church* (English trans.; Ligouri, MO: Ligouri Publications, 1994): 839–845.

41. In this connection, see the intriguing recent publication by the noted economist Amartya Sen, *The Argumentative Indian: Writings on Indian History, Culture and Identity* (New York: Farrar, Straus and Giroux, 2005).

42. See Françoise Jacquin, *Jules Monchanin prêtre 1895–1957* (Paris: Cerf, 1996); André Gozier, *Le père Henri Le Saux: à la rencontre de l'hindouisme* (Paris: Centurion, 1989); Judson B. Trapnell, *Bede Griffiths: A Life in Dialogue* (Albany: State University of New York Press, 2001).

43. See Enomiya Lasalle, *Zen: Way to Enlightenment* (New York: Taplinger, 1968); Donald W. Mitchell, *Spirituality and Emptiness: The Dynamics of Spiritual Life in Buddhism and Christianity* (New York: Paulist Press, 1991).

44. See Christian Destremau & Jean Moncelon, *Massignon* (Paris: Plon, 1994); Mary Louise Gude, *Louis Massignon: The Crucible of Compassion* (Notre Dame, IN: University of Notre Dame Press, 1996); Christopher Lamb, *The Call to Retrieval: Kenneth Cragg's Christian Vocation to Islam* (London: Grey Seal, 1997).

45. See Fethullah Gülen, *Advocate of Dialogue* (comp. Ali Ünal & Alphonse Williams; Fairfax, VA: The Fountain, 2000).

46. See Muslim-Christian Research Group, *The Challenges of the Scripture: The Bible and the Quran* (Maryknoll, NY: Orbis Books, 1989).

Chapter Five

Judaism

B. Barry Levy

The modern Hebrew word for "crisis" is *mashber*, which derives from a root meaning "break" or "smash." This suggests that any crisis includes a significant dimension of destruction and negativity, but, already in biblical times, *mashber* also referred to a pregnant woman's breaking water shortly before entry into labor.[1] While "breaking" remains an important component, this usage significantly broadens the word's semantic range and suggests that "crisis" contains a serious amount of potential for creative good. As painful and challenging as any crisis may seem, it surely need not be all bad, and it has the potential for very positive outcomes; perhaps it also contains the notion of being temporary, but severe crises, even if short-term, can be cataclysmic.[2]

The crisis of which I speak here is a modern one, born of the ongoing evolution of Judaism and the interplay between its constituents and between it and the cultures in which its practitioners have found themselves. To be sure, there is nothing specifically modern about this situation or the presence of an accompanying crisis; with rare exception, it has been an ever-present facet of Jewish life since antiquity. Rarely has there been uniformity of thinking on any major issue, but only in a few situations was the Jewish people divided into dozens of polarized sects. The modern era has added its own features: the concomitant shrinking of the global community; the development of extremely negative attitudes to Jews and Judaism by non-Jews (and even by many Jews) that are perceived to be more universally legitimate than ever before and transferable to the Land of Israel; and the pressures resulting from new technologies that invade every dimension of sacred life. These are exacerbated by the media, which know no bounds in exploring the negative side of humanity in general and religion in particular but cannot seem to find the time and interest to explore regularly and to sustain interest

87

in the positive things religions do. Instead, they try to express complex and nuanced ideas in thirty-second sound bites, thereby reducing everything to oversimplified and polarized extremes. Many other factors differentiate this crisis quantitatively and qualitatively from all previous ones, however frequently they have occurred and however troubling they have been to those who lived through them.

Judaism has survived for thousands of years, in part because Jews understood how to cope with crisis. To paraphrase a song popularized by Kenny Rogers, they have known when to hold, when to fold, when to walk away, and when to run.[3] Perhaps they did not always run fast enough, but Jews are still around after more than three thousand years. Whatever they have accomplished—and there is much to their credit—they have prioritized their survival as Jews. While their varied expressions of Judaism have mutated and evolved, commitment to survival itself really has not; indeed, in some ways it has become emblematic of Judaism.

The decade between 1939 and 1948 witnessed the two most important Jewish events in at least two millennia, the Holocaust and the creation of the State of Israel. One is viewed as largely negative; the other, largely positive, though we have reached the point where even which is which is the subject of a great deal of public debate, particularly among some non-Jews. But Jews dare not imagine that the former is the sole source of the crisis Judaism presently faces or that the latter provides the only potential solution. The contemporary forces that, in many ways, result from these two events but, in others, remain largely independent of them have placed Jews in a new and unfamiliar position that requires ongoing attention and careful negotiation of potential pitfalls. Rather than dwell on past successes and failures, which would exhaust the available space and accomplish very little, I move to offer some historical descriptions, some related analysis, and some questions that may help contemporary religious leaders formulate the specific challenges to which they choose to direct their short-term and long-term attention.

In its classic form, Jewish religious life is a cooperative effort that enlists the participation of all members of society. These efforts are not identical for priests and laymen, men and women, adults and children, or other categories of societal members; indeed, in some cases the expectations of them differ substantially. But the overarching assumption is that the totality of their efforts—not only the individual parts—is what maintains the covenant between God and the Jewish people. This covenant, a crucial aspect of biblical religion and of post-biblical philosophical consideration, is both a personal and a national one.

In the following pages, I discuss many dimensions of "The Crisis" confronting contemporary Jews, perhaps more accurately described as a series of interlocking crises and related challenges and pressures. While many different forces combine to influence the current situation, and in many ways it is impossible to differentiate among them in a clear and systematic way, most of my concerns relate to two themes: the implications of individualism in a religious system that is only partly individualistic, and the pervasive fragmentation and disunity of Jews and of Judaism that result from them. Specific crises in education, leadership, the nature and integrity of change, the survival of small or isolated communities, the conflict of traditionalism and modernism, the nature and quality of public worship, the alienation of women, and the quality of religious authority affect almost every aspect of Judaism. External pressures for change on all religious communities include globalization, the breakup of the family, the power of the media, secularism, modernity, and the development of technology.

To be sure, all is not in crisis, nor is the Jewish situation deteriorating beyond hope of recovery. Surely things have been worse than they appear today, even in the recent past. But even as positive forces gather strength to solve problems, others give life to new challenges. And so I believe that there is a multi-faceted and distinctly Jewish Crisis of the Holy that I will now attempt to describe. For the sake of simplicity, each individual example is highlighted as a separate entry to facilitate future reference, not to suggest that this is a definite list of problems to the exclusion of all others.

THE CRISIS OF EXCESSIVE INDIVIDUALISM

Modernity is a culture of the individual. Individuals often travel in packs, but ultimately Western societies and their laws are about individuals; they are concerned primarily with individual rights and freedoms and are not dedicated to group values, practices, or beliefs, or to conforming to them. As one simple Canadian example, I advance the evidence from a legal decision about a Jewish matter rendered in July of 2004.[4] After a series of challenges to an issue about the nature and obligation of a particular religious requirement, in a five-to-four decision the Supreme Court ruled that the definition of one's religious obligations could not be determined by court consultation with formal religious leaders. (Indeed, in this case, religious authorities had defended two opposing positions regarding the precise nature of a particular religious obligation, but that was not the point.) What was paramount in this case was the belief of the individual. In other words, in Canada, formal religious requirements, the teachings of scriptures, and the writings of recognized religious leaders, even the testimony of contemporary experts cannot determine the nature of anyone's personal religious obligation. Only the independent practitioner is so empowered, which effectively turns every layman, however lacking in formal religious education, into his or her own founder, legislator, theologian, priest, and prophet. The absurdity of this secular and allegedly liberal decision notwithstanding, it is self-evident that it reflects the mood of the contemporary Western world. Ours is a generation of individuals and individualists. The standards, expectations, rules, and teachings of the founders, transmitters and contemporary leaders of religions have been subjugated to those of every individual.

In response to the same forces that ultimately produced this Canadian situation, over the past century or two, many Jews have become very supportive of the optional quality of religious observance. For many, Judaism is like a perpetual smorgasbord, from which one chooses as much or as little of whatever one wishes at any time. According to such thinking, observing the Sabbath, for example, is difficult and restrictive; why not make the biblical principle of its being "a joy" the overriding value and apply contemporary standards of joy to defining its practices and ignore the rest? Or why not observe only the prescriptive rituals and not the prohibitions from various forms of work? Or why not confine Sabbath observance to the public arena and ignore the private one? Or limit it to Friday night or Saturday, but not both?

In like fashion, some argue, dietary laws are complex and seemingly unnecessary; why not abandon them or replace them with commitments to healthy eating, vegetarianism, and the like? Given how they have developed, dietary restrictions are complex and omnipresent, as much because of the laws as the contemporary methods of food production. Rather than follow these laws in detail, some people have opted to imagine that they do not matter; to observe them only at home and to eat food cooked improperly in restaurants; or to assume all pots and plates are equally permitted for use. Some rely on food labels that, according to the governmental bodies that legally endorse them, do not meet required religious standards. They imagine that a "pure" ingredient means 100 percent of it, when the law has a very different definition that legally permits substitutions without requiring label changes and has nothing to do with the totality of allowed ingredients (it is more about the lack of contamination than consistency of the product). Others simply live as vegetarians—however that is actually done—without regard to the details of other dietary restrictions. And remember, this includes many who are considered observant by themselves and by others. Those who have officially rejected the entire dietary system or all of Jewish law are not under discussion now.

THE CRISIS OF PUBLIC WORSHIP

Synagogue communities are composed of groups of individuals with different needs, expectations, and abilities, who often press their local groups to conform to their individual expectations and thus turn individual changes to group ones; others fight to prevent any change, regardless of need. Sometimes *de facto* changes are introduced by those who eschew them. Over the past several centuries, there has perhaps been no greater arena of religious change than public worship, which has seen the creation of entire movements of Jews who rewrote the prayers and prayer books and changed almost everything that touches on public worship in an attempt to modernize prayer and make it more acceptable to those troubled by it traditional forms. Whether this is ultimately good or bad remains to be seen, but despite traditionalist sentiments opposed to most of these changes, modernists continue to seek to make worship meaningful. But what has happened to those who generally oppose such changes in their own lives but at least understand the possibility of their being meaningful to others?

In many diaspora synagogues, the Sabbath morning service often approaches four hours in length; for many people that is a very long time to sit and be attentive to worship in a foreign language. Many nonorthodox synagogues have shortened the service, but those that have not often share in the following situation, endemic of Orthodox synagogues outside Israel. As a result of the long service and failure to identify fully with it, many find it convenient to arrive after the official early morning service (during the second hour of the four); to talk during the Torah reading (much of the third hour); to then attend the Kiddush Club (a brief optional collation held by a group of individuals who assume the cost of the affair, held during the conclusion of the Torah service in some synagogues); to follow, read during, or sleep through the sermon, and to spend the rest of the service in close social engagement with the others in attendance. This is neither an exaggeration nor a caricature; such a Sabbath morning is routine for many thousands of regular synagogue goers; it is more social than spiritual.

As new situations call for new prayers, the old ones that most people no longer recite remain part of the official and formal community worship but not of many individuals who attend. Thus a real and ever-increasing gap between the many attendees and the few participants has developed, which has people filling slow points in the service by doing all sorts of things other than praying. Some study classical religious texts, or read translations of them, or read other books or the omnipresent printouts from daily and weekly Jewish Web-based news and study services that are available. Others merely socialize or conduct business that was not finished on Friday.

Despite what the people themselves might admit, a wide segment of the religious population—and I must emphasize that, for the most part, these people see themselves and others see them as Orthodox—attends worship to witness it, *i.e.,* to see that it has been conducted properly and to share visually in it through a psychological process somewhat akin to ancient participation in Temple worship, conducted solely by priests. Most of these people actually participate in the four-hour service for less than five minutes. Prayer is in crisis, at least for many who seem by their attendance to wish to take it seriously. And the system of formal public worship is deteriorating for many who value it. Those who make substantial changes are criticized by traditionalists, but traditionalism prevents many of its adherents from acknowledging and confronting the real problem. Individuals and groups may attempt to correct this situation, but their solutions often lead to isolation from others. These dividers among Jews and Jewish groups are one of the most troubling results of systematic fragmentation of the community, to be addressed below.

THE CRISIS INHERENT IN FAILING TO RECOGNIZE THE LEGITIMACY OF DIFFERENT FORMS OF JEWISH RELIGIOUS EXPRESSION: TRADITIONALISM VERSUS MODERNISM

At the same time, some individuals and their followers have created identities and postures through which they challenge other groups within the international Jewish constellation. It is reported that the Toronto Police Department once wanted to organize a meeting of synagogue administrators to discuss matters of security. There is a long history of some Orthodox rabbis refusing to enter non-Orthodox synagogues, and some of their non-Orthodox colleagues have learned to reciprocate in kind. Accordingly, the police department could not find a synagogue able to host the meeting; ultimately it was forced to organize four of them. Similar segregation has been evident at sessions of the Canadian National Bible Contest, where members of one or another Jewish community refused to enter the sanctuary of an "offending" alternative group. In good Canadian spirit, accommodations were provided by the organizers to insure no student would be forced to violate any principles by participating, but this kind of control prevents well-intentioned members of communities from behaving as they might want to and encourages extremism and separation at a time when both should be avoided. Corporate politics thus control individual lives, encourage further antagonisms, and divide an already small and fragmented group even further.

Exclusionist policies benefit no one and stand to harm many. They are maintained in order to remain officially critical of co-religionists. As globalization shrinks the world, one hears ever-increasing calls for religious people everywhere to rethink their attitudes toward other religions. The process might begin with or at least include internal Jewish consideration of how individual interests are dominating those of the community and how all Jews treat all other.

THE CRISIS OF THE ALIENATION OF WOMEN

Recent decades have seen a frontal assault by some groups on what seems to be the male monopoly on Jewish religious life, and this has resulted in all sorts of pressures for change and shifts in allegiances and practices. The issue is not directed to any specific ritual, though there are serious objections to some practices and the way they are controlled, but rather what appears to be the entire system of traditional male priority in the spheres of public worship, ritual practice, and study. Recent years have witnessed revolutionary changes of attitude and practice in both the Orthodox and non-Orthodox communities, some to allow greater equalization of opportunities for both males and females and, in some rightist circles, a move to counteract this trend.

In part, the problem results from the modernization of family life, changes in economic and social expectations, the abandonment of many traditional observances, and the radical technological advances that have influenced the Jewish home and the potential roles of the Jewish woman (and man) in it, and created a very different environment in which people find themselves. The modernization of the home substantially reduced the labor-intensive nature of being a housewife and mother; concomitantly it eliminated many of the spiritual components and traditional practices associated with these activities, leaving the modern woman in need of some other form of religious expression. The need to satisfy inherent and valued spiritual needs naturally led to imitating male roles, while many men drifted further from the base of commitment and observance. One of the primary arenas in which this is playing itself out is public worship, which continues to evolve in ways not anticipated in even the recent past.

The egalitarianism of Western democracies strengthens this position and keeps it in the forefront of Jewish discussion. Even so, some traditionalist women have taken to defending the status quo ante,[5] but this defense of traditionalism by women is itself a modern innovation. Personal observation suggests that, in general, Orthodox men and women share commitments to religious values and practices, while, in the non-Orthodox communities, women are responsible for the lion's share of Judaism's survival. If correct, this single fact serves to necessitate and justify the importance of female influence on the non-Orthodox religious realm, but the unrest that still surrounds the issue and its resolution remains a crisis of major proportions.[6]

FAMILY IN CRISIS

Traditionally, the family has been the basic unit of Jewish social existence. It is where people live together, share in life's joys and sorrows, eat, sleep, reproduce, and die. It is also the primary locus of religious life and religious education, though both also have become the foci of larger group practices. Every modern interference in a family's religious life impacts on the individual-family-community nexus and on the global Jewish situation, not to mention the religious values and behaviors that traditionally were taught and practiced there.

Many aspects of personal life are family-based, and Judaism is famous for its strong family bonds. Young children and aging elders are among the many concerns of the family, and in earlier times the family was the social unit in which one played out many of life's challenges and developments. Modern reorientation of the expectation that people will marry, sustain a family, live in a family context, and both contribute to and benefit from the family structure affects the delivery of these services and also the very mechanism by which they were provided and the prospect of continuing to provide them in the future. Rituals and observances that were or are family-based usually seem strange, if not bizarre, to those attempting to follow them outside the family context; the table fellowship of old and the Sabbath and holiday meals of later times are the most prominent examples. Interestingly, recent studies have confirmed that eating dinner together is one of the best ways to insure a family's values are transmitted to its children and to prevent drug use, poor schoolwork, involvement with undesirable individuals and influences, etc. Incremental increases or decreases are visible for every day of the week in which families do or do not eat together. The family is a very powerful but only recently appreciated vehicle for teaching values.

To be sure, everyone did not always live in a family setting, but far more people did in the past than do today, and that change has created a crisis for the contemporary Jewish community. Things formerly done by and in the family are now the responsibility of the community, including match making, hosting community Shabbat and holiday meals, arranging a community-wide Passover Seder, providing centers for baby care, organizing bar and bat mitzvah celebrations, and the like. The community provides these opportunities, because many individuals cannot; and their contacts with sustained family activities are often negligible. For these reasons, rituals traditionally conducted in or by the family are under immense pressure to change or to disappear. Children are educated in families, and even when given a solid grounding in school, often it is only through the family's reinforcement at home that the child internalizes the importance of what is being taught, and the responses are not limited to specific movements within the Jewish fold. All are equally affected; only those who doggedly maintain full commitment to the family can hope to escape.

Of course, the concern over the loss of the family as a conveyor of religious values is only one small part of the global attack on the family as an institution. Changes in attitudes about extramarital sex, having children out of wedlock or having none at all, living only for oneself with an obligation to work and pay taxes but not to contribute otherwise to society have changed the nature of the family in many places. Now it is recommended that one live, enjoy life, and be removed expeditiously from the arena of the living before becoming a burden on one's relatives or the society in which one lives. Euthanasia is the ultimate affront to the individual, who in the present system must resist all challenging forces alone. Families help to do that also, but the contemporary crisis of the family suggests it needs global support and willing parents need new coaching in how to raise their children are needed, even as communities need ways to convey the values formerly deemed a part of parental responsibility.

CRISIS OF SMALL AND CULTURALLY ISOLATED JEWISH COMMUNITIES

At no time in history did all Jews live in centers that provided all ideal forms of Jewish life, and, in response, various levels of cultural independency, isolation, and assimilation have resulted. In many modern contexts, norms and patterns of classical Jewish life are constantly under pressure both from inside and out. Standards of religious observance in the Jerusalem and New York Metropolitan areas are generally considered to be totally different from those in most other Israeli or North American communities. High school students who apply to study in Israel are treated differently if they come from New York or elsewhere. Religious leaders will do almost anything to attain a posting in the New York area. Standards of observance differ from those in many other places, particularly small outlying communities, where similar concentrations of Jews do not exist. For this reason, some parents send their high-school-aged children to study and live in distant places, potentially fomenting additional personal crises. Some outlying communities have all but disappeared, as committed families have educated their children in the cities and encouraged them to move there. This concentration of people and wealth provides main centers with enviable resources, but it often has a less positive effect on demographic realities and their political implications in the other regions, creating a crisis of the Jews there, if not of the Holy.

Extensive efforts to maintain and to develop active communities outside the major metropolitan areas do succeed. I know of places where the local teaching staff includes members of the legal, medical, and agricultural professions; and by any standard the students are well-educated in traditional texts and issues. I once attended the Saturday afternoon synagogue service in a relatively isolated American town where the audience for the rabbi's class regularly included at least one-half dozen internationally known (and observant) scholars of Judaica who worked at local universities. Together they were so broad in their intellectual strengths and so intimidating in their knowledge that the rabbi found it necessary to write out the weekly presentation and read it like a conference paper, and even then they challenged, corrected, and augmented his words at every turn.

But these situations are highly exceptional. The rhythms of Jewish life in many small or poorly educated communities often permit Buddhist, Native American, and Christian forms of worship to influence synagogue services and be called Jewish. In such places, it is far from exceptional for the beginning and end of the Sabbath, for example, to be determined by means that have no relation to any religious definitions of the time of sunset and the like but are merely selected for the convenience of those who make the decisions. In such contexts, Jewish life has become largely what the Jews do to express their Jewishness, whether or not it has any base in the tradition or even is compatible with it. Clearly the pressures of isolation, distance from the core communities, lack of adequate education, diluted commitment, a shortfall of leadership, and many other factors influence what is considered Jewish life.

For some, eating bagels qualifies as a Jewish act and doing so on Sunday morning is a religious ritual; if done in a synagogue, it is an act of deep piety. Modern technology has the potential to change much of this, but only if people want it to. Arguably, Jews have the existential right to worship any way they choose, and if they deem eating bagels or sitting atop flag poles more sacred than observing the Sabbath or the dietary laws, they can make that decision; but would this then be Judaism? Conceivably these new acts could be done in truly sacred ways, but probably there is no greater crisis of the Holy than to see Judaism move in this direction.

A CRISIS OF COMPLEXITY AND THE RESULTING CRISES OF EDUCATION AND LEADERSHIP

For thousands of years, Judaism existed in what is often understood as some normative state but actually was a constantly evolving constellation of religious communities that shared many ideas and commitments but differed on others. Regardless of many minor and major differences in the details of practice, generally the members of an individual constituency conformed to and shared in local norms. Today, the right of the individual to choose to follow the laws or not—recognized and discouraged in Deuteronomy 18:19 but rarely acted upon broadly—has become the Western, secular ideal. The individual has been empowered to choose, to accept or to reject, to modify, to augment, and to delete elements from any aspect of religious life, as he or she sees fit.

Most individuals are not encumbered by the need to find a new title for their new personal religion; they merely consider it a personalized version of an old and established one.

Such attitudes present all contemporary religions in their classical forms with a true crisis; Judaism is no different. Concomitantly, it has grown so complex that many potential adherents are at a loss to follow its details, and many others are not even motivated to try. In the West, every man is king in his house, and whether or not every woman is also queen, both have the right to observe, not to observe, to not observe, or to change any aspect of any observance any way they desire. All may not be able to alter formal public worship carried out under the auspices of an incorporated religious body, but they can create their own and then do virtually anything as they wish. In fact, non-Orthodox Jews have been doing this quite successfully for several centuries; some would suggest Orthodox Jews actually do so also but that they are much less candid about it.

Two important factors in countering these trends—and not only in isolated contexts—are proper education and competent leadership. Most communities have educational activities and leaders, but do the former truly satisfy their needs and are the latter recognized as legitimate by all the insiders to any group, much less by outsiders? This is a complex issue, as segments of the Jewish community demand to be led by people with whose messages they can identify, but there is also a general tendency to choose leaders who are somewhat to the group's ideological right; rarely to the left. Thus Reform schools may hire Conservative or Orthodox teachers, but Orthodox ones will not reciprocate. Modern Orthodox synagogues often seek increasingly traditional rabbis to replace the relatively liberal minded ones they formerly employed. Non-Hasidic Yeshivot may engage Hasidic teachers, but rarely will the reverse happen. The global community lacks universally accepted leaders, and individual communities seems to prefer leaders who are more representative of the community's ideals than its realities. In some cases this has led to increased interest in and care for the sanctity of Judaism, but at least as frequently it contributes to tension and ill will, as people who have lived their lives one way suddenly find the changes they once made or the standards by which they always lived unacceptable.

Early and more extensive identification of potential lay leaders is crucial and must be accompanied by a grassroots movement to discuss and educate all Jews in how one makes Jewishly informed decisions. I speak not only of halakhic decision making, which many people insist be done by their official religious leaders, but of the need to inculcate in everyone, but especially the youth, a commitment to seeing Jewish values as a global part of all decisions they make. Decisions made at the personal, family, institutional, community, national, and international levels must reflect Jewish values, and this cannot happen without a conscious attempt to train all Jews to think this way, so that those who eventually assume leadership roles can behave accordingly.

THE CRISIS OF JEWISH EDUCATION

Rabbinic law requires that a new community build a school before a synagogue[7] and invest immediately in educating its youth, but each individual is
mandated to study the Torah "day and night,"[8] which does not mean all day
and all night, but often has been observed that way. Literacy is a given in
Jewish communities, and while in some times and places it was limited to
Hebrew or a "Jewish" language, a generation ago Jews who spoke between
six and ten languages were far from a rarity (sometimes because persecutions
and wanderings made that learning inevitable). In medieval times, Jews contributed extensively to an international and inter-confessional commerce in
ideas that included many personal efforts to translate books written in Arabic, Hebrew, or Latin into one or both of the others. While many of the
contemporary Orthodox cannot fathom the extent or even the historicity of
this activity, which was a cherished aspect of Jewish learning, study is undoubtedly the classic rabbinic activity; not even prayer can compete in some
contexts.

It is therefore reasonable to assume that Jewish identity has been strengthened and maintained through study and education, and the failure of either,
which would result in widespread ignorance, is a plague perceived by many
to be more serious than almost all others. How do the pressures of contemporary life affect Jewish education? In some countries, Jewish private schools
are rapidly increasing in popularity, and while the trend originated with the
Orthodox, it no longer is limited to them. An impressive range of Conservative, Reform, and nonsectarian schools dot the North American landscape,
and a new model, the "pluralistic" school, largely a development of Conservative educators anxious to attract a broader clientele, is poised to give many
others a run for their money. In other places, Zionist schools may be the
norm; some also have Hasidic ones.

Orthodox Jews often fancy themselves to be the continental leaders in
Jewish education, because they are relatively successful in keeping their
children within the religious fold, but I believe that the long-term title–
holders are really the members of the Conservative movement. To be sure,
all the others are also committed to education, and many have highly successful records with which to bolster their claims, but the Conservative
movement has surpassed all others in its creative, pedagogically sound, universally accessible forms of Jewish education. In the 1960s, for example, the
Ramah camps were probably the most powerful Jewish educational institution in North America. As they became more closely aligned with Conservative, particularly leftist Conservative ideologies, they lost much of their appeal to the broader Jewish community (not to mention some more traditional
elements in the Conservative one and many of the children they had so
successfully educated), but one of their successes was to spawn a series of

non-Conservative institutions that carried out some of their goals in different ideological communities.

The Ramah camps and USY (and NIFTY, NCSY, and Bnei Akiva) also legitimated informal education as a powerful contributor to Jewish education. In fact, today one of the weaknesses in many Jewish day schools—which now claim the role of Judaism's most influential educational institutions—is that they have become too informal and camp-like. While it is foolish to hold the Ramah camps responsible for this development (the looseness of contemporary society and a lack of sophisticated education-based decision making in the schools deserve a much larger share of the blame), ultimately this development can be traced to the educational success of the camping movement. The opportunity to live a total or even partial Jewish life for two months a year for many consecutive formative years transformed the lives of many students who did not attend day schools, and often it provided them with strong working skills in spoken Hebrew. It also provided an alternative model of educational success that in many cases involved the same staff during the school year and the summer. For the students who did not attend a Jewish day school, camp was an intense experience of Jewish living; for those who did, it was merely a religiously acceptable form of summer relaxation that inevitably spilled over into school.

Many elementary schools are found across North America, and, while secondary schools are significantly less plentiful, many cities are blessed with a range of institutions from which potential students and their parents can choose. When one considers that in many places annual day school tuition for one child can exceed $18,000 and many families have three or more children, an annual bill of $50,000 pre-tax is not unusual. Multiply that for twelve years and one can see why some communities have not been able to sustain high schools (not only why Jewish parents are very concerned about earning and preparing their children to earn substantial sums of money). Many parents prefer to rely on public education and to save their limited financial resources for the all-important college years and even higher costs; others simply want the Jewish education, feel there is no other alternative, and make whatever sacrifices are required to insure their children have it. Very often, their schools—particularly those not populated by the rightist religious community—owe their survival to academic success in secular subjects, not only Jewish ones. But whether families accept the Jewish Studies because accompanied by a good secular education or the reverse, or they are avoiding what is often perceived to be the less desirable culture of public schools, they are equally committed to both aspects of the dual curriculum, or some mix of the above, they often prioritize college admission, particularly to Ivy League institutions and other excellent schools.[9]

In theory, Jewish education should not be devoted to the continuity of the Jewish community. It should teach the languages and texts of Judaism and work to inculcate a commitment to its religious values, to its practices, and to the Jewish people. The goal should be to create educated Jews who are able to grapple with the inevitable challenges life throws their way and to nego-tiate a meaningful Jewish life around or through them. We need serious, thinking Jews, not warm fuzzy ones. My greatest fear is the trivializing of Jewish education, not the possibility that it is overly rigorous. The idea is not to work for continuity but something much more important—meaningful commitment. Continuity is a necessary by-product, not the primary goal. If Jewish education succeeds to teach meaningful commitment, Judaism will continue to flourish. If not, it will not; and one might ask if, under those circumstances, it even should.

Successful calls for more education often produced a ritualized form of study, itself a part of the crisis of education of which I speak, though of a very different order. Less than a century ago, one European rabbi created a plan for men to study a daily page of the Babylonian Talmud (called *daf yomi*, "daily page," in Hebrew). This effort, which runs to completion in about seven-and-a-half years, had a slow start, but today hundreds of thou-sands identify with the program and many tens of thousands actually fulfill it. A new seventy-three-volume English translation and commentary has been produced[10] to help those who need it (with Hebrew, French, and Spanish translations on the way), and *daf-yomi* Talmud classes are now found in synagogues all over the world. People from all walks of life participate in this effort, and even if they do not actually study every page, they do cover many. To assist in this endeavor, some cities provide access to a dial-a-*daf* phone service, whereby one calls in at any time and listens to a presentation of the daily page. Classes in synagogues, sometimes two or three a day, work through the text. Other classes are presented on line, through Web sites, on CDs, and on tapes. Some cars of the Long Island Railroad are full of riders who study Talmud there daily on the way to work, alone or in groups.

Technology, to return to one of the discussions above, has become a major contributor to Jewish education, which is not limited to children, of any particular age but is considered a daily obligation for every individual. The ease of publishing, the coordinated efforts of agencies, schools, rabbis, teachers, and financial backers have created a huge market and successful following for study. There is no doubt that technology has greatly enhanced the popular interest in Talmud study and helped further or actually begin the educations many people never had or never appreciated. Of course, even with all the technology, the nagging question is whether this kind of hasty routin-ized study—almost review, perhaps more akin to a public scriptural reading than a serious class—serves any general need, especially for beginners. Most admit it is not a perfect system, but they defend it as better than any other available program or motivator. One can debate whether this form of study is what the general population needs, indeed, whether it is truly beneficial for anyone other than the teacher who must prepare and deliver the class seven days a week for more than seven years.

THE EXTERNAL COMPONENTS OF THE CRISIS

Failures of education and leadership are internal problems that may be shared by other religions but whose correction can be effected only by Jews. However external forces also shape these issues and contribute to these and other forms of crisis. What are the precise identities and natures of some of the forces affecting relations of individual and community, and how do they contribute to the contemporary crisis? Globalization presses in on all sides. Communities that in previous eras could anticipate the possibility of independent, even isolated survival are now swept into the global tidal wave with increasing rapidity. In theory, technology allows all people to see all things in all places, in real time. Everyone, everything, and everywhere are now essentially one commodity. Privacy, seclusion, and slow quiet are things of the past; they must be cultivated and actively preserved in order to experience them. How many vacation and housing advertisements seek customers by promising to provide them? The public sphere has come to define and to control most of the private one.

Some forms of worship that used to be limited to specific houses of prayer are now available on TV or online. Indeed, one can log in, adopt a personal identity that may be totally different from one's biological persona—indeed, we have difficulty speaking of one's "real" persona any more—and participate as anyone who might be conjured up, as a figment of the imagination. Jews have not been as creative in doing this as the members of some other religions, but they are learning quickly; and even some Orthodox leaders have created websites for occasional prayer and routinized study opportunities. So what is the crisis?

During the nine days in August before the ninth of the month of Av, it is traditional to eat no meat unless it is consumed as part of a religious celebration. Completion of the study of a book of the Bible or a tractate of the Talmud qualifies, and in many places it has been common for individuals to study for months in order to finish during this week and even to invite friends to the occasion. The practice was encouraged by those who prioritized study, which obviously is increased and enhanced in the process. Recently a number of restaurants and educational institutions advertised that you could call in or log-in and participate, virtually at any time. While such services provide instant access to mechanized, ritualized learning and technically give license to eat meat during these days, there is no justification for the damage being done to the system of learning that had developed. Undoubtedly a similar pattern of accessibility will be provided for exclusion of the first born from the fast held on the day before the Passover Seder.

The development of technology has had a profound impact on religious life. Not only can one travel anywhere to participate in virtually any particular ceremony or occasion, whatever goes on there can be broadcast around the world instantly. Memory is becoming irrelevant, as recording replaces it. Not only is a potentially infinite amount of contemporary information being stored continually, its preservation for the future (if organized in some sustainable and recoverable way) means that the amount of data available will surpass what any individual or group can actually control. Before long, the sheer quantity of it will totally overwhelm the system. We are already creating an ever-growing workforce to create and preserve it.

The foregoing observation applies to everyone, but perhaps it challenges Jews in a unique way. For at least two millennia and probably for much longer, Jews have made the study of religious texts one of their highest priorities. And because learned people both studied and taught these texts, they preserved a huge literature of explanations and derived teachings. Thanks to technological advances, the availability of Jewish textual resources is far greater than ever before. A generation ago, a collection of one hundred books was considered a good home library. One could find thousands of books in particularly well-equipped homes (the limit used to be in the ten-thousand range) and tens of thousands or more in important university or seminary libraries, but a few hundred volumes was considered a fine collection, and owners of them prided themselves on controlling the books and their contents. Now for a few thousand dollars, any individual can purchase a CD containing a vast library of standard rabbinic texts, including thousands of individual documents that almost no one read a generation ago, and a hard drive that holds upward of fifteen thousand texts and is constantly being augmented. The first group of texts is concordance-searchable and occupies virtually no space; the second is not and is the size of one book; both require the use of a computer, a virtually ubiquitous tool.[11]

Not only is access to this library of materials now a universal opportunity and possibility—not the privilege of the wealthy or the learned—it provides untold challenges to those who seek to determine or to practice what the Jewish religious tradition demands of them in any situation. In many contexts, oral tradition, family practice, and community models have given way to vast text searches that, in a few seconds, scour entire literatures for information and provide it in usable form. Gone is the need for an expert who has studied this material for a lifetime; also gone is the limited reliance on a few standard texts and handbooks from which to derive most needed information. More important, gone is the confidence in any form of Jewish life that relies primarily on the living traditions and expressions of Judaism and the formerly dominant confidence in their authenticity and authority. They have been replaced by reliance on "sources," a poorly defined term that basically means any book or electronic datum available, regardless of the traditional emphasis on its relevance or its pecking order in the hierarchy of texts and arguments. Moreover, given the theoretical commitment to study and the reliance on such materials, the conclusions supported by computer-based searches for information are virtually impossible to challenge.

Anyone can search and find answers, as well as render decisions, or, at the very least, challenge those whose professional status has traditionally allocated such power to them. Texts that literally no one looked at a generation ago are now accessed daily, and their contents—however ignored or pigeon-holed they once were—are freely consulted at every turn by anyone so inclined. Rabbinic consensus used to be determined on the teachings of between six and twelve major writers. That figure has multiplied many times over, as other perhaps no less important but often less consulted writers become more accessible and more influential. Knowing how to negotiate this sea of information and texts is now as important as, perhaps more important than, knowing what to do in any given situation or how to decide. Knowledge has become a universal commodity; authority now resides not with those who possess the information but with those popularly perceived to know how to apply it correctly.

THE CRISIS OF MEDIA ATTENTION, SCRUTINY, AND MISREPRESENTATION

Another pervasive influence on all aspects of religious life (and nonreligious life also) is the media. Because the media have access to all aspects of Jewish life, they are able to present and to critique them constantly. When the critiques are favorable they provide additional political sustenance to the Jewish cause; when negative, the community quickly grows wary and weary of a world with an infinite number of searching eyes and critical mouths. [12]

The media can and do literally make mountains out of molehills. Tentative solutions to problems, new trends in care giving or supporting those in need, archaeological discoveries, corrections of previously held erroneous positions, and the like are easily shared with all but often are not. Problems, political errors, weaknesses, the personal failures of leaders, conflicts among political groups supposedly of a single mind and minor events that, in previous eras, might have gone unreported or unnoticed and, in any case, were not acted upon, are often treated in public, sometimes with all the sensitivity and finesse of a tornado.

Just as politicians have learned to finesse the impact of the media, so too must religious leaders and religious communities. But often this is difficult. Find a crime or a compromise deemed worthy of attention, and it will be shared immediately and universally by the media, and if it appears to be religiously motivated it will get even more attention than it might otherwise. Unfortunately more significant events of a positive nature often receive far less if any attention, leaving the average well-intentioned reader or listener with the impression that the evil in the world far outstrips the good and that the forces of religion are among the former's major architects. This dimension of the crisis applies to all religions, and the Jews are far from immune.

THE CRISIS OF JEWISH IDENTITY

In past generations, some Jews were known by their region of origin: Ashkenazim, from Central Europe; Sefaradim, from Spain, North Africa, or the Ottoman Empire; Litvacks, from Lithuania; or Galitzianers, from the Galician region of today's Poland. The reason for this is not difficult to divine. As Jewish communities crystallized in various locations, different cultural and ethnic entities began to take shape. Of course more than these four labels were in use; indeed almost every North African, Middle Eastern, European, and Asian community or cluster of communities had its own. Though difference was assumed and sometimes became a source of internal ethnic pride and of external derision, it was real. Even in antiquity, distinct Jewish identities ranged over the entire Middle Eastern and Mediterranean region. There were cultural as well as religious differences between the Jews represented in the Babylonian Talmud and the Palestinian one, in all likelihood even greater ones between them and the various outlying regions that were less connected to rabbinic culture. And if we press backward to shortly before the Christian era, Hellenistic Judaism differed greatly from what might be called its parallel Semitic equivalent. Jews of the Mediterranean, Elephantine, the Levant, India, the countries surrounding Mesopotamia, and many other places all have a different story to tell about their ethnic and religious differences. In biblical times, the same is true. Even the northern and southern kingdoms of the biblical monarchs did not see eye-to-eye on all issues, especially religious ones.

Local differences in Hebrew pronunciation, in religious customs (*minhagim*), in climactic responses to seasonal holidays, in choice of foods, and the like are largely a function of the cultural contexts in which Jews lived. Custom reigns supreme, augmenting, reinforcing, or challenging, halakhic considerations, as demonstrated by the Jewish treatment of American Thanksgiving. Most American Liberal Jews and numerous Orthodox ones observe American Thanksgiving, and a generation ago the number of Orthodox rabbis who actively included themselves in their number seems astounding by contemporary standards. They did this to acknowledge formally the many noble acts of American goodness from which they and their communities benefited, and their ranks included Rabbi Joseph Soloveitchik, Rabbi Pinhas Teitz, and a number of close associates of Rabbi Moses Feinstein. Contemporary objections[13] see this as adoption of some non-Jewish religious practices and grow stronger from year to year. In many circles, observing Thanksgiving has come to be seen as inappropriate, to say the least; in others, its observance remains strong. Thanksgiving is observed far less enthusiastically in Canada (and a month earlier); expatriate Jews in Canada usually observe it, if at all, on the following Sabbath. Jews elsewhere know nothing of this practice.

Just as has happened with the adoption of Thanksgiving by American Jews, others have juxtaposed various Jewish values and commitments with related but sometimes opposite ones derived from the surrounding culture or state. Were Jews in Germany and elsewhere fully German enough to serve in the army? Were early Canadian Jews Canadian enough to hold office, and if so could they take an oath on the Hebrew Bible or only on a Christian one? At times Jews fought for cultural equality, even while some of their religious leaders prayed that the quest would fail, because they believed that such Jewish success would ultimately undermine the community and its religious values.

The twentieth century saw most Western democracies accept the idea that Jews could be proper, productive, and loyal servants of the state, and they acted positively on this assumption; it also saw the strengthening of Jewish commitment to the idea. Whether they are called American Jews or Jewish Americans, few doubt the sincere commitment of many to both identities. Is there a similar distinction to be made between Israeli Jews and Jewish Israelis? Between Israeli and Jew?

Israel is the traditional homeland of the Jewish people. While many of its values derive from classical Jewish roots and many others are shared with Western democracies, other cultural and ethnic elements in its society are neither and of no particular value to Jewish living. What if anything should be their role in a Jewish value system or culture? And how can they be divorced, if that is the goal, from the total mix of attitudes and practices we associate with life in that country?

And what of the inevitable mix of cultures that the ingathering of exiles has produced and that grows daily outside Israel where even more forms of culture and identity are regularly in contact? Families that contain, for example, an Ashkenazi husband and a Sefaradi wife are Jewishly intermarried, but there is little rabbinic objection to such matches. Medieval texts bear witness to Rabbanite-Karaite intermarriages,[14] which were accompanied by contractual commitments that spelled out what the spouses would or would not do in order to both make the marriage work and remain faithful to differences of law and custom that derived from their home communities and religious practices. Today Jewish families are often constructed from many different ethnic pieces, and even when halakhic conversion has taken place—which means a formerly non-Jewish partner is now unquestionably Jewish—issues of multiple identity still arise. In traditional societies, the husband's practices theoretically became those of the family, but who says that is the ideal? One can be sure that if a wife spoke a language other than her husband's the children learned it; the mother's influence was always paramount.

In some cases, the optimal situation has been to allow all aspects of one's cultural background to remain as visible as possible. And so, to create a fictitious but highly realistic example, when an American male whose parents came from Russia and Morocco marries an Israeli female whose parents are from Ethiopia and Italy, which of the six operative Jewish ethnicities is (or are) to be followed in any particular situation? More importantly for our purposes, how will the decision be made? The problem is far from new or insurmountable, but as the Jewish global village shrinks and people become less racially and ethnically limited, the number and complexity of the problem's permutations will continue to increase.

As other nations and religious groups continue to mix with Jewish ones (either through formal conversion or in other ways) and the Jewish cultural baggage of one partner manages to survive or evolve, to what extent will a new symbiotic relationship between two or more religions play a role in Jewish life? It is no longer unusual to find a university student with parents from different religious communities; intermarriage between Hindus and Muslims or Christians and Jews, for example, did happen, but that is old news. Now we see students whose mother is Jewish (from a Jewish grandmother and a Christian grandfather) and whose father is Muslim, for example (with one Muslim grandparent and one Hindu). According to Jewish law, the student in this example is Jewish; what is her cultural identity? And whom will she marry? And should she decide to live as an observant Jewess, what then? The issue is not one of legitimacy or of acceptance; in any case, that will be *ad hominem.* The question is the cultural and religious identity of the woman and her offspring.

The above situation can lead to and support a range of symbiotic relationships, but from some perspectives they would be deemed syncretistic. Is this good or bad? To ask the question differently, can Judaism survive on a global playing field without relying on the social glue that holds together its many religiously committed adherents, regardless of the many differences among them and without the walls that keep out unwanted influences?

THE CRISIS OF RELIGION WITHOUT SPIRITUALITY

Many of the other crises mentioned above converge and pale in significance when compared to the multi-faceted crisis Jews and Judaism face over Jewish spirituality. On the one hand, when confronted with challenges or problems, many well-intentioned people with little or no understanding of the rationales behind various aspects of Jewish life simply change or abandon it. And modeled on the Nike slogan, we may describe the contemporary religious response to these preferences for change and avoidance as an amalgamation of "just study it," "just do it," and "just continue it." *I.e.,* change nothing. All religious behaviors, even the intellectual ones, have been ritualized; few responses are focused on the need to "just feel it" (without regard for anything else), and only exceptional people are able to "just understand it" (once the slogan of even the un-observant secularists, who valued classical learning even if not accompanied by a commitment to practice).

An understanding of human psychology that tries to regularize specific behaviors has been coupled with a mystical assumption that these behaviors have cosmic significance. Whereas Judaism is, in theory, a way to serve and worship the deity, it is rapidly becoming a mechanistic serving and worshiping of its codes of religious practice. In a rush to reconstitute the European communities lost in the Holocaust and to capture a maximal number of potential returnees to religious life (a truly unanticipated positive development of the late twentieth century), the purposes behind many acts have been lost, and relationship with God has been relegated from the goal of religious life to the status of a catalyst for what is claimed to be required Jewish behavior. One year, after I taught about the Kinot, relatively obscure medieval poems recited annually in the Tisha Ba'Av liturgy but never properly understood by most synagogue-goers, one regular attendee shocked me by observing that he was surprised to learn that these texts were supposed to mean anything. He figured he just had to mumble them every year to fulfill some religious obligation. Has modernity convinced Jews that the final words of Ecclesiastes are the best we can do, "When all is done, everything having been heard, just fear God and observe his commandments, because this is the entirety of what humanity is capable"?[15]

Spiritual concerns are authentic and pervasive aspects of Jewish religious life, and they need to become a more prominent aspect of its maintenance. The responses to sacred time and space, to study, to pilgrimage, and to many other aspects of religious life need to be reconsidered in the light of the strengths that have been developed of late and the imbalances that may accompany them in certain contexts. Sabbaths and holidays are times for religious growth—by which I do not mean only for study and discovering the details of required and prohibited religious behaviors, however important they are.

THE CRISIS OF THE LAND OF ISRAEL

The Land of Israel, the ideal Jewish homeland for well over three thousand years, was reconstituted in the twentieth century as a spiritual oasis, a center of holiness; but it was to be real, not only ideal, perhaps even a model of what an inspired human society could be. Everyone acknowledges that it has not achieved that nearly impossible task, but visiting it should at least acknowledge these ideals and find place for them in the tourist's reality. When its holiest sites are surrounded by equipment and supplies, plagued by the sounds and smells of busses and cars (not to mention great numbers of the vehicles themselves), and guards are posted to inspect all visitors lest they be the bearers of wanton destruction, a great deal remains to secure their sanctity.

The sacred center known as the "Temple Mount," contested not just between religions but between Jewish religious authorities, [16] is a metaphor for Israeli society in general, and the rabbinic leaders themselves have become implicated. While many do everything in their power to assist those in their care, they frequently do it only on their own terms, forcing the removal of religion from contemporary culture farther than it need be or indeed than many "average Israelis" wanted it to be. The crisis has seen a divide between the "religious" Israeli and the "secular" one that is nothing short of astounding. Some religious people will have nothing to do with the nonreligious other than to allow them to serve in the army; some even object to that. Some truly pious people refuse to call themselves "religious," because they cannot bear the negative associations. Israeli society has been divided into two groups.

One prioritizes study and worship, invests itself in the performance of the commandments, maintains a position of cultural and religious isolation, and claims to be opposed to change of any sort. Many males devote their lives to study and do little to support their families; in avoiding contemporary materialism, they can err to the other extreme by denying their wives and children the basic necessities of life and themselves the physical and psychological benefits of gainful employment. Or they manage to engage with the secular state just long enough and frequently enough to remain supported by it. They challenge the state at every turn, influence its political decisions to serve their needs, and many have de-legitimated the state both at home and abroad.

The second, larger group is polarized in the opposite direction. Most basic classics of Jewish literature are unknown, widely practiced religious rituals are totally unfamiliar, holy sites—even in Jerusalem—are never visited, materialism is rampant, and openness to most of those things held so dear by the first group is hardly part of the culture any more, even though it was as recently as one generation ago. Israeli educational systems were devised to provide opportunities for both secular and religious education. The rightists created their own system, moving away from the merely "religious," leaving the secularists even further from any fallout of religious activity. The middle group, the Orthodox who are still anchored in the real world, used to provide a model of compromise and synthesis; they were believed to have it all. Now, in many cases, the rightists refuse to relate to them because they have compromised with modernity, while the secularists cannot abide their religious commitments. Extremism breeds extremism. Perhaps most troubling, this situation has been normalized and institutionalized in Israel, and for a decade or more it is being exported to other centers of Jewish life.

The crisis of the Jews has become the crisis of their Judaisms, and however one defines "The Holy"—holy books, holy people, holy land—of that too. To speak in a highly anthropomorphic way, even "The Holy One, Blessed Be He," must be in crisis over this sacrilege. Somehow the inchoate abstraction we call "The Holy" should help unite contemporary Jews, but it has been enlisted only to force them further apart. What could be a greater crisis? Outside Israel, the tensions are perhaps less, but that is true mostly in places where the number of Jews is small and they badly need each other. Once positioned in larger communities where corporate posturing is accepted as the norm, all sorts of less positive situations result.

THE CRISIS OF SPIRITUAL FRAGMENTATION

The fragmentation of the Jewish people, the specialization of commitments to various religious and anti-religious postures, the forces of contemporary society and its leaders that are generally hostile to religion, and distractions—both neutral and negative—conspire to pressure Jews and their Judaisms in unprecedented ways. And the failure to develop a strong middle that enables everyone to feel part of the whole exacerbates an otherwise bad situation. What evolved over the millennia into a complete religious system and spiritually sophisticated entity has been fragmented and re-shaped. The states of its religion, of its land, of its practices, of its belief system, and of its practitioners have been set on paths of perpetual evolution but in divergent rather than convergent directions. The external pressures, the religious complexities, the internal conflicts, and the divergent interests of those committed to them mean that few people ever have the option to experience the richness of Judaism in any theoretical or practical way.

The past is a valuable component in setting goals for the present and planning for the future. In all likelihood, the balance between these needs, potentials, and challenges will be negotiated in many different ways, which at least suggests that if some models fail, others may succeed. Some will prefer to change what they can and mothball the rest; others will use every resource to preserve even fossilize what they have in an attempt to thwart the inevitable forces of change. For better or worse, the goal of Judaism is neither to undo the past nor to preserve it. It is to enable Jews to build a closer relationship with God, with themselves, with each other, with other people, and with the world we share. Perhaps it is the time to insure that these goals are more mutually compatible.

NOTES

1. Isaiah 37, 3.
2. Editor's note: See parallels in the Buddhist perspective on page 40.
3. Kenny Rogers's song, "The Gambler."
4. Syndicat v. Anselem [2004] S.C.R. 551. Seehttp://aaron.ca/columns/2004-07-17.htm.
5. See, for example, http://www.chabad.org/thejewishwoman/default_cdo/jewish/Women.htm and http://torah.org/learning/women/archives.html.
6. Editor's note: Compare to the Buddhist experience on page 49.
7. http://www.chabad.org/library/article_cdo/aid/74339/jewish/Who-Invented-the-Synagogue.htm.
8. Joshua: 1, 8.
9. Editor's note: See parallels in Christianity on page 78.
10. The Artscroll edition of the Talmud.
11. Editor's note: See the parallel trend in Hinduism on page 118.
12. Editor's note: Compare to Islam on page 128.
13. For some typical popular discussions, see http://5tjt.com/thanksgiving-and-halachah/, and http://www.shemayisrael.com/parsha/halacha/Vol8Issue8.pdf.
14. See M. A. Friedman, *Jewish Marriage in Palestine: A Cairo Geniza Study II*, Tel Aviv-New York, 1981, 2, 290–301. Also in Judith Olszowy-Schlanger, "Early Karaite Family Law," in Meira Pollack (ed.), *Karaite Judaism* (Leiden: Brill, 2003): 277–278.
15. Ecclesiastes 12, 13.
16. Some Jewish religious authorities permit Jews to visit the Temple Mount and strive for Jewish rights there but other regard the ground as too sacred and forbid Jewish pilgrimage to the site.

Chapter Six

Hinduism

Deepak Sarma

In recent times, the global landscape has changed irrevocably. Many of these changes have challenged the ways that religions are conceived and the ways that religious people put their beliefs into practice. These challenges confront all of the world's religions and peoples. What kinds of moments of crisis face the Hindu communities? What kinds of responses have worked well? What kinds have not? How have these challenges and threats been reinterpreted as opportunities for growth?

To answer these questions, I will paint a broad picture of these moments of crisis as they pertain to Hinduism, both in India and in the ever-growing diaspora. I will first address the most significant issue faced by Hinduism, namely the history and use of the term "Hindu" itself. Next I will turn to the ways that the global landscape has changed the social world of Hindus in both India and beyond in the context of reform movements. Third, I will examine issues pertaining to education and the dissemination of doctrine in diaspora communities. Fourth, I will concentrate on the rapidly changing media and technology sector and its impact on Hinduism. Fifth, I return to the issue of the divide between the secular and the sacred. I will close with some suggestions for ways that religious leaders can confront these crises and resolve them.

HINDUISM, "HINDUISM," AND HINDUISMS

Perhaps the most significant crisis that faces Hinduism today is its name, the very category "Hindu." Unknown to most insiders and outsiders, the term "Hindu" is not an entirely indigenous one.[1] Unlike Christianity, Buddhism, and Islam, Hinduism did not have a founder or a specific birthplace. There is no "Hindu" who was the first to proclaim an adherence to the so-called Hindu tradition or who is a figure around whom adherents orient themselves. Instead, as studies of the history of the usage of term indicate, it was first developed as a geopolitical designation invented by outsiders to refer to the lands east of the Indus River. According to von Stietencron, authors in the eighth century CE used the term to distinguish between Hindus and Muslims.[2] Hindus, in fact, did not self-identify using the term until very recently. By colonial times the term was further invented as a result of a dynamic interaction between "Hindu" intellectuals, such as Rammohan Roy and their British counterparts.[3] Their shared desire to reform and to unify the multiplicity of traditions led to the continued invention and propagation of the umbrella term, a rubric under which diversity could be reduced and syncretism could be achieved. This was made especially problematic after 1947, when the framers of India's Constitution sought to address concerns from Muslim and "Hindu" constituencies, further entrenching the fabricated term. The end result was the establishment of "Hindu" as a fairly broad category. In fact, the Indian government offers a definition of "Hindu" in the Hindu Marriage Act of 1955, which includes any person who is "Buddhist, Jaina or Sikh by religion and to any other person . . . who is not a Muslim, Christian, Parsi, or Jew by religion."[4]

The first significant challenge for Hinduism thus concerns its self-definition. With so many varieties and beliefs and (given the Hindu Marriage Act) religions included in it, its utility as a meaningful, significant, and distinctive term comes into question. What ought to be included? Excluded? What ties these various "Hindu" groups together? One may argue that all Hindus believe in the mechanism of *karma*. Though this is true, the same can be said of Buddhists and Jains; this definition, then, would be too broad. Given the history of "Hindus" who have left the subcontinent, one also cannot maintain that the defining characteristic of Hinduism is that its practitioners are found in India. Are there beliefs that tie together all Hindus that distinguish them from Buddhist and others (this of, course, is irrelevant if we follow the definition found in the marriage act)?

Others suggest that having a belief in the authority of the Vedas is required of all Hindus. Though this is true for some Hindus, not all hold the Vedas to be authoritative. A large number of people who consider themselves Hindu do not pay much heed to these texts that they consider primarily *brahmin*-oriented ones (the *varna*, or four-fold class, system was organized around *brahmins*, or priestly class; *ksatriyas*, or warrior and ruling class; *vaisyas*, or merchant class; and *sudras*, or laboring class). Though all Hindus *orient* themselves around the Vedas, some of that orientation is merely rejection and not acceptance of the sacrality of these texts.

The breadth and imprecision inherent in the categorization lead to many questions. Who, for example, speaks for Hinduism?[5] Is there a Hindu perspective on any given topic? These challenges, which have confronted the Hindu population since 1947, have become even more central in recent times given the numbers of Hindus who have left India and are living in Western and other countries, where identification with well-known and reified traditions is the norm ("I am Jewish," "...Christian," and the like). Though some would like to consider *Svamis* (religious leaders) of *Brahmin*-dominated communities to be the voice of Hinduism, the *Svamis* do not speak for those outside of their community and especially for those outside of the *brahmin* fold. Often training of the *Svamis* is in the Vedas and other texts that, as already mentioned, are not held to be sacred by all.

While these are challenges that are faced by all of the world traditions in their desire to find a unifying and all-encompassing "essence," the challenge to "Hinduism" is heightened by the history of its name. Moreover, when the Indian government takes up such concerns and attempts to put forth an agenda based on an allegedly unified Hindu population, the issues become even more confused.[6] Such reification has resulted in tensions between Muslim and "Hindu" groups and has led to much religious strife in South Asia.

This ongoing crisis is at the core of many of the issues faced today. It is inextricably connected with a host of other complexities, including the relevance of some controversial beliefs (class, caste, etc.) in a global context, the often-conflicting ideas inherent in the difference between individual and collective freedom, and the difficulties stemming from the desire for leadership and to provide religious educations especially in the Diaspora communities. It is to these ancillary challenges I will now turn.

TO REFORM OR NOT TO REFORM? INTEGRITY AND CHANGE

There have been many attempts to "reform" Hinduism, first by the British then by Hindu intellectuals (most notably Rammohan Roy), and then by the framers of the Indian Constitution. Articles 15, 17, and 25 of the Constitution, for example, concern the abolition of the indignities and discrimination of the class system. In an attempt to reply to the principle of equality adopted and developed by Enlightenment thinkers and embraced by Europeans, Hindu leaders and others sought to modify or even to eliminate what they perceived to be non-essential doctrines and practices pertaining to *dharma* (dutiful behavior).[7] Roy, for example, along with the British, put an end to *sati*, the controversial practice of self-immolation by widows on their husband's funeral pyres.[8] More recent issues concern the relevance of the class and caste system in Hinduism. The social system in India prior to 1947 was built around the *varna*, or class, and *jati*, or caste, system that revolved around one's purity in comparison to others. The lower three classes and those marked as outside of the class system with the least amount of purity, were restricted from activities and places where they might taint the purity of those higher up, such as the *brahmins*. The so-called "untouchables," who were renamed by Gandhi as the "Harijans" or Children of God, now identify themselves as *Dalits* (The Oppressed/Broken), are part of this reform movement. Foreseeing a crisis, the framers and others doubted that either India or Hinduism could compete with their Western counterparts (First World, Enlightenment-based countries, and all-inclusive and purportedly egalitarian Christianity) and thus proposed Articles 15, 17, and 25 of the Constitution, which specifically eliminated discrimination based on class.[9]

In response to one crisis, a new one developed: how were communities whose identities were bound to their place in the class system to function? A social system that sought to be comprehensive was altered by means of these constitutional articles in an effort to reduce its scope and impact. How were those whose livelihoods were intimately connected with practices permitted only to the purest to conceive of themselves? This crisis has led to significant changes in all of the Hindu communities and is not exclusively a crisis for *brahmin* communities. After all, anyone of any class can work in whatever capacity s/he can and is not limited to the jobs and behaviors traditionally held by members of that class, caste, or even gender. A male *brahmin* need not be a priest and a female *sudra* need not be a laborer. The attempt to achieve social equality gave rise to a moment of crisis when an all-embracing worldview was modified and no longer so complete.

This development is certainly a double-edged sword. If Hinduism were not to reform, ideals of equality and the visions of the power and dignity of the individual would overrun it. On the other hand, if it were to reform, as it has, the required changes are significant doctrinal ones that some would argue are at the essence of this amorphous religious tradition. Without these central doctrines and dictates, what remains? Could, for example, one take Jesus Christ out of Christianity? The Pope out of Catholicism?

Consider, for example, how these reforms have changed and continue to change the Madhva community, a traditional school of thought that has its origins in thirteenth-century southwestern India.[10] Like other traditions of Vedanta, the Madhva School of Vedanta has historically limited the ways and the degrees to which the uninitiated and, more importantly, the ineligible, can receive teachings of Madhva doctrines. Non-*brahmins* and women of all classes and castes were not permitted access to the doctrines of the Madhva community as they were found in sacred texts. A select few male teachers taught a select few male students in prescribed settings such as *mathas* (monasteries) and the like. Others, who did not have *adhikara* (eligibility) were not permitted to learn in these (or any other) settings. Madhvacarya wrote, "For women, *sudras*, and unworthy *brahmins* (*brahmabandhus*), there is eligibility with regard to the knowledge of the *Tantras* but only when a portion is spoken and not with regard to study from a text."[11]

All women were eligible to be taught only a portion of the *Tantras*. According to Jayatirtha, a Madhva commentator, "The term '*tantra*' refers to the *Pancaratras* and so on."[12] These *Pancaratras* were sectarian texts that were merely prescriptions for ritual behavior, temple construction, and the like.[13] Even then, they were not allowed to learn directly from the text; women required *brahmin* teachers for limited instruction of sections of the Madhva canon. Those who had power over the knowledge thus restricted knowledge and the degree of understanding that could be attained by listeners. Although women were only partially excluded, the degree to which they had access to the texts greatly limited the scope and depth of their learning.

These restrictions were altered by reason of the Constitutional reforms, most notably Article 25(2b) which threw open "Hindu religious institutions of a public character to all classes and sections of Hindus."[14] The end result is that formerly esoteric doctrines are, by law, available to all, and the degree to which traditional teachers can function according to their traditional roles has somewhat diminished. The impact is now being reflected in the theology and pedagogy of Madhva Vedanta. It is possible that in the next decade the issue of eligibility will become obsolete, and outsiders will be made privy to root texts and concealed teachings. Hence, there may be no limitations on the kinds and extent of educations that are available to outsiders. This possibility, though, is bittersweet; will the changes be so massive that the new version of the traditional one barely resembles its antecedent?

Concomitantly, traditions like Madhva Vedanta, which are restrictive, risk dying or becoming irrelevant. The numbers of students in the Madhva monasteries is shrinking, as is the number of traditionally trained experts in the tradition. The logical outcome of this trajectory is a time when the last expert is no more and no one who can claim complete understanding of the Madhva root texts will remain. Like the dodo bird, the virtuoso reader of Madhva texts could become extinct. The restrictiveness could thus be the cause of its demise.

The predicament as it pertains to the Madhva community is just one example among many that confronts Hindu communities in India. To reform or not to reform? To enhance individual rights at the expense of collective ones? Either way the impact is as devastating as it is fruitful. The tension is heightened because of the advent of new technologies that further alter the integrity of religious traditions, which I will address below.

Though the reformations are indeed prevalent in Hinduism in India such changes are much larger, more substantial, and much more challenging for Hindu communities in the diaspora.

Deepak Sarma

DIASPORA LEADERSHIP AND THE SEARCH FOR UNITY IN DIVERSITY[15]

The Diaspora Hindu communities, especially those in the United States, are forced constantly to confront the pressures of reforms. Hindus have been taken out of the social context within which their beliefs such as class and caste had meaning. They have had to ignore sectarian differences among Hindu groups and to embrace the idea of a unified and syncretistic "Hinduism." Individual and community identities that formerly relied on differences of class, caste, and associated purity have been rejected in favor of identification with "Hinduism" and "India." Many of these problems originate from a distinction between the "secular" and the "sacred," or, alternatively, between the "church" and the "state." As already mentioned, it stands to reason that class and caste social distinctions have meaning only within comprehensive social contexts that are dominated and defined by class and caste.[16] In America, for example, where there is purportedly a separation between church and state, daily civic life has little or nothing to do with a religious motif such as class. It is nearly impossible to institute such segregation that is demanded by the class system when Hindu communities are few, far between, and relatively isolated. Though I will return to this, it is important to note that class and caste, which seems to have been one of the few, shared, beliefs of pre- "Hindu" Indian religions are irrelevant in the non-Indian landscape.

Perhaps the largest crisis that confronts the Hindu Diaspora communities concerns the degree to which Hindu beliefs can be inculcated in second and, now, third generation Hindus. The problem revolves around the vacuous nature of the term "Hindu" and the kinds of leadership roles lay people are forced to embrace in North America. First, the term "Hindu" is not a good definition, as it fails to identify some set of practices that are followed universally by all Hindus. Children of immigrant Hindus confront their confused identities every day when they are bombarded with the systematized doctrines of the world's religions.[17] Countless Hindu children return from schools during Christmas holidays unable to construct for themselves in Hinduism a parallel to the centrality of the celebration of the birth of Jesus Christ in Christianity. The children are continuously immersed in an inter-religious dialogue, albeit a simplistic one, where conversations with Christian and Jewish peers force them to search with futility for comparable holidays and events in their own religion. Given the enormous number of traditions held to be Hindu, only a few rituals and events are universal. Several holidays that are now being used to bind together all Hindus are Divali, Navaratri, Ganesa *caturthi* (celebration of the god Ganesa), Ugadi (New Year's), and Holi. Though there are many other holy days, such as Krishna-*jayanti* (the birthday of Krishna) they are often linked to particular gods whose importance may not be shared by all Hindus. Thankfully, a few festivals are currently shared by many.

Hindu parents have been heroic in their attempt to synthesize what is inherently diverse in order to create Hindu catechisms for their children. Almost all of these Hindu parents are lay people, certainly not authorized experts in Hindu beliefs and practices. Not surprisingly, purportedly cultural groups in India such as the Vishva Hindu Parishad, that also seek to combine elements from different forms of Hinduism into one, have capitalized on this and have produced Hindu textbooks for the diaspora laity, which essentialize that which, of course, was always without an essence. The result has been the continued invention and reification of Hinduism. While other groups, Catholics, for example, can turn to priests for authorized teachings, Hindu *purohits* or priests are largely ritual experts, not doctrinal ones. Though many have been recruited by eager parents or have themselves seen the need for regular catechisms, they are often not much better than the parents, especially given their deficient abilities to communicate with young adults and the fact that their training is in the ritual rather than the philosophical side of things. Parents of immigrants also serve similar capacities when they visit their children and grandchildren.

These complexities are further enhanced in light of the pooling of resources by members of the Indian Diaspora to build shared temples and cultural centers. The vast majority of temples in North America are conglomerations of various strands of "Hinduism." Deities and their sectarian devotees, for example, who would never cohabitate in traditional temples in India, are found side-by-side in temples in North America. Where only one god reigned supreme, now several do. In line with the definition of "Hindu" given in the previously mentioned Hindu Marriage Act, there are even Hindu temples wherein one finds images associated with Jainism. This is especially odd because Jainism's origins lie in the rejection of Hinduism! The melting pot of America is manifested on a smaller scale in the melting pot of the temple. The temple is now awash with diluted "Indian" spirituality. Diversity has been replaced with a bland unity. Again, like the Hindu reform movements, such attempts at syncretization are a mix of opportunity and threat. On the one hand, religions and religious people are brought together and can develop intra-religious dialogues. On the other hand, religions begin losing their distinctiveness. Religious identity is thus replaced with a broader, vaguely ethnic, one.

MEDIA, TECHNOLOGY, AND CHANGE

Hindus in India and North America have played an important role in the development of new forms of media and technology, and not surprisingly, such technologies have been incorporated into Hinduism. They have had both positive and negative effects on Hinduism. Take, for example, travel technology and its effect on the meaning of pilgrimage to Tirupati, a central pilgrimage site for members of the Sri Vaisnava sect of Hinduism. The Sri Venkatesvara temple in Tirupati is located on the seventh peak, Venkatachala (Venkata Hill) of the Tirupati Hills. It is only in recent times that access to the temple has been made much easier via motorcars and buses that can take pilgrims to the top of the hill. In the past, pilgrims made the eleven-kilometer journey to the top, and their labor was an obvious sign of *bhakti* (devotion). The technological advances have substantially reduced the difficulty in getting to the top and softened the commitment required of the ardent devotee. How does this technology change the religious experiences of the pilgrims? Does the meaning of the pilgrimage change in light of the relatively easy access? Once an experience of a select and dedicated few, *darsan* (vision) of Sri Venkastevara is no longer as exclusive as it was and perhaps is even diminished. On the other hand, such conveniences make access possible for those who are differently-abled. While one community, the devotees who reached Tirupati by walking, shrinks, that which simply has received on-site *darsan* grows.

But does one even need to go to Tirupati? The advent of the internet has made it feasible to perform *sevas* (worship ceremonies) and to get *darsan* of Sri Venkatesvara from the privacy of one's own home (whether it is in India or abroad). Pilgrimage thus becomes transformed, thanks to technology. This same technology has distinct benefits, as it keeps diaspora Hindus connected with temples in India. The actual and the metaphoric distances are reduced significantly, which is especially helpful for these diaspora Hindus who, as I mentioned above, are negotiating a difficult space between the various cultures and worlds they inhabit.[18]

One can return to the Madhva community described above for further dimensions of the crisis. The restrictiveness of the tradition has since been lessened given the advent of publication and Internet technologies. A great deal has changed in the South Asian subcontinent since the thirteenth century CE and it should come as no surprise that the contemporary Madhva tradition reflects these new innovations and has risen to the challenge of modernization, in particular, the inevitable change in the technology of duplicating and disseminating texts. In reaction to these the Madhva tradition was forced to reduce the severity of its restrictions, thereby undermining the culture of knowledge upon which it was based. An elite world of oral transmission of texts and commentaries has been opened up to the masses. Since book publication technology entered India, Madhvas have published texts that were formerly restricted. The largest number of publications of Madhva root texts has occurred since India became independent in 1947.[19]

Since the mid-1990s, Madhvas have also made use of the newest form of publication, the Internet. Numerous sites devoted to Madhva materials have been constructed by Madhva practitioners in India and in the Indian diaspora. Some were even developed by the scholars of the *mathas* (monasteries) under the auspices of their *Svamijis*. These sites contain in both English and Kannada introductions to Madhva doctrines, translations and summaries of root texts, downloadable recordings of discourses of Madhva teachers and religious leaders, and even downloadable copies of Madhva root texts. These are available to the masses and are not restricted in any way; they do not require passwords and there are no charges for accessing the sites. Unlike hard copies, there are neither limitations on the number of books published nor any ways to control their distribution. Anyone, and this, of course, includes outsiders, can learn basic Madhva doctrine and can download the root texts. Scholars who developed the first site in 1995 were not unaware of the potential problems of making the texts available to the masses. The following was found on the site in 1999: "It is recommended that you not recite either the *Brahma-Suutra*, or the *BalitthA Suukta* [*sic*], unless instructed in the proper procedure by a Guru [teacher]. It is of course the rule that no *stotra* [hymn], including these and others on this page, be recited whimsically, disrespectfully, or uninterestedly [brackets are mine].[20] Though no reason has been given, the reference to the Madhva restrictions has since been removed. This may indicate that the tradition has given up on the restrictions.

It would seem that the Madhva restrictions have broken down and that the boundaries are now permeable or merely nominal. This moment of crisis has been both a challenge and an opportunity for the Madhva community. On the one hand they have had to rethink their restrictive rules. On the other hand, they have made their doctrines available to more people, perhaps assuring the survival of a new *avatara* (incarnation) of the tradition itself.

COMPREHENSIVE WORLD

Religions seem to offer comprehensive views of the universe to adherents. That is, a religion seems to adherents to take "account of everything" and "that nothing is left unaccounted for by it."[21] This, of course, would include divisions of time. There are innumerable daily, weekly, monthly, and yearly rituals by which Hindus orient themselves. Some Hindus, for example, orient themselves toward a lunar calendar in which every few weeks a day of fasting is prescribed. Others make decisions on when to begin a project based on auspicious and inauspicious times. As India becomes more secular, the importance of these time frames is reduced. This situation is enhanced for Diaspora Hindus who must acclimatize themselves to the time orientations of their "host" country. Hindus in North America, for example, imitate their

Christian counterparts when they establish Sunday as the best day of the week to go to the temple. Sunday, in fact, has become the *de facto*, religious day in North America. Not all non-Christians bow to the Christian structures. Jews, for example, have maintained the importance of their religious calendar and celebrate it regardless of the dominant time frames. The strength of any religious tradition, Hindu or otherwise, is affected when there are other, more dominant, religious paradigms present. These challenges are quite daunting and are faced by nearly all traditions in their attempt to integrate themselves into a global economy. This challenge, as Jews have shown, is not insurmountable.[22]

The Hindu community in America is slowly recognizing this need. One group, for example, petitioned the U.S. Postal Service to include a Divali (spelled Diwali below) stamp in its collection:

> To: Citizens Stamp Advisory Committee, c/o Stamp Development, U S Postal Service, Washington, DC
>
> Dear Dr. Norlke, Chairman—Citizens Stamp Advisory Committee:
>
> We are requesting you to issue a US postal stamp commemorating "Diwali", the ancient and joyous festival of lights celebrated universally by Hindu and several other faiths, reflecting the unity and multi-cultural rich diversity of the people of USA and India. Freedom of religion is a hallmark of United States of America. The U.S. Postal Department has befittingly honored Christmas, Hanukkah, Kwanzaa and Eid by issuing commemorative stamps depicting these festivals. According to former President William J Clinton, "Diwali" presents all of us with an opportunity to reflect on the many ways, the talent, the history and the traditions of the Indian people who have contributed to our national life and cultural heritage. President George W Bush, this year- even though he was traveling in Asia-, made sure that "Diwali" was celebrated in The White House and he sent personal greetings and felicitations to the community on "Diwali". "Diwali" constitutes a medium to express gratitude and appreciation for the extraordinary diversity that is our nation's greatest strength. "Diwali" symbolizes our incessant prayers and endeavor to be led from darkness (ignorance) to light (knowledge). It is celebrated to signify the victory of truth and righteousness over evil. We request you to approve issuance of a US postal stamp commemorating the festival of lights "Diwali".[23]

Their perseverance resulted in legislation on April 20, 2005, in the U.S. House of Representatives to consider the stamp. The Bill has been tabled but has certainly caught the eye of those who can help make Hinduism a part of the American landscape.

SUGGESTIONS FOR THE FUTURE

In this brief chapter I have outlined a variety of challenges that confront Hindus and Hinduism today. But are there any suggestions for ways to deal with these challenges? Ways to convert them into opportunities rather than threats?

The first step toward resolution is accepting and analyzing the challenges. Presumably this essay itself is part of this process but a mere catalyst. As I have shown, the greatest challenge concerns the definition of Hinduism itself. Now that the term has taken hold and has a life of its own, it cannot be replaced or eliminated. My recommendation is for Hindu religious leaders to embrace the diversity of these traditions rather to perpetuate the myth of unity and syncretism. The need to develop a "Hindu voice" is reduced if one recognizes the futility in the search itself. Many of the challenges I have outlined here will fall to the wayside if leaders developed the integrity of their own traditions rather than invent the integrity of an invented one.

Reforming Hinduism, though possible, is contingent upon an agreement concerning which doctrines are essential and which are not. The central and most controversial issue is *varna* and *jati* (class and caste). Though one can certainly claim that class is not hereditary, proving it is fraught with difficulty. In any event, inheritability has become part of the popular consciousness. In the history of Hinduism, *bhakti* (devotion) was part of a complicated response to class and caste exclusion. Religious systems, which were founded on texts limited to a few, were changed significantly when they reoriented themselves towards *bhakti*. Devotion to a deity, and not simply textual knowledge, was given equal if not greater importance. Surely the changes brought about by the media that make formerly restricted practices available to all can be paralleled to the revolution in Hindu ideology brought about by *bhakti*. The threat may thus be an opportunity.

Diaspora leadership patterns are also changing given the growing numbers of students of Hinduism in Western and non-Western academic contexts who are second- and third-generation Hindus. If these young people are supported by their communities, in both India and America, they surely will take on leadership roles in Diaspora temples and the like. The issues concerning the development of Hindu catechisms are still problematic and directly related to those concerning the definition and scope of the term "Hinduism" itself.

There are, of course, many ways to answer to these challenges, and I have outlined only a few. I am confident that the leaders of the various Hindu communities can find ways to rise to these challenges and to take advantage of these opportunities. I am simply posing questions with hope of inspiring conversation among Hindu and other leaders of the world.

122   *Deepak Sarma*

NOTES

1. For more, see Von Stietencron, Heinrich, "Hinduism: On the Proper Use of a Deceptive Term," in G. Sontheimer and H. Kulke (eds.) *Hinduism Reconsidered* (Delhi: Manohar, 2001) 32-53 and Pennington, Brian K. *Was Hinduism Invented? Britons, Indians, and the Colonial Construction of Religion* (New York: Oxford University Press, 2005).

2. Von Stietencron, 33.

3. Pennington, 60.

4. Hindu Marriage Act of 1955. Application of Act: "This Act applies-to any person who is a Hindu by religion in any of its forms or developments, including a Virashaiva, a Lingayat or a follower of the Brahmo, Prarthana or Arya Samaj, to any person who is a Buddhist, Jaina, or Sikh by religion, and to any other person domiciled in the territories to which this Act extends who is not a Muslim, Christian, Parsi or Jew by religion, unless it is proved that any such person would not have been governed by the Hindu law or by any custom or usage as part of that law in respect of any of the matters dealt with herein if this Act had not been passed."

5. For more, see the articles in the special edition of *Journal of the American Academy of Religion*, 2000, vol. 68 concerning "Who Speaks for Hinduism?"

6. For more, see Thapar, Romila "Syndicating Hinduism" in G. Sontheimer and H. Kulke (eds.) *Hinduism Reconsidered* (Delhi: Manohar, 2001) 34–81.

7. See Derrett, J. D. M. *Religion, Law and the State in India* (New York: The Free Press, 1968).

8. See Pennington, 97–98, 140, 155–156 and Paul B. Courtright, "Sati, Sacrifice and Marriage: The Modernity of Tradition," in Harlan and Courtright (eds.) *From the Margins of Hindu Marriage* (New York: Oxford University Press, 1995).

9. Article 15. Prohibition of discrimination on grounds of religion, race, caste, sex or place of birth. (1) The State shall not discrimination against any citizen on grounds only of religion, race, caste, sex, place of birth or any of them. (2) No citizen shall, on grounds only of religion, race, caste, sex, place of birth or any of them, be subject to any disability, liability, restriction or condition with regard to—(a) access to shops, public restaurants, hotels and places of public entertainment; or (b) the use of wells, tanks, bathing ghats, roads and places of public resort maintained wholly or partly out of State funds or dedicated to the use of the general public. Article 17. Abolition of Untouchability. "Untouchability" is abolished and its practice in any form is forbidden. The enforcement of any disability arising out of "Untouchability" shall be an offence punishable in accordance with law. Article 25. Freedom of conscience and free profession, practice and propagation of religion (1) Subject to public order, morality and health and to the other provisions of this Part, all persons are equally entitled to freedom of conscience and the right freely to profess, practise and propagate religion. (2) Nothing in this article shall affect the operation of any existing law or prevent the State from making any law—(a) regulating or restricting any economic, financial, political or other secular activity which may be associated with religious practise; (b) providing for social welfare and reform or with throwing open of Hindu religious institutions of a public character to all classes and sections of Hindus.

See Derrett, Seervai, H. M., *Constitutional Law of India: A Critical Commentary* (Bombay: N. M. Tripathi Pvt. Ltd., 1967); Smith, Donald E., *India as a Secular State* (Princeton: Princeton University Press, 1963); and Pylee, M. V., *India's Constitution* (New York: Asia Publishing House, 1967).

10. See Sarma, Deepak, *An Introduction to Madhva Vedanta* (Great Britain: Ashgate Pub. Ltd. 2003), *Epistemologies and the Limitations of Philosophical Inquiry: Doctrine in Madhva Vedanta* (Great Britain: Routledge Curzon Limited. 2005), "Regulating Religious Reading: Access to Texts in Madhva Vedanta," *Journal of Indian Philosophy*, 1999, vol. 27, 583–635, "Modernity and Madhva Vedanta: The Beginning or the End of an Esoteric Tradition?" *Journal of Vaisnava Studies*, 2005, vol. 13, no. 2, 5–22.

11. Madhvacarya, *Brahma Sutra Bhasya*, 1.1.1.

12. tantram pañcaratradi | Jayatirtha, Tattvaprakasika, 1.1.1.

13. Sarma, *Epistemologies*, 27–28.

14. Article 25(2b) of the Indian Constitution.

15. For an in-depth study of the types of Hindu leaders in North America, see Deepak Sarma, "Hindu Leaders of North America?" in *Teaching Theology and Religion*, forthcoming.

16. For more on this comprehensive aspect of religions in general, see Paul Griffiths' *The Problems with Religious Diversity* (Oxford: Blackwell, 2001).

17. See further, Padma Rangaswamy's *Namaste America: Indian Immigrants in an American Metropolis* (University Park: Pennsylvania State University Press, 2000).

18. Editor's note: See parallels in the Christian experience on page 75.

19. Editor's note: See the parallel trend in Judaism on page 102.

20. This was found on the Dvaita home page (http://www.dvaita.org/stotra/index.html) but has since been removed.

21. Griffiths *op cit*, 7.

22. Editor's note: See similar examples in Buddhism on page 60.

23. http://www.petitiononline.com/diwali03/petition.html.

Chapter Seven

Islam

Vincent J. Cornell

EPISTEMOLOGICAL CRISIS

The Crisis of the Holy in Islam is, first and foremost, an *epistemological crisis*. The term, "epistemological crisis" was coined by the philosopher Alasdair MacIntyre to describe what happens when a tradition of inquiry—such as the theological or philosophical tradition of a religion—fails to make progress by its own standards of rationality. In a situation of epistemological crisis, formerly trusted methods of inquiry become sterile, "conflicts over rival answers to key questions can no longer be settled rationally," and forms of argument that have worked in the past now "have the effect of increasingly disclosing new inadequacies, hitherto unrecognized incoherencies, and new problems for the solution of which there seem to be insufficient or no resources within the established fabric of belief."[1]

According to MacIntyre, "the dissolution of historically founded certitudes" is the hallmark of an epistemological crisis, such that former answers to key questions no longer seem sufficient. If the crisis is to be resolved, new concepts and frameworks for the tradition must be developed. These concepts and frameworks must meet three conditions. First, *they must constitute their own tradition*: they must provide a systematic and coherent solution to problems that have proved to be intractable in the crisis situation. Second, *they must be critical*: they must provide an explanation of what it was that rendered the original tradition, before acquiring the new resources, sterile or incoherent or both. Third, *they must be authentic*: they must exhibit continuity with the shared beliefs that served to define the original tradition. However, authenticity does not necessarily mean that the new concepts introduced by the revised tradition must be derived from the earlier tradition. Instead, their justification will lie in their ability to engage with the previous tradition and resolve contradictions that had not been resolved previously.[2] The opportunity posed by an epistemological crisis lies in the prospect of coming up with new approaches to tradition that provide innovative solutions through a critical engagement with the past. As the historian of Christianity Jaroslav Pelikan said, "A 'leap of progress' is not a standing broad jump, which begins at the line of where we are now; it is a running broad jump through where we have been to where we go next."[3]

However, an epistemological crisis poses a threat as well as an opportunity. Not all epistemological crises can be resolved successfully. When a historically founded tradition confronts another historically founded tradition, it may be that the original tradition's claims to truth can no longer be sustained; this threatens the integrity of the tradition as a whole. Such a situation of crisis may be created through the challenge of a completely new epistemology, or it may occur when social and historical conditions change such that the perspective of the rival tradition provides a better explanation of why one's own tradition has been unable to solve its problems or restore its original coherence. In some cases, the conceptual language of the rival tradition may become, in MacIntyre's words, a "new and second first language" for the tradition in crisis.[4] This happened, for example, in the second and third centuries of Islam (mid-eighth through mid-tenth centuries CE), when, because of the epistemological crisis precipitated by Christian theological polemics against Islam, Greek works on logic provided new conceptual tools for the developing tradition of Islamic theology (*'ilm al-kalam*). Muslim theologians re-contextualized the logical formulations of Greek and Hellenistic thinkers such as Aristotle and the Stoics in ways that rendered them newly "Islamic." A similar process occurred in Islamic philosophy (*falsafa*), where the philosophical concepts of Platonism and Aristotelianism were recast as Islamic concepts.

Much the same thing is happening today. Muslim scholars who live or have studied in the West are seeking ways to incorporate critical structures and frameworks of inquiry into a new vision of Islamic tradition: Mohammed Arkoun, Khaled Abou El Fadl, and Ebrahim Moosa use the tools of critical analysis to interrogate the traditions of Islamic reason and authority; Seyyed Hossein Nasr and Vincent (Mansur) Cornell seek philosophical and theological grounds for Islamic pluralism within the Qur'an and the works of the Sufis; Farid Esack, Omid Safi, and Abdolkarim Soroush are developing models of "Progressive Islam" along the lines of Liberation Theology; Sadiyya Shaikh, Scott (Siraj al-Haqq) Kugle, Abdullahi An-Naim, and Sherman ('Abd al-Hakim) Jackson interrogate theological and legal traditions pertaining to gender, human rights, and minorities.

However, today as in the past, many Muslims see only confrontation between the revealed knowledge of Islam and the intellectual heritage of the West (although it was not called the "West" prior to the Colonial period). For example, traditionalist Muslims did not recognize that the encounter between Plato, Aristotle, and the Qur'an gave new life to Greek philosophy by reconfiguring it in Islamic terms. Instead, Muslim purists rejected Greek philosophy because its roots could not be traced directly to the Qur'an and the traditions of the Prophet Muhammad. This negative reaction necessitated veiling the new "second first languages" of Greek logic and epistemology behind traditionally Islamic, "first language" discourses of authenticity. Thus one finds, for example, that Aristotelian logic is a ubiquitous but unacknowledged presence in Islamic jurisprudence. Similarly, the teachings of Platonism and Neo-Platonism are visible but not identified as such in the writings of famous Sufis such as Muhyiddin Ibn 'Arabi (d. 1240) and Jalal al-Din Rumi (d. 1273). The names of pre-Islamic Aristotelian, Stoic, or Neo-Platonic thinkers were seldom, if ever mentioned by Muslim writers who were concerned about maintaining an image of authenticity. The mistake of *falsafa*, the philosophical tradition of Islam, was that it openly acknowledged its debt to the alien epistemologies of the Greeks without adequately making the case that the same or similar epistemologies were also present in the Qur'an. This inattentiveness to the relation between epistemology and tradition left *falsafa* open to accusations of inauthenticity by the very same Muslim jurists who ironically depended on Aristotle's logic and concepts for their own reasoning.

A similar situation exists today, where those who seek a new vision of Islamic tradition face challenges to their authenticity because of the epistemological threat posed by modern critical methodologies. This is particularly true of Muslim participants in interfaith projects sponsored by non-Muslim organizations such as the Elijah Interfaith Institute, the Shalom Hartman Institute, or the Church of England. Many Muslims believe that the comparative study of religion opens the way to religious pluralism, which will erode Islam's exclusive claim to the truth. When Muslim thinkers use the tools provided by secular Post-Enlightenment methodologies such as historical or comparative analysis, the critical outlook of such methodologies is seen as a threat to the integrity of Islam. It is no accident therefore, that most of the critical Muslim scholars mentioned above reside in the West, where critical approaches to knowledge are more accepted and where the political pressures of traditionalist or fundamentalist counter-discourses are less threatening.

However, it is still rare for Muslims to define the Crisis of the Holy in epistemological terms. More commonly, the Crisis of the Holy is viewed as a cultural crisis, which is seen as a specifically Western threat to the integral purity of Islam. This response can be found in all Muslim societies but it is particularly prevalent in traditionalist Muslim communities in Europe and the Americas. In these regions, a large minority population of nearly 50 million believers (counting Russian Muslims) struggles to retain a sense of tradition in an environment that poses the double threat of a dominant missionary religion (Christianity) and a missionary form of ideological secularism. Secularism, which in its most extreme form acts as a sort of fundamentalism without God, has turned its sights away from Catholicism and now targets Islam as the main enemy in its critique of institutional religion. For the secular fundamentalist, Islam epitomizes the social oppression and religious obscurantism that the rationality of the Enlightenment was supposed to dispel. In both Europe and the United States, and especially in political discourse and the media, epistemological fault lines have become political battle lines, causing many Muslims to perceive the confrontation between Islamic values and secular worldviews as a state of siege. Given such a siege mentality, it is little wonder that the politics of identity plays a large role in contemporary Muslim communities. It is also no surprise that not only Muslim modernists but also Salafists and other neo-traditionalist rejecters of modernity are found in these communities.[5]

CORPORATISM, TRADITION, AND CULTURE

To restate the point made above, among Muslims "The Crisis of the Holy" is most often expressed not as a crisis of epistemology, but as a crisis of tradition or culture. Typically, this crisis is viewed as a value conflict between Islam and the West or between the religious culture of Islam and the "secular" culture of modernity. There is much that is wrong with a perspective that takes a monolithic view of Islam, the West, secularism, and modernity all together. In the first place, Muslims tend to ignore the important difference between the ideological secularism that grew out of the French Enlightenment, which indeed has an anti-religious bias, and the more purely political secularism of England and the United States, which seeks to separate religious and governmental institutions for the sake of freedom of belief. In the Anglo-American version of secularism, it is possible to be both "secular" and "religious" at the same time, as the comparatively high level of religious belief and attendance at places of worship in the United States shows. Second, many Muslims tend to forget that modernity is no longer only Western. Not only is it misguided to assume that Japanese, Chinese, or Indians are "modern" in exactly the same way as Westerners are, but it also will be argued below that the very concept of "modernity" itself may be part of the problem. Whatever the term "modernity" may mean in different national contexts, it is now so imbricated within global culture that often it is no more than another way of referring to "the current times."

Finally, when the Crisis of the Holy is expressed as a crisis of tradition and culture, from a theological standpoint, neither of the dichotomies mentioned above engages directly with God or with the Holy. Nor are they much concerned with the individual's relationship to God. Despite calling for a reengagement with faith, modern ideologies of Islamic reform are largely temporal (one might even call them quasi-secular) and are mostly concerned with issues that a medieval Muslim theologian would deem accidental rather than substantial. This is equally true of both liberal Islamic and conservative Islamic critiques. Despite the reformist call for an ideological separation between religion (which is praised as pure, ageless, and unchangeable) and culture (which is condemned as historically contingent), the culture war with Western modernity implies that Islamic religion and normative Islamic culture go together like the warp and woof of a seamless garment.

The epistemological aspect of the Muslim culture war with the West lies in the fact that Islamic tradition is not viewed as one tradition among others; rather, it is seen as the *only* tradition that contains normative truth. Because this view of normative truth goes beyond religious belief alone and includes cosmology and justice as well, it is appropriate to call it fundamentalist. As Jaroslav Pelikan said of Christian fundamentalism, it is a view of tradition that "has undergone a frontal lobotomy."[6] On the one hand it has lost sight of the Qur'anic concept of the universality of revelation and on the other hand its perspective of the world is badly skewed. Little or no interest is shown in the history that Islam shares with other civilizations or in the common challenges it shares with other belief systems that face modernity. Instead, Islam is conceived in socio-cultural terms as what the Ottoman Empire called a *millet*: a hermetic, self-contained religious community that exists concurrently with but in nearly total separation from the *millets* of other religions.[7] Conceiving of Islam as a *millet* implies that the theological understanding of Islam is less important than its social or political meaning.[8] All that is left of the theology of Islam is a creed. As a socio-cultural entity, Islam is seen as a *normative society or cultural tradition whose normativity is proven by its religious claim to truth.* By contrast, the West is seen as a *dissident society or cultural tradition whose dissidence is proven by its secularism, which has infected its religious values.*

Although there is arguably much truth to the claim that secularism has altered the concept of religion in the West, the culture war of Islam versus the West is clearly a reflection of epistemological crisis. This can be seen in the ironic fact that the Islamic critique of modernity is undertaken in modern terms. To the extent that it is expressed theologically, the critique of Western modernity is a modern gloss on the dichotomies of religion versus unbelief (*Islam* vs. *kufr*) and the Non-World versus the World (*al-akhira* vs. *al-dunya*) that have long been important to Islamic thought. However, the key element that makes this critique modern is the reified concept of culture, which allows religion to be defined ideologically in corporate terms. In fact, the very notion of "Islamic culture" would have seemed strange to medieval Muslims. The reformist view of religion that sees an epistemologically unsullied Islam combined with an ideologically defined cultural tradition is a largely modern creation that is based on the worldview of nineteenth-century social science. This can be seen when one compares anthropologist Edward Burnett Tylor's famous 1871 definition of culture ("That complex whole which includes, knowledge, belief, art morals, law, custom, and any other capabilities and habits acquired by man as a member of society") with the reformist understanding of Islam. [9]

The corporate understanding of Islam that undergirds the ideologies of modern Islamic reform movements corresponds to Tylor's definition of culture almost exactly. All that one has to do to make Tylor's definition fit this model is to insert the word "Islam" or its derivatives wherever "culture" appears in the original: "[*Islam* is] that complex whole which includes, knowledge, belief, (art is ignored by most Islamic reformists) morals, law, custom, and any other capabilities and habits acquired by man as a member of [*Islamic*] society." This view of Islam is so tautological as to be virtually meaningless: Islam includes the domains of x, y, and z, but Islam itself is never defined. To put it another way, Islamic culture embodies an ideologically normative *Islamic* knowledge (often called "Tawhidic"), a normative *Islamic* belief (the Creed or *'Aqida*), a normative *Islamic* Law and moral code (the *Shari'a*), and a finite set of normative *Islamic* customs (the *Sunna*). Note how all of the key Arabic terms in the corporate definition of Islam are in the singular. Furthermore, as the second half of the definition implies, one can also Islamize any other "capabilities and habits" that one wants. Conceptually, it is a small step from this definition to the "Islamization of Knowledge" movement that was popular among modern Muslim reformists from Egypt to Malaysia between the 1960s and the end of the twentieth century.

It is also important to note that in the corporatist vision of Islam, the theological concept of the oneness of God (*tawhid*) is subjected to two major revisions: first, it is redefined in social terms as the oneness (*wahda*) of Islam as a community; second, it is redefined in political terms as the union (*ittihad*) of Muslims under the *Shari'a* or some form of "Islamic" government. [10] This reification of Islam in ideological and cultural terms makes the corporate vision of Islam both modern and nontraditional. In fact, it is the key factor that transforms Islam into *Islamism*. Strikingly absent from the concept of a reified Islam is any mention of personal salvation. The relationship between man and God is more often spoken of in terms of corporate relations (i.e., of humanity or Muslims as a whole) than of individual piety. It is thus more than a rhetorical question to ask whether there is any spiritual authenticity at all in a version of Islam that speaks of identity, social justice, and utopian political ideals while ignoring the human being's personal relationship with God. Ironically, the feeling of difference or alienation that has caused Muslim minorities in the West to approach Islam in terms of identity politics seems to have entered the Muslim consciousness to such a degree that traditional Islam itself seems alien.

The theological confusion that results from the reification of culture and religion in contemporary Islamic reformism can be seen in a statement by the English Muslim intellectual Abdul Hakim Murad on the subject of Islam and capitalism: "Is the engagement of Islamic monotheism with the new capitalist global reality a challenge that even Islam, with its proven ability to square circles, cannot manage?"[11] Murad identified this question as a central issue of the Islamic "Crisis of the Holy" in a paper given at an interreligious conference at Hartford Seminary in 2005.[12] After considering the statement carefully, one is led to ask: What does Murad mean by the terms he uses? What does Islamic monotheism, which is a theological concept, have to do with "capitalist global reality," which is primarily an economic concept? In other words, what does *tawhid*—the theological doctrine of the oneness of God—have to do with globalization? Does Murad mean to say that capitalism is a new quasi-religion and that globalization is a form of quasi-polytheism? Does he mean that economic and cultural unification under capitalism and consumerism are threats to the existence of the One God? This would make sense only if capitalism were viewed as a sort of anti-theology, in the same way that Marxism was once viewed as an anti-theology. Perhaps this is what Murad intends to say, but the relationship is not clear. According to the traditional theological understanding of *tawhid* in Islam, nothing in the material universe can affect the nature of God. According to the traditional perspective, neither capitalism nor a globalized "McWorld" can threaten God, no matter how ubiquitous they are.[13] However, they could threaten the integrity of traditional societies and other corporate entities. This begs a follow-up question: Is the "Crisis of the Holy" a threat to God, a threat to Islam as a religion, or is it only a threat if Islam is viewed as a corporate entity? Each of these issues posits a different crisis and each requires a different answer.

Central to the culture war between Islam and the West is what some scholars have termed "Occidentalism." Inspired by Edward Said's famous book *Orientalism* (1979), this is a critique of the West that utilizes the bipolar model of Orientalism but reverses the polarity such that an idealized image of a spiritual East is valued over a hypercritical image of a secular and soulless West.[14] According to Ian Buruma and Avishai Margalit, in Occidentalism,

> The mind of the West is often portrayed by Occidentalists as a kind of higher idiocy. To be equipped with the mind of the West is like being an idiot savant, mentally defective but with a special gift for making arithmetic calculations. It is a mind without a soul, efficient, like a calculator, but hopeless at doing what is humanly important. The mind of the West is capable of great economic success, to be sure, and of developing and promoting advanced technology, but cannot grasp the higher things in life, for it lacks spirituality and understanding of human suffering.[15]

When a Muslim reformer such as the Iranian intellectual Abdolkarim Soroush writes, "The modern world is the ethical inverse of the old world. The ancient apocalyptic prophecies came true: Reason is enslaved to desire, the external governs the internal, and vices have supplanted virtues," he is practicing Occidentalism.[16] Occidentalism is a polemical strategy that uses *ad hominem* arguments to turn the tables on a Western culture that is conceived as the moral inverse of Eastern culture. According to this perspective, the foundational values held by religiously based civilizations such as Islam are denied to the secular West.

An ironic aspect of Occidentalism as practiced by modernist Muslim intellectuals such as Soroush is how little this approach depends on the Qur'an and how much it depends on the Greek philosopher Plato. The cynical, utilitarian, and worldly ethic that is attributed to the West is very similar to the ethic attributed to the Sophists in Plato's *Dialogues*.[17] A Sophistical ethic is an ethic of expediency rather than of virtue: it is an ethic of pragmatism, political rhetoric, and the mere fulfillment of needs. According to Plato, the problem with this ethic is that it ignores the possibility of transcendence by overlooking the ends to which a moral life aspires. Muslim Occidentalists view the West in much the same way. For them, competition, moral realism, and pragmatic liberalism can never be compared to a life that is lived with a higher purpose in mind. This view of Western values ignores the Protestant religious background of the Northern European Enlightenment and focuses more on the anti-religious secularism of the French Enlightenment. If Voltaire's project of undermining the foundations of institutionalized religion is taken as fundamental for Western values, it becomes much easier to posit a stark difference between Islamic tradition and secular reason. However, it is more difficult for the religious polemicist to deal with the Scottish Enlightenment, whose concept of the privatization of belief was based in part on the Christian notion of the "inner voice," which was first made famous by St. Augustine. It was this tradition, and not that of the French Enlightenment, that inspired the American philosopher Ralph Waldo Emerson to state in his Divinity School Address of 1838 that the wisdom that dwells in the human spirit will become a "newborn bard of the Holy Ghost," which will lead humanity to transcend the "dead faith of the living."[18] Similar traditions can also be found in Islam, but only if one looks beyond the corporatist spirituality of modern Islamic reformism.

"SECULARISM," CHANGE, AND "MODERNITY"

However, corporate Islam is not only obsessed with the West; it is also obsessed with modernity. What is meant by "modernity"? Which aspect of modernity allegedly poses the greatest threat to Islam? Is it Universal Reason, Progressivism, Scientism, Moral Autonomy, Individualism, Nationalism, Democracy, Capitalism, Globalism, Consumerism, or the Technological Society? A clear definition of modernity is seldom included in Islamic critiques of the West. If Islam is supposed to be in opposition to "modernity," it is important to specify exactly which aspect of modernity poses the greatest threat to the Holy. Otherwise, modernity has no meaning and becomes just another straw man in the polemical discourse of Occidentalism. In the logic of its argument, the reformist problematic of Religion versus modernity is similar to that of Religion versus Culture. Both culture and modernity are historically conditioned, whereas religion is supposed to be epistemologically and ideologically pure and unblemished. However, as noted above, this view of religion is unrealistic. Just as religions are contained within one or more cultures, contemporary religions are also situated within one or more contexts of modernity. Pre-modern Islam can no longer exist as a practiced religion, despite the best efforts of Al Qaeda, the Taliban, and other pseudo-traditionalists to the contrary. However much we may decry our present condition, we are all born into modernity.

Although they cannot define what "modernity" is, Muslim critics of the West are convinced that it is fundamental to Western civilization and that "secularism" is part of the package. In the 1940s, Muhammad al-Bahi, the Rector of al-Azhar University, decried the "cultural venom" of secularism as the ideological component of Western colonialism. Bahi, whose notion of Islamic cultural integrity was a forerunner of corporate Islam, claimed that already in his day modern secular values had polluted the Muslim consciousness. The primary goal of Western Colonialism, he argued, was to weaken Islamic religious values, which would eventually lead to the dissolution of Islamic society and culture. According to Bahi, Colonialism's most effective tactic was to spread Western intellectual and cultural hegemony throughout the Islamic world, first by encouraging Muslim intellectuals to reform Islam along secular lines, and second to establish centers of critical scholarship whose task was to highlight differences and schisms among Muslims. Bahi's answer to this threat, anticipating the later writings of Sayyid Qutb (d. 1966), was to reformulate Islam as a total system that would counteract secular movements of liberation in the Arab world. Although political independence was an important goal for Muslim peoples, in Bahi's words, secular liberation movements permitted "atheist and Orientalist Western thought to infiltrate and consolidate both polarization and vacuum."[19]

This view of the West as both secular and worldly (and hence dissident and profane) still persists among Muslims today. It lies behind Ayatollah Khomeini's (d. 1989) view of America as the "Great Satan" as well as the Pakistani Islamist Abu al-'Ala al-Mawdudi's (d. 1979) view of Western society as *jahili*: a society in willful ignorance of the Truth. As John Esposito has pointed out, one source of this view was a positivist theory of development, popular under Colonialism and in the immediate post-independence period, that equated modernity and progress with secularization and Westerniza-tion.[20] Perhaps the starkest example of this model was the French colonial notion of the secularized and Westernized Muslim as *evolué*, "evolved." Under French Resident General Louis Hubert Lyautey in Morocco (1912–1925), the "unevolved" or traditional Muslim in urban areas was physically relegated to the medieval sector or "Old City" (Fr. *la vielle ville*, Ar. *al-madina al-qadima*), a living museum of Islamic life that was physical-ly separated from the modern colonial city (Fr. *la ville nouvelle*) by a "sani-tary cordon" (*cordon sanitaire*) that could be as much as a kilometer wide.[21]

Not just in Morocco, but throughout the Muslim world, the experience of Colonialism inscribed the dichotomy of Tradition versus modernity as a form of apartheid whose traces can still be seen in the Muslim consciousness. The continued popularity of the colonial development model in Muslim countries after independence meant that for those who sought to retain the historical and cultural authenticity of Islam, "progress" meant denuding Islam of its inherited traditions. Often, saving the integrity of Islam meant one of two things: one could either try to hermetically seal off the world of Islam from the secular West, as Al Qaeda or the Taliban try to do, or one could essential-ize a particular aspect of inherited tradition as the key factor in the preserva-tion of Islamic values. Corporate Islamists have exercised this second option by reifying and idealizing the Shari'a ("Islamic Law") while discarding most of the jurisprudential (*fiqh*) tradition through which the Shari'a was original-ly interpreted. As one Muslim activist in the United States once told me, Islam today "is all about Shari'a."

Both of the aforementioned strategies—the attempt to hermetically seal off the Islamic world from the influence of modern global society and the fetishization of the Shari'a as the embodiment of all Islamic values—are further symptoms of the epistemological crisis of Islam. What those who attempt such solutions fail to recognize is that meeting the challenges of modernity cannot be accomplished by fleeing from it. Modernity—whatever it may be—is now part of the human condition, even in the most out-of-the-way villages of Afghanistan or northern Nigeria. Without coming to grips with the modern condition, the attempt to restore an idealized or pristine Islamic Tradition becomes a false front (Ar. *talbis*), the fetishization of an ideal, and an artificial reinvention of Tradition. This creates a simulacrum of tradition, not tradition itself. The British social historian Eric Hobsbawm similarly described the reinvention of tradition as "a process of formalization and ritualization, characterized by reference to the past, if only by imposing repetition."[22] The Moroccan feminist Fatima Mernissi characterizes contem-porary Islam's obsession with Tradition as a *mal du présent* (literally, "sick-ness of the present"), which is expressed as "a desire for death, a desire to be elsewhere, to be absent, to flee to the past as a way of being absent. A suicidal absence."[23]

Sufi Muslims in particular should see the fetishization of the past as antithetical to the spiritual values of Islam, for the true seeker of God is encouraged to live in the present time and become a "Son of the Moment" (Ar. *ibn al-waqt*). Peter Coates, a British writer on Sufism, has found an answer to the *mal du présent* of which Mernissi speaks by referring back to the Ash'arite theological notion of perpetual recreation (*al-khalq fi kull al-waqt*). According to this perspective, because the world is recreated at every moment, each era can provide a new opportunity to contemplate and understand the process of divine self-disclosure. As Coates puts it, each era is a "theatre of manifestation in the infinity of world process." According to the Sufi Muhyiddin Ibn 'Arabi, "God appears *in* the era, and He appears *as* the era. According to the Hadith, 'God is called Time,' we are advised not to be disappointed by time, or to curse time, for God *is* time. In another rendering, we are cautioned to 'Revile not the era for I [God] am the era.'"[24] To restate the point that Coates makes, the tradition to which Ibn 'Arabi refers contains two teachings: First, "modernity" is just another name for the present, and today's present is no more important to God than yesterday's present. The second teaching is a corollary to the first: to run away from the present era by trying to resurrect an idealized past is to run away from God Himself.

EMPIRICISM, EVIDENTIALISM, AND EVOLUTION

Despite the many forms in which modernity appears, most students of modernity have identified science, technology, and economics as the cultural forms whose dominance most characterizes the contemporary era. Epistemologically, the greatest threat posed to Islam by these forms of modernity is the valuation of empiricism above both revelation and theoretical inquiry. For premodern Muslim thinkers, theoretical knowledge was superior to empirical knowledge, which was conceived mainly as a way of acquiring a skill. This corresponded to a view of the intellect in which the theoretical intellect, which made use of theoretical wisdom, was superior to the practical intellect, which utilized practical or "common-sense" wisdom. It is highly difficult, if not impossible, to square this theory of knowledge with the Enlightenment notion of empirical reason, which refuses to place ultimate truth-value in inherited beliefs, traditions, or empirically unsubstantiated theoretical notions.

In *Essay Concerning Human Understanding* (1690), John Locke graded assertions of truth on a scale of probability that was based not on theoretical reason, but on the practical reason of legal inquiry. Knowledge based on religious traditions or revelation was, for Locke, low on the scale of evidential probability. Since the claims of revealed religion could not have the highest degree of truth-probability, they could not attain factual certainty. Instead, they could only attain "moral certainty." Locke's attempt to privilege empirical truth over moral truth could not be farther from the perspective of traditional Islam.[25] For Muslims, the truth-value of the Qur'an as a revelation from God is *a priori*. Furthermore, the arguments of the Qur'an, instead of relying on empirical notions of truth, are largely theoretical, and include categorical arguments, syllogisms, and conditional and disjunctive arguments.[26] If they were to debate, Locke and a medieval Muslim theologian such as Abu Hamid al-Ghazali (d. 1111) would likely argue past each other, with Locke appealing to a notion of truth dismissed as insufficient by the Muslim, and the Muslim appealing to a notion of truth dismissed as unprovable by Locke.

This contrast would be even starker if the Muslim theologian were to debate Thomas Reid (d. 1796), a Scottish Enlightenment philosopher who influenced Thomas Paine and other intellectuals of the American Revolution. Reid, the founder of the so-called "Common-Sense Realism" school of philosophy, was a great admirer of Francis Bacon (d. 1626), who taught his students "to despise hypotheses as fictions of human fancy." Reid also saw himself as a follower of Isaac Newton (d. 1727), who taught that "the true method of philosophizing is this: from real facts ascertained by observations and experiment, to collect by just induction the laws of nature."[27] Reid attempted to harmonize empiricism and religion by appealing to the truth of basic empirical observations, such as cause and effect, the regularity of nature, and the predictability of human behavior. Reid, a Presbyterian Christian, felt that empirical common-sense rationality would lead to belief in God without recourse to either first principles or theoretical wisdom.[28] Reid's epistemology fundamentally disagrees with the epistemological premises of medieval Islamic theology. It is also different from the epistemology of medieval Islamic philosophy, for this system of thought asserts the primacy of empirical observation over first principles. In light of the beliefs of this moderate Enlightenment thinker, the contrast between the epistemology of classical Islamic theology and the epistemology of the Enlightenment could hardly be more striking. This contrast becomes even more significant when one discovers that Reid's common sense empiricism provided the foundation for American Pragmatism. If the epistemological break between classical Islamic theology and post-Enlightenment "moderate" Protestant theology is so significant, imagine the gulf that separates classical Islamic thinkers from the real "godless materialists"—the ideological secularists!

A similar epistemological break characterizes the Islamic response to Darwin's theory of evolution, which has become an obsession for many Muslim traditionalists. From a classical Islamic perspective, the theory of evolution is a philosophy of gross materialism. Since modern Muslim theologians still refer back to medieval schools of thought such as Ash'arism and philosophical Neo-Platonism when making their arguments, Islamic theology in the post-Darwin age has not fully assimilated the epistemological implications of evolutionary theory.[29] Current Islamic thinking about empirical science is similar to that of American Evangelicalism prior to the publication of Charles Darwin's *Origin of Species*. Most evangelicals up to the middle of the nineteenth century believed that the findings of modern science would reveal not only scientific laws, but God's laws as well. So-called "Evidentialist" evangelicals accepted secularism as part of an epistemological division of labor, in which science and religion coexisted as separate but equal domains of knowledge. Although science was independent of religion, it was thought that the laws discovered by the scientific method could be viewed as evidence of the wise design of the Creator. According to George Marsden, a "rickety compromise" was thus created between Christian faith and the ideal of free scientific inquiry.[30] Mark Hopkins, a well-known mid-nineteenth century evangelical teacher, asserted, "Truth is one. If God has made a revelation in one mode, it must coincide with what he has revealed in another."[31]

My experience with Muslim communities in the United States has demonstrated that Muslim professionals in the technological fields—chemists, aerospace engineers, software developers, and the like—feel much the same as Mark Hopkins did in the nineteenth century. Muslim technological professionals live in two separate worlds. On one side is the world of their professional lives, which is governed by the empirical epistemology of their secular technological careers. On the other side is the world of the local mosque or Islamic center, which is governed by traditional views of truth that have little or no relation to the professional lives of its members. "Mosque World" has its own mode of discourse, its own epistemology, and its own reality. The Mosque World mindset governs a web of relations that connects members of Islamic centers and their families in a virtual Islamic village that can be stubbornly resistant to outside influences. It is here where the siege mentality that resists cultural and epistemological change is the strongest. Such resistance is particularly strong when the majority of mosque members share the same ethnic background or the same corporatist ideology.

Because of the compromise that they made between the truths of science and religion, the main theological issue for nineteenth-century Evangelicals was the authenticity of the Bible as a repository of truth. The same is the case for the Qur'an among contemporary Muslims. Much effort has been devoted to demonstrating that the Qur'an does not contradict the findings of modern science but in fact often anticipates science in ways that the Bible does not. This can be seen in the wide popularity of the book, *The Bible, Qur'an, and Science* by the French physician Dr. Maurice Boucaille (d. 1998), or the 1986 Malaysian film, *The Book of Signs*.[32] Like the nineteenth-century Evangelicals before them, Muslims in the West have tended to ignore the rational arguments for God presented in the Qur'an and classical works of Islamic theology in favor of evidentiary arguments, which often appeal to personal witness as testimony to the truth of divine revelation. While both theoretical and evidentiary arguments can be found in the Qur'an, the rejection of formal rational proofs in favor of the evidence of personal testimony is a recent phenomenon (possibly influenced by modern Evangelical Christianity) that marks a significant departure from classical Islamic thought. What seems to be most important for Muslims today is not a theoretical understanding of God, but external signs and tokens of divine favor.[33]

The weakness of Islamic Evidentialism, as it was for nineteenth-century American Evangelicals, is that this approach depends on a view of truth and the world that is essentially static. The argument for God from design works best when the design of the universe appears as a painting or a vast tableau. In this tableau, the will of God is revealed in the regularity of natural phenomena. This view can be found in Qur'anic verses such as those of *Surat al-Rahman* (Sura 55), which argue for God from design. Even the Occasionalist worldview of Ash'arite theology posed no threat to this argument, for despite the fact that Ash'arism taught that reality was created at every moment, the world was in fact recreated more than it was created anew. For non-Sufi Ash'arite theologians, God created the world as a series of still pictures in which change was accidental rather than essential. The closest thing to revolutionary change was miracles, which were phenomenal rather than substantial in nature. Thus, they did not contradict the overall schema of the divine plan.

The Darwinian theory of evolution undid all of this. What is unacceptable about Darwinism for Muslim traditionalists is not just the idea that human beings evolved from apes, but that creatures evolve at all and that they evolve not according to a divine plan, but as part of a natural process of adaptation that occurs randomly, without intelligent design. Darwinism did more than simply assert that one cannot prove that the Creator exists. His system allows no room for a creator at all. Darwinian Evolutionism is thus a fundamental issue for the Islamic Crisis of the Holy, because its premises make it impossible to prove the existence of God. Equally importantly, evolutionary theory also introduced the idea of continuous change and transformation, not only of creatures and the physical universe, but of human society as well. In the medieval Islamic worldview, created things changed too. But change occurred mainly as an accidental process, linked to the rhythms of birth, growth, and decay. Change was not a universal principle, and it did not apply to all aspects of existence. This was despite the fact that the Qur'an refers to the universe as having its own life cycle leading from creation to destruction. The modern universe, which is governed by impersonal forces such as relativity theory, chaos theory, and Heisenberg's Uncertainty Principle, would seem sinister to a medieval Islamic philosopher such as Ibn Sina (Avicenna,

d. 1037), whose universe was motivated by the forces of love and attraction, and who sought perfection in order and equilibrium. As George Marsden has pointed out with respect to Evangelicalism, the modern view of physical reality seems to leave the believer with no solid ground on which to stand: "With process rather than design as a basic category for thought, 'truth' tends to become far more relative to the observer, his time and place. 'Facts' commonly are regarded as not fixed, but as some combination of an objective reality and interpretation imposed by the observer."[34]

POST-MODERNITY AND ITS DISCONTENTS

With the concept of truth as a process, we arrive at the epistemology of what has come to be called post-modernity. For Muslims who do not regard reality as a kaleidoscopic theater of divine manifestation as the Sufi Ibn 'Arabi did, post-modernity can create a profound crisis of the Holy because nothing can be thought of in static terms. post-modernity is governed by the epistemology of what Anthony Giddens has termed *wholesale reflexivity*: "We are abroad in a world which is thoroughly constituted through reflexively applied knowledge, but where at the same time we can never be sure that any given element of that knowledge will not be revised."[35] A world where knowledge and truth are contested and relativized makes it nearly impossible for the individual to make the right choices or to successfully thread his or her way through the moral labyrinth of the human condition. A world where critical reflexivity must always be practiced is a world of stress for the believer because the traditional certainties of community, society, and even family can be cast into doubt. This inability to confront critical self-reflection and constant change is one of the factors that lie behind the *mal du présent* that Fatima Mernissi speaks of, a malaise that leads not only Muslims, but also many Buddhists, Hindus, American Christians, and others to find solace in a nostalgia for a time when the world was simpler and the choices were easier.

In *The Labyrinth of Solitude* the Mexican Nobel laureate Octavio Paz (d. 1998) observed, "Man is nostalgia and a search for communion."[36] The price of man's invention of himself by saying "No" to nature is a nostalgic longing to find communion with someone or something more meaningful than himself. In Islam, this nostalgia has led to the development of a religious outlook in which an idealized and anti-modernist view of tradition is explained by the very reflexivity it purports to reject. As Anthony Giddens notes, a constructed tradition is a "tradition in sham clothing [because it] receives its identity only from the reflexivity of the modern."[37] Especially in corporate views of Islam, believers seek refuge in a traditionalistic yet fully modern utopia that falsely offers Muslims protection from the storms of change raging around them.

According to the philosopher Karl Popper, the construction of such utopias is a "tribal" response to the stresses created by modern open societies, which are feared as individualistic, depersonalized, and overly competitive. By contrast, the corporate or "tribal" ideal is collectivistic, traditionalistic, and conservative with regard to custom. Its social order is governed by convention and taboo and society as a whole is seen as an organism, where naturalized ideologies of human relations support the group as a whole at the expense of individual forms of expression.[38] Although Popper's critique of corporatism was originally meant to apply to Fascism and Communism, his model of nostalgic utopianism accurately characterizes the worldview of corporate Islam, especially in its appeal to idealized tradition and in its contention that the social order be governed by social conventions and taboos. This is the hidden subtext that lies behind the notion stated above that "Everything is about the Shari'a." Although we must keep in mind that there is an element of corporatism in every institutionalized religion, the reification of religion that is engendered by the epistemology of modern empiricism (and even by the modern study of religion) has made the tendency toward corporatism more universal, and hence more totalitarian in nature.

Here we can add another irony to the many ironies discussed in this chapter. As Popper predicted, in the ideological confrontation between modernity and corporately defined Tradition—and despite attempts to conceptually separate religion from culture—tribalism most often emerges as a by-product, if not the actual outcome. The result of this dialectic can be seen in the widespread phenomenon of ethno-religious nationalism, an ideology that characterizes such diverse societies as Orthodox Russia, Hindu India, Buddhist Thailand, the Jewish state of Israel, and the Islamic state of Malaysia. Ethnic tribalism also characterizes many movements of corporate Islam, despite their claims of universalism. Many Islamist movements covertly support culturally patterned forms of religion, while outwardly calling for a meta-cultural Islam whose ideology transcends local forms of religiosity and other supposedly "cultural" accretions, such as Sufism.

To cite just a few examples: the ideology of identity expressed in Yusuf al-Qaradawi's "Jurisprudence of [Muslim] Minorities" (*fiqh al-aqalliyyat*), is as much about Arab cultural heritage (*turath*) as it is about creed ('*aqida*).[39] Similarly, when Ayatollah Khomeini translated the Qur'anic term *khimar* (woman's head-covering) with the Persian term *chador* (a blanket-like veil), he conflated creed and culture in an ideology that was ostensibly universalistic but actually culturally Iranian. In the same vein, the Al Qaeda view of Islam, despite its claim of universalism, is based socially on early Islamic Arab values and customs. In each of these cases, cultural practices have been reified and converted into ideological precepts.

In a popularly recounted *hadith qudsi* (non-Qur'anic divine saying), Allah says: "I am whatever my servant thinks of me" (*ana 'inda zanni 'abdi bi*).

Today, it seems that Allah is mainly a symbol in Islam, like the calligraphic icon on the Iranian flag. Corporate Islam in particular conceives of God less as a theological construct than as an ideological icon. *Islam*, a word that originally meant "individual submission to the will of God," is now defined as a system (*nizam*) that unites culture and creed in the context of a divinely guided society of the righteous. Proof that this vision of Islam is essentially modern can be found in the fact that metaphysics is largely absent in contemporary Sunni thought.[40] What passes for metaphysics in Sunni Islam today are usually variations on Sayyid Qutb's concept of the Divine Shari'a.[41] Personal belief has been reduced to a creed and on the level of practice the content of one's Islam is measured by means of an engineer's blueprint of steps to paradise. What is most important for Sunni Muslim reformists today is the engineering of society, not the spiritual development of the human being.

The corporatist worldview of modern Islamic reformism recalls not only anthropologist Edward Tylor's definition of culture, as we have seen, but also sociologist Emile Durkheim's (d. 1917) view of religion as the symbolic representation of the social group. This is significant, because as Anthony Giddens remarks, "modernity is itself deeply and intrinsically sociological."[42] Even more than the natural sciences, says Giddens, sociology reflects the culture of modernity: "[T]he chronic revision of social practices in the light of knowledge about those practices is part of the very tissue of modern institutions."[43] Especially in the United States, sociology—in the form of statistical surveys and demographic studies—has become the most generalized type of reflection on modern social life. The administrative control achieved by the U.S. government is inseparable from the routine monitoring of sociological data. In American universities, theory has largely disappeared from departments of sociology, which tend to focus on demographics. Even political science has become quantitative, in order to become more "scientific." A similar process of sociological reductionism is at work in corporate Islam. The reduction of the religion of Islam to a system, the reduction of theology to ideology, and the reduction of community to a simplified normative tradition has led Islamic reformism to largely become a plan for social engineering, where individual needs are subordinated to those of the group in a totalitarian fashion.

Individual needs are overlooked in the sociological perspective of corporate Islam. This is also part of "The Crisis of the Holy," because the original goal of Islam, like that of all religions of salvation, was to prepare individual souls to meet God. When religious leaders who stress the importance of individual salvation are criticized for being socially irresponsible, one must ask whether the World has taken over Islam in the name of the Non-World.[44] The Qur'an states: "Thusly has Allah shown you the signs so that you may reflect upon them" (2:266). The rise of corporate Islam is a significant portent of these times, although it is not mentioned in Hadith collections. It suggests to the self-reflective believer that many Muslims have forgotten the admonition of the Qur'an that "Each soul is the hostage of its own deeds" (74:38). This verse does not say that we should be hostage to political ideologies or the actions of the collectivity. By following this precept more faithfully than we do today, premodern Muslims were able to avoid the mistake of believing that the fate of the individual soul was dependent on the fate of the community.

TECHNOLOGY AND EDUCATION

The present chapter and book came out of an Elijah think-tank retreat on the Crisis of the Holy held at Mount Sequoyah Assembly in Fayetteville, Arkansas, in July 2005. Apart from the issues discussed above, two other "moments of crisis" were identified that pertain to the epistemological aspect of the Crisis of the Holy in Islam. These were the issues of technology and education, and they deserve at least a brief mention.

In general, Muslims have not regarded technology as a problematical issue for nearly a century. On the contrary, modern Islamic ideologies tend to view technology and the applied sciences as epistemologically neutral domains of knowledge that do not threaten fundamental Islamic worldviews. Most Muslims have eagerly adopted technological change and are often among the first to apply technological innovations. In fact, one could even say that the problem for Islam is not resistance to technology but its unqualified acceptance. By not problematizing the social and epistemological consequences of technology, modern Muslims have in many cases allowed technological thinking to shape their worldview. Epistemologically, this has contributed to the rise of *instrumentalism* with respect to both knowledge and ethics.

Instrumentalism, which, like sociology, is integral to modern culture, is an "ends justifies the means" ethic that values technical efficiency above other values. Almost fifty years ago, the French philosopher and culture critic Jacques Ellul identified instrumentalism as one of the hallmarks of the modern Technological Society.[45] In the Technological Society, power and reproductive capacity are no longer solely dependent on capital; instead, they are fundamental values of technology. According to Ellul, the promotion of technical efficiency in all areas (including the physical and social sciences) has contributed in the modern era to the erosion of spirituality and the blurring of ethical boundaries. Technological thinking and the instrumentalism that goes with it are double-edged swords: they are necessary for survival in the modern world, but they can erode humanistic values if they are allowed to develop unhindered along the lines of their own logic. The loss of spirituality and the distortion of ethical values discussed earlier in this chapter are closely related to instrumentalism and technocratic thinking. As such, the problematic of technology deserves to be part of "The Crisis of the Holy" in Islam, even though the issue is not one of resistance to technology. So far, the critique of instrumentalism and the Technological Society suggested by Jacques Ellul has not yet entered the critical discourse on Islam and modernity.

The issue of education is significant both with respect to the Occidentalist culture war with the West and to the problem of the cultural assimilation of Muslims in Western countries. Its prominence in Islamist discourses is also a symptom of epistemological crisis. The issues of moral values and education have been closely intertwined since the beginning of Islamic history. An extreme response to this question can be seen in the Taliban *madrasas* of Afghanistan and northwest Pakistan, where epistemological purity is maintained through indoctrination in a closely monitored curriculum of religious texts. The interrelationship between epistemology and education was most famously highlighted in Sayyid Qutb's *Ma'alim fi al-Tariq* (Milestones), where Muslims were warned to avoid all Western views of "the interpretation of human endeavor . . . the explanation of the origin of the universe, [and] the origin of the life of man . . . It is . . . not permissible for a Muslim to learn them from anyone other than a God-fearing and pious Muslim, who knows that guidance in these matters comes from God."[46] The relevance of education for Sayyid Qutb to the issues of ideology and normative culture can be seen in the title of the chapter in which the above quotation appears: "The Islamic Concept and Culture" (*al-Tasawwur al-islami wa al-thaqafa*).

Sayyid Qutb's epistemological critique of the West in *Ma'alim fi al-Tariq* inspired the educational experiment known as the "Islamization of Knowledge," which from the 1970s through the early 2000s sought to create a fully modern yet Islamically pure and authentic worldview by Islamizing and thus epistemologically purifying Western philosophies and social sciences.[47] This movement has lost its vitality since the death of its founder Ismail al-Faruqi in 1986 and the removal of its main theorist, Syed Muhammad Naquib Al-Attas, from the directorship of the International Institute of Islamic Thought and Civilization (ISTAC) in Malaysia. However, the effects of Sayyid Qutb's warning against the influence of Western philosophy and speculative thought are still apparent in many Muslim communities. For example, until recently in the United States, few Muslim university students majored in the humanities or the social sciences. Although this can partly be attributed to the desire by immigrant parents to prepare their children for well-paying jobs, virtually every Muslim academic in the United States and Europe has heard complaints in local Muslim communities about the dangers of Western philosophy, social science, and "academic Islam."

What the partisans of the Islamization of Knowledge overlooked is that in every Muslim country the problem of youth education is complicated by the fact that Muslim youth are being educated in school systems that were designed under the influence of Western models of state-sponsored education. Religious leaders who seek to undo the influence of modernity are faced with the dilemma of closing the barn door after the horse has already left. As a result, their only real options are to replace modern education with totalitarian indoctrination or to scrap the modern educational system entirely, as the Taliban did, and artificially reconstruct a quasi-medieval system of education. Muslim youth would be better served, both politically and religiously, by an educational system that stresses critical and independent thinking instead of modern or pre-modern forms of indoctrination. A full discussion of this issue, while important to the epistemological crisis of Islam, would unfortunately take us beyond the scope of this chapter.

TRADITION AND THE PRESENT TIME

"Tradition is the living faith of the dead. Traditionalism is the dead faith of the living."[48] This maxim by Jaroslav Pelikan epitomizes the dilemma faced by Muslims who wish to retain an authentic sense of tradition in the face of modernity and post-modernity. The epistemological crisis of Islam impacts the believer on every level. Traditionalism is an inadequate response to this crisis because it is no longer possible to pretend that pre-Enlightenment epistemologies can still be maintained in their original form. In addition, the twentieth-century tragedies caused by nationalism, racism, and communism have proved beyond a doubt that ideologies founded on idealism and perfectionism oppress the individual by holding people to standards that they cannot attain. It is similarly foolish to try to resurrect medieval theologies such as Ash'arism by arguing, for example, that quantum physics describes a similar view of reality. Such similarities are superficial at best, and modern theoretical models of relativity, perspectivism, and the Uncertainty Principle are far from the divine Foundationalism that Ash'arite theologians had in mind. The Crisis of the Holy in contemporary Islam is abetted by the traditionalism that Muslims have employed in defending Islam against modernity. The task of the constructive theologian of Islam today is not to repeat the language of tradition out of context, but to engage critically with the legacy of tradition as it impacts the experience of Muslims in the contemporary world. To do so, Muslims must engage their traditional sources of wisdom—particularly the Qur'an—in new ways, "with both eyes open." The challenge is to maintain the integrity of God's teachings but at the same time to remain aware of the obstacles put in the way of understanding by a traditionalism that parodies, rather than duplicates the worldviews of the past.

The Greek philosopher Heraclitus of Ephesus (d. ca. 475 BCE) spoke of time as a flowing river in which one cannot step twice in the same waters, because fresh waters are forever flowing past the spot where one stands. Karl Popper disliked this metaphor because it led, in his view, to the notion of historicism, the idea that time moves forward according to inexorable laws that determine the outcome of human fate.[49] Others have interpreted Heraclitus' metaphor differently. In *The Passion of the Western Mind*, Richard Tarnas highlights the tendency of the River of Time to erode the foundations of tradition: "Many sense that the great determining force of our reality is the mysterious process of history itself, which in our century has appeared to be hurtling toward a massive disintegration of all structures and foundations, a triumph of the Heraclitan flux."[50]

This is a different kind of historicism than what Popper imagined; rather than leading toward a predetermined or teleological outcome, history for Tarnas means open-ended change, which is the historicism of post-modernity rather than of modernity. The "Heraclitan flux" that Tarnas speaks of is the notion of change itself, in which the world is in a continuous process of transformation and all notions of stability are illusions that will be dispelled by the flow of time. Many Muslims see the present age in the way described by Tarnas, in which traditions, values, moral precepts, and the truths of religion are all in danger of being washed away by the flood. Concurrently with the rise of Muslim pseudo-traditionalism has been a host of predictions and warnings about the End Times, in which apocalyptic passages from the Qur'an and Hadith are cited to attract adherents to the teachings of Wahhabi sheikhs and Sufi sages alike. The hysteria created in some quarters by this Muslim *mal du présent* is reminiscent of the attitude of the Aztecs of Mexico on the eve of the Spanish conquest. For the Aztecs, the present age is the Fifth Sun—the Sun of Change—in which the gods are overthrown and the world is transformed into a new and hitherto unknown reality.

But as we have seen, not all Muslims fear the unknown. While not denying the potential of destruction through change, the Andalusian Sufi Ibn 'Arabi saw time as a theatre of manifestation where different aspects of the divine reality are displayed according to the appropriate divine names. A similar attitude was held by the Egyptian Sufi Ibn 'Ata'illah of Alexandria (d. 1309), who wrote a remarkable treatise on the spiritual practice of trusting in God (*tawakkul*) entitled, *al-Tanwir fi isqat al-tadbir* (Illumination in the Abdication of Personal Agency). In this work, Ibn 'Ata'illah counseled his readers to avoid trying to control their destinies. Instead, he said, they should accept the time in which they live and see the consequences of the present time as a manifestation of the divine will. To be true servants of God they should adapt themselves to present circumstances, "go with the flow," and trust that God will see them through the changing times. In a striking use of the Heraclitan metaphor, Ibn 'Ata'illah summarized the essence of this spiritual attitude in a way that is very relevant for Muslims today:

> When I saw destiny flowing,
> There was no doubt or hesitation about it.
> So I entrusted all of my rights to my Creator
> And threw myself into the current.[51]

I find it significant that in my experience of debating Islamic spirituality with conservative Islamists and liberal Muslim modernists alike, no doctrine of the Sufis is more disparaged than *tawakkul* or entrustment of the self to God of which Ibn 'Ata'illah speaks. The spiritual practice of trust in God's will should not be seen as an obstacle to progress but as an essential Islamic attitude, the practical application on the level of the personal self of the God-consciousness that all Muslims profess to seek. If Muslims claim, following the Qur'an, that agency belongs to God, then "letting go and letting God" is an appropriate response of the truly faithful. However, this attitude has been derided as an abdication of personal responsibility, as socially insensitive, and as the example *par excellence* of the "isolated spirituality" (*ruhaniyya i'tizaliyya*) that renders Sufism irrelevant to the modern condition.[52] It is ironic, therefore, that those who think like Ibn 'Ata'illah appear to be the only Muslims who can chart a course through modernity without abdicating authentic Islamic tradition. Perhaps this paradox highlights the underlying problem of the Crisis of the Holy in Islam. Perhaps the root cause of the crisis is not modernity or post-modernity after all. Perhaps it is the loss of a sense of the sacred, a loss of that spirituality that makes Islam not just a tradition or an identity, but a true submission to God. If this is truly the case, then Muslims should stop exceptionalizing modernity because to God, the present time is no better or worse than any other. After all, as the famous hadith says, God *is* time. Thus, the answer to the Crisis of the Holy in Islam, as Ibn 'Ata'illah tells us, is to entrust all of our rights to the Creator and to embrace the river of time by jumping into its current.

NOTES

1. Alasdair MacIntyre, *Whose Justice? Which Rationality?* (Notre Dame, IN: University of Notre Dame Press, 1988): 361–362. MacIntyre's term, "epistemological crisis," first appeared in the article, "Epistemological Crises, Dramatic Narrative and the Philosophy of Science," *The Monist*, 69, 4, 1977.

2. MacIntyre, *Whose Justice?*: 362.

3. Jaroslav Pelikan, *The Vindication of Tradition* (New Haven and London: Yale University Press, 1984): 81.

4. MacIntyre, *Whose Justice?*: 364.

5. Editor's note: Compare to Judaism on page 103.

6. Pelikan, *The Vindication of Tradition*, 80.

7. The Turkish word *millet* comes from the Arabic *milla*. In the Qur'an, the Prophet Joseph says: "I have forsaken the *milla* of a people who do not believe in Allah and reject the Hereafter. Instead, I follow the *milla* of my fathers Abraham, Isaac, and Jacob. Never was it our practice to associate partners with God" (12:37–38). Although *milla* as used in the Qur'an is best translated as "tradition," in the Ottoman Empire it took on the meaning of a religious community, such that Muslims, Christians, and Jews each had their own *millet*.

8. Many Muslim advocates of religious tolerance do not call for true religious pluralism, but for what Kwame Anthony Appiah calls "millet multiculturalism," a form of *modus vivendi* in which Muslims and other religious communities are given virtual autonomy to decide their own affairs. Such arguments often involve the right to practice the *Shari'a* (the version of which is seldom specified). This lies behind attempts in the legislatures of North Carolina and other southern states in the United States to ban "Shari'ah Law." See Kwame Anthony Appiah, *The Ethics of Identity* (Princeton, N. J.: Princeton University Press, 205): 74–79.

9. For Tylor's definition of culture see the beginning of chapter 1 ("The Science of Culture") in idem, *Primitive Culture*, Volume 1: https://archive.org/stream/primitiveculture 01tylouoft/primitiveculture01tylouoft_djvu.txt.

10. In the 1982 edition of *al-Shibl al-Muslim* (The Muslim Lion Cub), a sort of Boy Scout manual for young Muslim Brotherhood members in Egypt, the anonymous author of an article on Islamic government writes: "Islam is not only a creed, it is a creed and a system. It is not only a religion but also a religion and a state. The unity of Islam in all of its meanings and manifestations includes the establishment of such a state. Social unity is established on the basis of the language of the Qur'an (Arabic) and the Qur'anic system. Political unity is found under the shade of the Commander of the Faithful and the banner of the Islamic Caliphate." Note how this passage promotes both a corporatist view of society and Arab nationalism.

11. Abdul Hakim Murad, "Faith in the Future: Islam after Enlightenment," http://www.masud.co.uk/ISLAM/ahm/postEnlight.htm, 2.

12. Basit Bilal Koshul, "Studying the Western Other, Understanding the Islamic Self: A Qur'anically Reasoned Perspective," Hartford Seminary, unpublished conference paper.

13. See Benjamin Barber, *Jihad vs. McWorld: Terrorism's Challenge to Democracy* (New York: Ballantine Books, 1996); this work sees "tribal" religious fundamentalism as the main enemy of globalization and global capitalism. 'Abd al-Hakim Murad seems to be arguing for what Barber would call the "tribal" view.

14. The first generation of Arab Occidentalists, such as Hassan Hanafi, who claims to have coined the term, "Occidentalism" in 1993, used this approach as a counter-discourse to Colonialism and Western Imperialism. See, Hassan Hanafi, "From Orientalism to Occidentalism," in idem, *Islam in the Modern World: Vol. II Tradition, Revolution, and Culture* (Cairo: Dar Kebaa Bookshop, 2000): 395–409. See also the Syrian writer Sadik Jalal al-'Azm, "Orientalism and Orientalism in Reverse," in A. L. Macfie, Ed., *Orientalism: A* Reader (New York: New York University Press, 2001): 217–38.

15. Ian Buruma and Avishai Margalit, *Occidentalism: the West in the Eyes of Its Enemies* (New York: The Penguin Press, 2004): 75.

16. Abdolkarim Soroush, "Life and Virtue: The Relationship Between Socioeconomic Development and Ethics," in Mahmoud Sadri and Ahmad Sadri, *Reason, Freedom, and Democracy in Islam: Essential Writings of Abdolkarim Soroush* (New York and Oxford: Oxford University Press, 2000): 43.

17. This point was first noted by Karl Popper in *The Open Society and Its Enemies: Volume One: The Spell of Plato*, (London and New York: Routledge, 2003 reprint of 1945 first edition). The contrast between Plato's idealism and Sophistical realism is drawn throughout the book, but it is most prominent in the chapters titled, "Nature and Convention," "The Principle of Leadership," and "Aestheticism, Perfectionism, Utopianism."

18. Ralph Waldo Emerson, "An Address," in *The Complete Essays and other Writings of Ralph Waldo Emerson*, Brooks Atkinson, ed. (New York: Modern Library, 1940): 81. Cited in Pelikan, *The Vindication of Tradition*.

19. Ibrahim M. Abu Rabi', *Intellectual Origins of Islamic Resurgence in the Modern Arab World* (Albany: State University of New York Press, 1996): 21–22. See also, Muhammad al-

Bahi, *al-Fikr al-Islami al-hadith wa silatihi bi-al-isti'mar al-gharbi* (Modern Islamic Thought and its Relation to Western Colonialism) (Beirut, 1970).

20. John L. Esposito, *The Islamic Threat: Myth or Reality?* (New York, 1992): 10.

21. Janet L. Abu Lughod, *Rabat: Urban Apartheid in Morocco* (Princeton: Princeton University Press, 1980): 131: "[Lyautey's urban planning] included one essential condition: the complete separation of European agglomerations from native agglomerations. The European population centers must be separated from those of the indigenous populations for political, economic, sanitary, and aesthetic reasons, as well as for town planning purposes." (This policy was first developed by Henri Prost, chief town planner of the French Protectorate in Morocco under Lyautey.)

22. Eric Hobsbawm, "Introduction: Inventing Traditions," in Eric Hobsbawm and Terence Ranger editors, *The Invention of Tradition* (Cambridge: Cambridge University Press, 1984): 4.

23. Fatima Mernissi, *Women and Islam: An Historical and Theological Enquiry*, translated by Mary Jo Lakeland (New Delhi: Kali for Women reprint of Basil Blackwell original, 1991): 15. This work was published in the United States as *The Veil and the Male Elite: A Feminist Interpretation of Women's Rights in Islam* (Reading, MA: Addison Wesley Publishing, 1991).

24. Peter Coates, *Ibn 'Arabi and Modern Thought: The History of Taking Metaphysics Seriously* (Oxford: Anqa Publishing, 2002): 82–83.

25. On John Locke's epistemology and views of religion, see Nicholas Wolterstorff, *John Locke and the Ethics of Belief* (Cambridge: Cambridge University Press, 1996). A summary of Locke's views on epistemological certainty can also be found in Ronald A. Kuipers, *Critical Faith: Toward a Renewed Understanding of Religious Life and its Public Accountability* (Amsterdam: Vrije Universiteit Amsterdam, 2002): 10–43.

26. On logical arguments in the Qur'an, see Rosalind Ward Gwynne, *Logic, Rhetoric and Legal Reasoning in the Qur'an" God's Arguments* (London and New York: Routledge Curzon, 2004).

27. George Marsden, "The Collapse of American Evangelical Academia," in Alvin Plantinga and Nicholas Wolterstorff eds., *Faith and Rationality: Reason and Belief in God* (Notre Dame, IN: University of Notre Dame Press, 1983): 224–25. On Thomas Reid, see also Nicholars Wolterstorff, "Can Belief in God be Rational if it has No Foundations?" in the same volume, 148–55.

28. Ibid, 226–28.

29. See, for example, Mehdi Ha'iri Yazdi, *The Principles of Epistemology in Islamic Philosophy: Knowledge by Presence* (Albany: State University of New York Press, 1992). This work is so traditionalistic that it ignores the findings of modern Cognitive Psychology in favor of medieval theories of perception.

30. Marsden, "The Collapse of American Evangelical Academia," 233.

31. Ibid, 235.

32. See Dr. Maurice Boucaille, *The Bible, the Qur'an and Science: The Holy Scriptures Examined in the Light of Modern Knowledge* (Elmhurst, NY: Tahrkie Tarsile Qur'an Inc., seventh revised edition, 2003). The documentary film, *The Book of Signs*, was produced by former Malaysian Prime Minister Tunku Abdul Rahman and released by Kechik Film Production, Malaysia, and Naas Limited, London, in 1986. It draws heavily from the theories of Maurice Boucaille. The film can be viewed in its entirety at https://www.youtube.com/watch?v=xLCxtUY9k4I.

33. Ironically for a theological argument, such signs and portents of divine favor are more often than not political. See, for example, Vincent J. Cornell, trans., "'Abduh and Afghani on Destiny and Fate," in John Renard, Ed., *Islamic Theological Themes: A Primary Source Reader* (Oakland, California: University of California Press, 2014): 358–67.

34. Marsden, "The Collapse of American Evangelical Academia," 243.

35. Anthony F. Giddens, *The Consequences of Modernity* (Stanford, California: Stanford University Press, 1990), 39. What I have called post-modernity is considered by Giddens to be merely another phase of modernity.

36. Octavio Paz, *The Labyrinth of Solitude and The Other Mexico, Return to the Labyrinth of Solitude, Mexico and the United States, The Philanthropic Ogre*, Lysander Kemp, Yara Milos, and Rachel Phillips Belash, trans. (New York: Grove Press, 1985): 195.

37. Giddens, *The Consequences of Modernity*, 38.

38. Popper, *The Open Society and Its Enemies: Volume One: The Spell of Plato*, 184–86.

39. See, for example, Abu Rabi', "*Turath* Resurgent? Arab Islamism and the Problematic of Tradition," in *Intellectual Origins of Islamic Resurgence*, 40–61.

40. Metaphysical thought still exists in contemporary Shi'ism, which has remained closer than Sunni Islam to its historical and philosophical roots.

41. See Sayyid Qutb, *Ma'alim fi al-Tariq* (Beirut: Dar al-Sharq, 2000), 46. In this passage Qutb states, "To act by the Divine Shari'a (*al-Shari'a al-Ilahiyya*) is an established rule. This stands even above the requirement to establish Islam as a creed."

42. Giddens, *The Consequences of Modernity*, 43.

43. Ibid, 40.

44. See, for example, the following statement by the South African Muslim academic Farid Esack: "Despite the regular reminders of the inevitable return to God, the spiritualizing of human existence, which regards earthly life as incidental, is unfounded in the qur'anic (*sic.*) view of humankind. The human body, being a carrier of a person's inner core and of the spirit of God, is viewed as sacred, and physical concerns are, therefore, not incidental to the Qur'an." Apparently, for the liberal modernist Esack, the practice of contemplative spiritually is un-Islamic. Farid Esack, *Qur'an, Liberation, and Pluralism: An Islamic Perspective of Interreligious Solidarity against Oppression* (Oxford: One World Books, 1997): 95.

45. See, for example, Jacques Ellul, "Faith or Religion?" in *Perspectives on Our Age: Jacques Ellul Speaks on his Life and Work*, edited by William H. Vanderburg (Concord, Ontario Canada: Anansi Press, 1997), 85–111. According to Ellul, "Man creates for himself a new religion of a rational and technical order to justify his work and to be justified in it." (85).

46. Seyyid (*sic.*) Qutb, *Milestones* (Damascus: Dar al-'Ilm, n.d.): 109–110. See also the Arabic edition of this work, *op. cit.*, 139.

47. The most extensive theoretical exposition of the Islamization of Knowledge idea is in Syed Muhammad Naquib al-Attas, *Prolegomena to the Metaphysics of Islam: An Exposition of the Fundamental Elements of the Worldview of Islam* (Kuala Lumpur: International Institute of Islamic Thought and Civilization, 1995).

48. Pelikan, *The Vindication of Tradition*, 65.

49. Popper, *The Open Society and Its Enemies* Vol. I, 7–14.

50. Quoted in Coates, *Ibn 'Arabi and Modern Thought*, 81.

51. Ahmad ibn 'Ata'illah al-Iskandari, *Kitab al-Tanwir fi isqat al-tadbir* (Cairo: al-Matba'a al-Maymuniyya al-Misriyya, 1306/1888-9): 11.

52. This is the term used by Hasan al-Banna (d. 1948), to criticize Sufism.

Chapter Eight

Concluding Reflections

Alon Goshen-Gottstein

One of the challenges that has faced us as we have reflected upon the "Crisis of the Holy" has been how to present our descriptions and analyses in ways that are helpful and that offer a handle and a perspective upon the phenomenon, seen in its broadest aspects. The challenge is complicated given the need to take account of the realities of diverse traditions, each with its own particularity, history, and specific challenges. As stated in chapter 1, we attempted this through two means. The first was the identification of key notions that can serve as handles to conceptualizing the broader crisis. Here we noted, in particular, the problem of individualism and the axis of individual/collective approach to religion. The second was by identifying core issues that confront all of our traditions, through which we could recognize the crisis as common to all our traditions.

Having heard the voices of the different traditions, it seems that we can group the most important concerns that have emerged along an axis representing a process that allows us not only to describe the problem but also to analyze it and to point to the potential it contains. We noted at the outset that the "Crisis" of the Holy is a confluence of threats, challenges, and opportunities. The axis, as presented here, highlights the ways in which we may conceive of the crisis in terms of opportunity.

At the one pole of the axis stands the term "Identity." So much of what has been discussed in this collection of essays touches upon issues of identity. The most obvious instances are those of Islam and Hinduism, both struggling with corporate, or syndicated, identities and the ways in which these threaten the authenticity of historical tradition. Judaism, too, experiences identity at the core of its crisis, as suggested in my summary of Barry Levy's paper. Issues of unity, of teaching and more all revert to concerns for identity. While these issues were less prominent in the first two chapters, they are still applicable to them, as far as the construction of the present conceptual matrix is concerned. This will be seen from a consideration of the relationship of identity and the integrity of tradition.

Concerns for the integrity of tradition have been most prominent in our discussion. This could be broken up into two. On the one hand, concern for the integrity of the tradition itself and on the other hand, concern for the integrity of the community. Both are subjects of discussion, and distinctly so, in the case of Judaism. Both are also the focus of discussion in the case of Buddhism. The teaching, the Dharma, is challenged in new ways. New religious forms arise and the question is to what extent are they true to the original teaching of the tradition and to what extent does the classical tradition succeed in leaving its impact upon present-day reality. Hence, questions arise regarding the integrity of the teaching. Similar questions may be raised regarding the community. Concern for protecting the venerable structures of old while accommodating new structures, the shifting balances between lay and monastic, and the challenges of gender all touch upon the core issue of the integrity of the community of practice.

A similar point may be made in relation to the Catholic tradition. Issues of change, acculturation, and dialogue all throw into the limelight the concern for the integrity of tradition. The carriers of tradition are also challenged. As authority structures are challenged and shift, as individual-community balances are redefined, concern is shown for the integrity of the community itself. As suggested in my own presentation of Griffith's chapter, what is at stake is ultimately the question of the Church's mission in the world, its continuing purpose and functioning. Who will act on its behalf and to what ends—these questions sum up the broader concerns of the Catholic tradition. These are, in important ways, issues of identity. Thus, all our traditions are concerned in some significant way with preserving their identity, while allowing that identity to adapt to contemporary circumstances and to find new voice, new expression and new purpose under present day challenges.

At the other end of the axis stands "Spirituality." While the term may support different definitions, it suggests an affinity to that which makes the present project unique—concern with the Holy as the heart of religion and its purpose. In some sense, all our traditions are implicated in a quest for spirituality. The quest may be that of the members of tradition seeking their own spiritual fulfillment, in conjunction with or independently of, religious structures. Or it may be the quest of the tradition itself to discover its deeper purpose and the contemporary voice and expression of its spiritual meaning. Spirituality is used here to designate not simply the subjective inner feeling or the experience of religion, but that entire domain that is conditioned by some direct relationship to God, by relating the memory of His presence and awareness of His purpose. Naturally, as God (or ultimacy captured in other terms) becomes the center of awareness, the experiential dimension of religion will become more prominent.

Ideally, all our traditions contain the balance appropriate for them between these two poles—identity and spirituality. In a noncrisis situation, identity constitutes spirituality, and spirituality in turn constructs and reinforces identity. A sign of the crisis is that there is much tension between these two dimensions. Thus, spirituality is sought at the expense of traditional understanding of identity and outside it. This tension allows us to introduce two more elements on our axis. For most of our discussion these elements have stood on their own. Indeed, we may continue to consider them as a self-standing axis, that provides insight into the crisis. In the present context, I shall attempt to integrate them into the axis of identity and spirituality. I refer to the two core concepts that have occupied our attention time and again—the collective and the individual.

According to this attempt to integrate these two axes into a broader holistic analysis, the corporate dimension would follow identity on the axis, while the individual should precede the keyword spirituality.

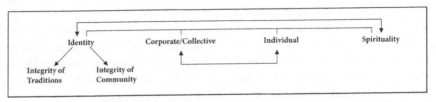

What this suggests conceptually is that corporateness plays an important role in the construction of identity. It is developed, in part, in order to foster identity and the need to develop identity is in and of itself a strong corporate need. Thus, those forms of religion that highlight corporateness do so for the sake of identity construction. While there is an ideal "collective" element that is important for the purposes of spirituality, what sets "corporateness" apart from what we shall call here "collective" is precisely the fact that it serves the one pole, that of identity, more than it does the other, that of spirituality.

By contrast, the individual is closer to the pole of spirituality. Concern for the individual is concern for spiritual salvation and well-being. Cornell's chapter demonstrates how the corporatness of Islam comes at the expense of concern for the spiritual welfare of the believer and how the sense of personal submission to God that provides the basic definition of Islam is transformed into a system in which this personal dimension is lost sight of. My own knowledge of Judaism allows me to testify how valid this association is there as well. The need to uphold collective identity allows political, national, and group concerns to dominate and to define the agenda of organizations, communities, and individuals. It provides an alternative framework for identification, replacing the ultimate purpose of the system, pointing to God, with identification with the corporate body, either in relation to the People of Israel or in relation to the state of Israel. The crisis of membership and affiliation in the Catholic Church can also be attributed to a significant extent to the felt sense that Church practice upholds identity, understood collectively, rather than advancing the spiritual goals of the individual. One might pose the question of whether the success of various protestant and charismataic groups does not lie, in fact, in their ability to offer a different balance of these constitutive elements in their presentation of an alternative version of Christianity. It stands to reason that Buddhism may be less implicated in identity politics, because of its upfront rejection of identities of various kinds as forms of attachment. Nevertheless, as it becomes involved in local cultural identities, upholding the tradition and the community and their own preservation act, de facto, as forms of identity preservation. The individualistic impact within traditional Asian societies, described in the chapter on Buddhism, enacts the kinds of tensions we encounter in relation to other traditions also in relation to Buddhism.

What all this suggests is that the forms of tradition, the ways they are reified, constructed, and defended are things we need to consider. On the one hand, the maintenance and protection of traditions is an act of caring for the vehicles that serve us in our quest for the ultimate. These vehicles safeguard tradition and protect it from the whims and capriciousness of individual choices and the factors that motivate them. On the other hand, forms can become encrusted, concerned with their own propagation and maintenance, and ultimately may prove to be as much a barrier as a carrier to the ultimate purpose of the tradition.

If the crisis is also an opportunity, then it would seem that the opportunity it provides us with is to examine our traditions and the degree to which they are faithful and able to serve as effective carriers for their ultimate purpose. Growing individualism and tension between individual and community push us to reexamine the ways in which group identity politics shape our agenda and influence how our religions are constructed. At the same time, the quest for spirituality, spearheaded by the individual quest for meaning, forces us to consider the tension between form and purpose as it applies to our traditions and to the ways and degrees to which they are able to effectively mediate spiritual reality and lead believers to it.

Before moving on to other lessons and suggestions indicated by our essays, a word is in order concerning the theoretical possibilities that emerge from a broad analysis spanning multiple religions. Considering these issues in an interreligious context is first and foremost an exercise in understanding. The first step in understanding is self understanding. If these suggestions are valid and useful, one might examine one's own tradition in light of this presentation. Following that one may gain a better grasp of processes that take place in another tradition. Great insight may be discovered when we ask how other traditions negotiate this axis. Rather than dealing only with the specific Crises of the Holy (authority, women, youth, etc.), we might ask the question of how the tension between identity and spirituality is played out in other traditions, and what mechanisms, constructive steps, and practical actions are taken in relation to it. The significance of this may go beyond curiosity and interest. There may be genuine lessons for all to learn.

Having moved from conceptual analysis to practical application, I would like to revisit some points that appeared in most of the chapters and to suggest they can be extremely helpful also in the formulation of action and policy as these emerge from an interreligious conversation, such as ours. Three issues seem relevant here.

The first concerns knowledge and education. All traditions assembled here place a great premium on knowledge and upon education. Education is the key to shaping leadership as well as to shaping the understanding of the community of believers. Education, and youth in particular, have been recognized in all of our chapters to be in some sense in crisis. Usually, one considers the crisis in terms of quantity—not enough education for not enough people. Hence the endless quest to broaden the network of schools and to increase exposure to our educational efforts to the maximum. However, as the discussion of technology has made plain—knowledge is nowadays easily accessible in forms previously unimagined. The concerns of education are not simply quantative but qualitative. What do we want our communities to know? What do we deem most essential for knowledge? To what extent is our choice of what is deemed important to know responsible for the alienation and distancing of our communities from our religions? And are we providing our communities with the kind of knowledge that is going to best serve them in their life quest? Only so can we ensure their deep affiliation with our traditions and the sense of their continuing relevance to our religious lives.

One might examine all of these questions independently of the previous discussion. However, one may readily pose the question of education and the dissemination of knowledge in terms of the identity-spirituality axis. Seen in this context, we must ask to what extent does our teaching seek the spiritual illumination and welfare of others, and to what extent does it seek to uphold existing identities. If there is value in the conceptual construct offered above, then education could be an immediate arena for its application.

A second arena that was discussed in most of our chapters is the family. Because this issue did not receive as much attention in all chapters, I shall not dwell upon it at length. I would like to raise the question here of whether in relation to the family similar dynamics apply as in relation to our religions. Are we witnessing the same kinds of crises and are they attributable to related sources? One specific application of this question would be whether the identity-spirituality matrix could be relevant to work in the family. There is no need to discuss family and identity. Family is our most basic unit of identity and breakdown of family has implications for identity. The question here is whether the identity-spirituality axis can be of relevance to our treatment of family-related concerns. To what extent are we sufficiently aware of spirituality as a component of family life and of family as a component of spirituality? To what extent might we focus our efforts in family education, counseling, therapy, etc., along lines that are informed by the above analysis?

The third arena for consideration in practical terms is the role of interreligious dialogue. Several of our chapters highlighted the importance of dialogue and learning from one another. The chapter on Buddhism suggests the wisdom of Buddhist as a resource for others. The chapter on Christianity suggests the need for better study of the Other as part of our own growth. In the present context I wish to raise the question of the value of interreligious dialogue and study of other traditions for more than just community peace. Interreligious dialogue might take on particular significance when seen along the identity-spirituality axis. Could this not itself be a focus of study? Could we not be challenged by other traditions precisely on the issue of the balances we keep, in theory and in practice, in each of our traditions, in relation to our ultimate stated goals? It is not only that we can learn from each other in practical ways. Ultimately, the other tradition might serve as a mirror through which we may examine ourselves. If we have intuited correctly the import of the identity-spirituality axis, then perhaps the most helpful way to take stock of our tradition may be by going beyond our tradition. As long as we are ensconced in our tradition, we will uphold that which we love, and justify that which we have come to know. The Crisis of the Holy is also an invitation to broaden the perspective through which we examine the world and its crises, including the individual crises that our own communities face. Could it be that by opening ourselves up to the study of the Other we might obtain better self-understanding on how we ourselves negotiate the core axes of identity and spirituality, as well as of individual and collective? Dialogue, thus understood, is not simply about understanding the Other or dispelling mistaken notions. Rather, in this instance it offers us the possibility to learn to see ourselves, in relation to a fundamental issue that touches upon how we function in the world as well as to who we are in ourselves, through the light refracted from the experience of the Other.

Selected Bibliography

Adams, Henry. *The Education of Henry Adams* (New York: The Library of America, 1983).

Bhikkhu Sugandha, Lumbini in the New Millenium: Youth in Buddhism (a theme paper for the International Buddhist conference at Lumbini, Nepal, Febuary 1–2, 2001).

Bloom, Harold. *The American Religion: The Emergence of the Post-Christian Nation* (New York: Simon & Schuster, 1992).

Buckley, Michael J. *At the Origins of Modern Atheism* (New Haven: Yale University Press, 1987).

Buckley, Michael J. *Denying and Disclosing God: The Ambiguous Progress of Modern Atheism* (New Haven: Yale University Press, 2004).

Cleary, Thomas. Transl. *Secrets of the Blue Cliff Record* (London and Boston: Shambala, 2000).

Clooney, Francis X. *Divine Mother, Blessed Mother: Hindu Goddesses and the Virgin Mary* (Oxford: Oxford University Press, 2005).

Clooney, Francis X. *Hindu God, Christian God: How Reason Helps Break Down the Boundaries between Religions* (Oxford: Oxford University Press, 2001).

Collins, Steven. *Selfless Persons: Imagery and Thought in Theravada Buddhism* (Cambridge: Cambridge University Press, 1982).

Congregation for the Doctrine of the Faith, *On the Unicity and Salvific Universality of Jesus Christ and the Church / Dominus Jesus* (English trans.; Boston: Pauline Books and Media, 2000).

de la Vallee Poussin, Louis. transl. *Abhidharma Kosa Bhasyam*, (Berkeley: Asian Humanities Press, 1988).

Derrett, J. D. M. *Religion, Law and the State in India* (New York: The Free Press, 1968).

Destremau, Christian & Jean Moncelon, *Massignon* (Paris: Plon, 1994).

Downing, Michael. *Shoes Outside the Door: Desire, Devotion and Excess at San Francisco Zen-Center* (Washington, D.C.: Counterpoint Publications, 2001).

Dupuis, Jacques. *Christianity and the Religions: From Confrontation to Dialogue* (English trans.; Maryknoll, NY: Orbis Books, 2002).

Dupuis, Jacques. *Toward a Christian Theology of Religious Pluralism* (English trans.; Maryknoll, NY: Orbis Books, 1997).

Fox, Thomas C. *Pentecost in Asia: A New Way of Being Church* (Maryknoll, NY: Orbis Books, 2002).

Gozier, André. *Le père Henri Le Saux: à la rencontre de l'hindouisme* (Paris: Centurion, 1989).

Griffiths, Paul. *An Apology for Apologetics: A Study in the Logic of Interreligious Dialogue* (Maryknoll, NY: Orbis Books, 1991).

Griffiths, Paul. *The Problems with Religious Diversity* (Oxford: Blackwell, 2001).

157

Gross, Rita. *Buddhism after Patriarchy. A Feminist History, Analysis, and Reconstruction of Buddhism* (Albany: State University of New York Press, 1993).

Gude, Mary Louise. *Louis Massignon: The Crucible of Compassion* (Notre Dame, IN: University of Notre Dame Press, 1996).

Gülen, Fethullah. *Advocate of Dialogue* (comp. Ali Ünal & Alphonse Williams; Fairfax, VA: The Fountain, 2000).

Habito, Ruben. *Experiencing Buddhism. Ways of Wisdom and Compassion* (New York: Orbis Books, 2005).

Harlan, Lindsey and Paul Courtright (eds.) *From the Margins of Hindu Marriage* (New York: Oxford University Press, 1995).

Horn, Robert. "Buddha Boys," *Time Magazine*, Asia, May 6, 2002.

Huntington, Samuel P., *The Clash of Civilizations and the Remaking of World Order* (New York: Simon & Schuster, 1996).

Jacquin, Françoise. *Jules Monchanin prêtre 1895-1957* (Paris: Cerf, 1996).

James, William. *The Varieties of Religious Experience: A Study in Human Nature* (Centenary Edition; London & New York: Routledge, 2002).

Jenkins, Philip. *The Next Christendom: The Coming of Global Christianity* (Oxford: Oxford University Press, 2003).

Kabilsingh, Chatsumarn. "Prostitutes and Buddhism," in *Thai Women in Buddhism* (Berkeley: Parallax Press, 1991).

Küng, Hans. *A Global Ethic for Global Politics and Economics* (Oxford: Oxford University Press, 1998).

Lama, Khandu. "Trafficking in Buddhist Girls: Empowerment through Prevention," http://www.childtrafficking.com/Docs/lama_and_bory_nodate_trafficking_in_buddhist_girls_dec.pdf.

Lamb, Christopher. *The Call to Retrieval: Kenneth Cragg's Christian Vocation to Islam* (London: Grey Seal, 1997).

Lasalle, Enomiya. *Zen: Way to Enlightenment* (New York: Taplinger, 1968).

Loundon, Sumi. Ed. *Blue Jean Buddha, Voices of Young Buddhists* (Somerville, MA: Wisdom Publications, 2001).

MacIntyre, Alasdair C. *Whose Justice? Which Rationality?* (Notre Dame, IN: University of Notre Dame Press, 1988).

Marsden, George M. *The Outrageous Idea of Christian Scholarship* (New York: Oxford University Press, 1997).

Marsden, George M. *The Soul of the American University: From Protestant Establishment to Established Nonbelief* (New York: Oxford University Press, 1994).

McGreevy, John T. *Catholicism and American Freedom* (New York: W.W. Norton, 2003).

Mitchell, Donald W. *Spirituality and Emptiness: The Dynamics of Spiritual Life in Buddhism and Christianity* (New York: Paulist Press, 1991).

Murray, John Courtney. *We Hold These Truths: Catholic Reflection on the American Proposition* (New York: Sheed and Ward, 1960).

Muslim-Christian Research Group, *The Challenges of the Scripture: The Bible and the Qur'ān* (Maryknoll, NY: Orbis Books, 1989).

Nattier, Jan. *Once Upon a Future Time. Studies in Buddhist Prophecy of Decline* (Berkeley: Asian Humanities Press, 1999).

Noonan, John T. *Contraception: A History of its Treatment by the Catholic Theologians and Canonists* (Cambridge, MA: Harvard University Press, 1986).

Otto, Rudolf. *The Idea of the Holy* (2nd ed., trans. Jown W. Harvey; Oxford: Oxford University Press, 1950).

Pennington, Brian K. *Was Hinduism Invented? Britons, Indians, and the Colonial Construction of Religion* (New York: Oxford University Press, 2005).

Pope John Paul II, *Encyclical Letter: Fides et Ratio; On the Relationship between Faith and Reason* (English trans.; Boston: Pauline Books and Media, 1998).

Pope John Paul II, *Mission of the Redeemer / Redemptoris Missio* (English trans.; Boston: Pauline Books & Media, 1990).

Pylee, M. V. *India's Constitution* (New York: Asia Publishing House, 1967).

Rangaswamy, Padma. *Namaste America: Indian Immigrants in an American Metropolis* (University Park: Pennsylvania State University Press, 2000).

Ratzinger, Joseph Cardinal. *Truth and Tolerance: Christian Belief and World Religions* (trans. Henry Taylor; San Francisco: Ignatius Press, 2004).

Ray, Reginald. *Buddhists Saints in India* (Oxford: Oxford University Press 1994).

Sarma, Deepak. *Epistemologies and the Limitations of Philosophical Inquiry: Doctrine in Madhva Vedanta* (Great Britain: Routledge Curzon Limited. 2005).

Sarma, Deepak. *An Introduction to Madhva Vedanta* (Great Britain: Ashgate Pub. Ltd. 2003)

Schmidt, Leigh Eric. *Restless Souls: The Making of American Spirituality:From Emerson to Oprah* (San Francisco: Harper San Francisco, 2005).

Sen, Amartya. *The Argumentative Indian: Writings on Indian History, Culture and Identity* (New York: Farrar, Straus and Giroux, 2005).

Sherwin, Byron L. & Harold Kasimow (eds.), *John Paul II and Interreligious Dialogue* (Maryknoll, NY: Orbis Books, 1999).

Smith, Donald E. *India as a Secular State* (Princeton: Princeton University Press, 1963).

Sontheimer, G. and H. Kulke (eds.) *Hinduism Reconsidered* (Delhi: Manohar, 2001).

Soothill, William E. *A Dictionary of Buddhist Terms* (London: Kegan Paul, Trench, Trubner & Co. Ltd., 1930).

Special edition of *Journal of the American Academy of Religion*, vol 68, 2000, special issue devoted to "Who Speaks for Hinduism?"

Swanson, Herb. "The Wiang Pa Pao consultation on Evangelism in the Northern Thai context,"https://www.yumpu.com/en/document/view/22249394/herbs-research-bulletin-revised-october-2011-number-11-.

Swearer, Donald K. *The Buddhist World in Southeast Asia* (Albany: State University of New York Press, 1995).

Thurman, Robert. *The Holy Teaching of Vimalakirt. A Mahayana Scipture.* (University Park: Penn State University Press, 1967).

Trapnell, Judson B. *Bede Griffiths: A Life in Dialogue* (Albany: State University of New York Press, 2001).

Trouvé, Marianne Lorraine (ed.). *The Sixteen Documents of Vatican II* (Boston: Pauline Books & Media, 1999).

Tsomo, Karma Lekshe (ed.). *Buddhist Women and Social Justice* (Albany: State University of New York Press, 2004).

Urs von Balthasar, Hans. *The God Question & Modern Man* (trans. Hilda Graef; New York: Seabury Press, 1967).

Visalo, Phra Paisan. "Spritueller Materialismus und die Sakramente des Konsumismus," Publication by Buddha-Netz Info.

von Brueck, Michael/Whalen Lai. *Christianity and Buddhism* (Maryknoll, NY: Orbis 2001).

Williams, Mary Alice. "Tensions in American Buddhism", in *Religion and Ethics Newsweekly*, July 6, 2001: 2.

Yuichi, Kajiyama. "Women in Buddhism", Eastern Buddhist, New Series No.2 (1982)http://www.kommundsieh.de/bni-7-8.htm.

Zangpo, Ngawang. *Sacred Ground. Jamgon Kongtrul on Pilgrimage and Sacred Geography* (New York: Snow Lion, 2001).

Zizoulas, John. *Being as Communion: Studies in Personhood and the Church* (Crestwood, NY: St. Vladimir's Seminary Press, 1985).

Index

authority, 9, 10, 11, 18, 24, 28, 46, 69, 88, 112, 126, 152

change (and integrity), 17, 25, 34, 44, 59, 94, 113, 121, 127, 144, 152
consumerism, 9, 25, 47, 131

dialogue, 30, 60, 70, 73, 80–82, 116, 156

education, 29, 34, 53, 56, 76, 77, 98–100, 115, 143, 155

family, 6, 10, 15, 27, 31, 39, 45, 50, 53, 60, 69, 88, 93, 93–94, 139, 155
feminism, 10, 19, 134. *See also* women
fundamentalism, 14, 39, 64, 127, 129

globalization, 8, 28, 62, 72, 92, 101, 131

identity: challenges to, 33, 35, 116–117; formation of, 98, 104, 112, 140, 153; purpose/mission, 2, 5, 6, 30, 151, 153, 154
image: in media, 20, 52, 103; outside image, 87
individualism 9, 12, 18, 24, 26, 31, 39, 46, 68, 89, 151; and community, 24, 37, 44, 48, 63, 68, 69, 71, 75, 79, 141
integrity. *See* change

leadership, 44, 46, 49, 52, 75, 97, 113, 116, 121, 155

media. *See* image
mission (and missionaries), 28, 30, 31, 49, 61, 63, 72–73, 127, 152
modernity, 2, 36, 60, 78, 89, 132, 135, 139. *See also* globalization
monasticism, 42, 46, 114

secularism, secularization, 9, 20, 54, 70, 89, 96, 108, 116, 119, 127, 128, 129, 133
spirituality, 13, 15, 24, 33, 43, 46, 51, 106, 117, 130, 131, 135, 146, 152, 153
social justice, social activism, social responsibility, 30, 47, 70, 71, 80, 81, 129, 130

technology, 8, 19, 35, 54, 60, 74, 100, 102, 117–119, 136–138, 142
tradition, 11, 59, 78, 91, 118, 129, 140, 144, 154

women, 25, 29, 41, 49, 57, 58, 76, 92, 93, 115. *See also* feminism

youth, 19, 47, 49, 50, 53, 55, 77, 144. *See also* education

About the Contributors

Vincent J. Cornell is Asa Griggs Candler Professor of Middle East and Islamic Studies and chair of the Department of Near Eastern and South Asian Studies at Emory University in Atlanta, Georgia. From 2000–2006, he was director of the King Fahd Center for Middle East and Islamic Studies at the University of Arkansas. From 1991–2000, he taught at Duke University. His published works include over forty articles, three books, and one book set, including *The Way of Abu Madyan* (Cambridge: The Islamic Texts Society, 1996) and *Realm of the Saint: Power and Authority in Moroccan Sufism* (Austin: University of Texas Press, 1998). His most recent publication is the five-volume set *Voices of Islam*, Vincent J. Cornell, general editor (Westport, CT, and London: Praeger, 2007). His academic interests cover the entire spectrum of Islamic thought from Sufism to theology and Islamic law. He is currently finishing *The Wiley-Blackwell Companion to Islamic Spirituality* with Bruce Lawrence of Duke University. He has often appeared on television and radio, including interviews on the National Public Radio show, "Speaking of Faith." From 2002–2012 he was a key participant in the Building Bridges seminars of Christian and Muslim scholars conducted by the Archbishop of Canterbury.

Alon Goshen-Gottstein is acknowledged as one of the world's leading figures in interreligious dialogue, specializing in bridging the theological and academic dimension with a variety of practical initiatives, especially involving world religious leadership. He is both a theoretician and activist, setting trends and precedents in the global interfaith arena. He is the founder and director of the Elijah Interfaith Institute (formerly the Elijah School for the Study of Wisdom in World Religions), and its rich Web site is testimony to his many and varied activities. A noted scholar of Jewish studies, he has held academic posts at Tel Aviv University and has served as director of the Center for the Study of Rabbinic Thought, Beit Morasha College, Jerusalem. Ordained a rabbi in 1977, he received his Ph.D. from Hebrew University of Jerusalem in 1986 in the area of Rabbinic thought. From 1989 to 1999, he was a member of the Shalom Hartman Institute for Advanced Studies, Jerusalem, where he also served as director for interreligious affairs. Stanford University Press published his *The Sinner and the Amnesiac: The Rabbinic Invention of Elisha ben Abuya and Eleazar ben Arach* in 2000, and the Littman Library published his coedited volume *Jewish Theology and World Religions*. His *Beyond Idolatry—The Jewish Encounter with Hinduism* is to appear shortly. Several other collective research projects and edited volumes complement more than fifty articles, published in such scholarly journals as *Harvard Theological Review*, *Journal for the Study of Judaism*, *Journal of Literature and Theology*, *Journal of Jewish Thought and Philosophy*, *Ecumenism*, and *Studies in Interreligious Dialogue*.

Sidney H. Griffith is professor of Early Christian Studies at the Catholic University of America. His main areas of interest are Arabic Christianity, Syriac monasticism, medieval Christian-Muslim encounters, and ecumenical and interfaith dialogue. He serves on the advisory board of the journal *Collectanea Christiana Orientalia*. In 2009, Griffith was awarded a Rumi Peace Award for his efforts in interfaith dialogue. His book *The Church in the Shadow of the Mosque: Muslims and Christians in the World of Islam* was awarded the Albert C. Outler Prize for the best book on ecumenical church history by the American Society of Church History.

Maria Reis Habito is the International program director of the Museum of World Religions and the Director of the Elijah Interfaith Institute USA. She studied Chinese Language and Culture at Taiwan Normal University in Taipei, and received her M.A. in Chinese Studies, Japanese Studies, and Philosophy at the Ludwig-Maximilians-Universitaet in Munich. She was a research fellow at Kyoto University and completed her Ph.D. at Ludwig-Maximilians-Universitaet. Dr. Reis Habito represents Dharma Master Hsin Tao on the steering committee.

B. Barry Levy is professor of Biblical Studies at McGill University in Montreal. Having taught some sixty different courses in Bible, the history of Biblical interpretation, Hebrew, Aramaic, Religious Studies, and Jewish Studies at McGill since his initial appointment in 1975, he also has served as a visiting professor at Concordia University and Yeshiva University, and as Shier Distinguished Visiting Professor of Judaica at the University of Toronto. In 1994–1995, he held a Starr Fellowship from Harvard University. Levy is the author of various books and shorter monographs, including two volumes on the *Neofiti Targum, Planets, Potions, and Parchments: Scientifica Hebraica from the Dead Sea Scrolls to the Eighteenth Century*; and *Fixing God's Torah*. He has served two terms as chairman of McGill's Department of Jewish Studies, thirteen years as director of McGill's program to train Judaica teachers, and more than a decade as dean of its Faculty of Religious Studies.

Deepak Sarma is professor of South Asian religions and philosophy at Case Western Reserve University, and the author of *Classical Indian Philosophy: A Reader* (2011), *Hinduism: A Reader* (2008), *Epistemologies and the Limitations of Philosophical Inquiry: Doctrine in Madhva Vedanta* (2005), and *An Introduction to Madhva Vedanta* (2003). He was a guest curator of *Indian Kalighat Paintings*, an exhibition at the Cleveland Museum of Art. He is a curatorial consultant for the Department of Asian Art of the Cleveland Museum of Art. After earning a BA in religion from Reed College, Sarma attended the University of Chicago Divinity School, where he received a PhD in the philosophy of religions. His current reflections concern cultural theory, racism, and post-colonialism.

Michael von Brück is head of the Interfaculty Program of Religious Studies at the Ludwig Maximilians University of Munich/Germany. He studied Theology, Indology, and Comparative Linguistics at Rostock University, Indian Philosophy and Religion at Madras University. He specializes in Advaita Vedânta and Mahâyâna-Buddhism. Besides, he received four years of training in Yoga at a Yoga Institute in Madras and studied Zen-Buddhism in theory and practice in Japan. After a visiting professorship at Gurukul Lutheran College in Madras 1980 until 1985 he became professor of Comparative Religion at the University of Regensburg in 1988. In 1991 he took over the chair of Religious Studies at the University of Munich.